A STEP ALONG THE WAY

A STEP ALONG THE WAY

Models of Christian Service

Stephen J. Pope

ORBIS BOOKS
Maryknoll, New York 10545

ORBIS ✪ BOOKS
Maryknoll, New York 10545

Second Printing, August 2016

Founded in 1970, Orbis Books endeavors to publish works that enlighten the mind, nourish the spirit, and challenge the conscience. The publishing arm of the Maryknoll Fathers and Brothers, Orbis seeks to explore the global dimensions of the Christian faith and mission, to invite dialogue with diverse cultures and religious traditions, and to serve the cause of reconciliation and peace. The books published reflect the views of their authors and do not represent the official position of the Maryknoll Society. To learn more about Maryknoll and Orbis Books, please visit our website at www.maryknollsociety.org.

Library of Congress Cataloging-in-Publication Data

Pope, Stephen J., 1955–
    A step along the way : models of Christian service / Stephen J. Pope.
      pages cm
    Includes bibliographical references and index.
    ISBN 978-1-62698-118-8 (pbk.)
    1. Christian life. 2. Service (Theology) I. Title.
  BV4509.5.P645 2015
  248.4—dc23

                                     2014047880

To Ruth Raichle and Kathleen Denevan, OSF,
Bethany House Ministries, and
The Our Lady of Mercy Chapter of the Lay Fraternities of St. Dominic,
Norfolk Prison, Massachusetts

Contents

Part 2
MODELS

Acknowledgments

I would like thank friends who read parts of this manuscript or helped me think through its topics: Kevin Ahern; Juliano Almeida; Gordon Burghardt; Lisa Sowle Cahill; Joseph Curran; Ellen Dabrieo, SND; Dave Fernandez; Anthony Ford; Claire Geruson; Tom Kelly; Maryanne Loughry; Marcus Mescher; Robin Lovin; Jim Petkiewicz; Barbara O'Brien-Miller; Mary Pope-Handy; Barbara Pope; Patricia O'Brien Rowell; Mark Potter; Timothy Radcliffe, OP; Colleen Shantz; Douglas Schuurman; and Daniel Vos. I owe a special debt of gratitude to Robert Ellsberg and Maria Angelini of Orbis Books for their patience in editing and producing this book. I would like express gratitude to Professor John Witte and the Center for the Study of Law and Religion at Emory University for allowing me to participate in an incredibly stimulating Pursuit of Happiness seminar that met periodically from 2007 to 2009. Some of what appears here reflects work conducted for that seminar. I also wish to thank Will Storrar and Robin Lovin from the Center of Theological Inquiry in Princeton, New Jersey, for allowing me to participate in the 2013–2014 Inquiry on Religious Experience and Moral Identity. The material of this book was shaped during that most exciting academic experience. I also want to express my heartfelt appreciation to my fine colleagues in the Theology Department at Boston College and particularly my fellow moral theologians Lisa Sowle Cahill; David Hollenbach, SJ; Kenneth Himes, OFM; Cathleen Kaveny; James F. Keenan, SJ; and John Paris, SJ. Finally, my greatest appreciation goes to my special family—Patti, Mike, Katie, Stevie—for the kindness, patience, and support they showed to me as I tried to complete this project. Finally, this book is dedicated to friends who belong to the Dominican lay community in the medium-security state prison in Norfolk, Massachusetts. Their care for one another has revealed dimensions of faith, service, and solidarity that I had never witnessed prior to our friendship. Jesus told his friends: "Everyone will know that you are my disciples, if you have love for one another" (Jn 13:35). He has true disciples in Norfolk.

Introduction

"How Service Can Save Us." This was the headline of the lead story of the June 30, 2013, edition of *Time Magazine*. Joe Klein wrote this story about the positive mental and physical health benefits that come from actively caring for others. He reported that combat veterans suffering from posttraumatic stress have been helped by engaging in community service facilitated by a St. Louis–based organization called Mission Continues. By June 2013, more than eight hundred veterans had volunteered to engage in a variety of activities from building houses and farming to teaching and helping in disaster relief.

Actively assisting other people helps to connect us to others, overcome isolation, and put our problems in perspective. People who spend time putting someone else's needs above their own, paradoxically, are more likely to feel good about themselves—a little more competent, needed, and self-confident—than people who spend all of their time focused on themselves. Altruistic commitments not only encourage us to be socially engaged, but also help to reduce our level of stress, boost our immune systems, and contribute to longer life spans.

Schools, universities, and churches provide ample opportunities for their members to engage in various kinds of service. There is nothing wrong with making a living by working in the "customer service" department of a store or in the "food-service" industry, but the term *service* here refers to ways of helping others for their own sake rather than primarily because it benefits the agent. This definition includes people who volunteer, either full or part time, in a vast range of activities from tutoring and coaching to teaching and working on political campaigns. It includes professionals like nurses and teachers, at least to the extent that they are motivated by empathy and altruism. Such people are drawn to a particular way of making a living because it enables them to use their talents to address important human needs in specific ways, for example, by teaching children, editing books, or representing clients. Many people earn a living by helping those who are lonely, lost, or marginalized, and they, too, are engaged in genuine service.

We are increasingly convinced that volunteer service is a good thing to do, but we are not always sure why. Religion has historically been the strongest motivator for service. Sociologists Robert D. Putnam and David E. Campbell tell us in *American Grace* that people who attend religious services are more likely to be engaged in service than those who do not.[1] Yet while religion based on biblical faith requires service to others, service to others does not require an explicit religious faith. Even as more Americans than ever refer to themselves as having no religious affiliation (the so-called Nones), many still appreciate the value of service.

If we step back for a moment, however, we might notice that there is something a little strange about viewing service as an admirable activity. The *Oxford English Dictionary* defines the noun *service* as the "condition, station, or occupation of being a servant." Our English word *service* is a modification of the Latin verb *servire*, which means "to act as a servant or slave"—one who obeys and labors in a state of bondage or who waits upon another person in order to provide for his or her comfort or more generally enact whatever the person wills. Who would want to do that, at least if one had other options?

Service has not, in fact, always been regarded as admirable. In large societies, modern as well as ancient, people at the bottom of the social hierarchy—slaves, serfs, the illiterate, and the powerless—serve those at the top. They perform mundane tasks like cooking, cleaning, and other chores that the wealthy and powerful don't want to do. Those who are "base" are supposed to serve the "noble," not the other way around. Only people with no better opportunities would be willing to work as servants, with its connotations of servility, subjection, lowliness, and powerlessness. When the "noble" do decide to help the "base," they often do so in a way that keeps them in their place and advertises their own superiority.

The fact that our culture places a special value on service has a lot to do with its ancient Jewish and Christian heritage. This tradition understood service primarily as directed to God, as we see expressed in the Book of Deuteronomy: "The Lord your God you shall fear; him you shall serve, and by his name alone you shall swear" (6:13, NRVS). This theme continues in the New Testament. Before he begins his public ministry, Jesus must go into the wilderness to be tempted by Satan. When tempted with political power, Jesus repels his tempter by recalling the primary religious command of the covenant:

> "Worship the Lord your God,
> and serve only him." (Mt 4:10; cf. Lk 4:8)

---

[1] Putnam and Campbell, *American Grace: How Religion Divides and Unites Us* (New York: Simon and Schuster, 2010), chap. 13.

Service as obedience is distinct from but related to service as caregiving. Responding to a conflict among Christians in Galatia, St. Paul tells them: "Through love become slaves to one another" (Gal 5:13). The Gospel of Mark also moves in this vein when it describes Jesus as teaching his disciples that "whoever would be great among you must be your servant and whoever would be first among you must be slave of all" (Mk 10:44; cf. Mt 20:26).

New Testament authors, in fact, used the least attractive social role in the ancient world as a metaphor for the Christian life. Early Christians expanded the meaning of service to include not only the fulfillment of menial tasks but also the more honorable role of acting as a messenger or emissary. In both cases one serves a higher authority. Early Christians believed that the highest honor comes from serving Christ. Jesus cared for the lowly, and so should we. Indeed, God became lowly in Jesus, and we can best serve Jesus by engaging in humble love. As theologian J. B. Metz puts it: "The God of the Christian gospel is, after all, not a God of conquerors, but a God of slaves."[2]

Many religions teach their members to act as servants of God or the gods. This was true of ancient Greek, Egyptian, and Babylonian religions. Christianity is unusual in seeing Jesus of Nazareth as the incarnation of a God who came in the form of a servant to care for us. Jesus says of himself: "The Son of Man did not come to be served, but to serve" (Mk 10:4; Mt 20:28). Jesus served the Father and sought to do his will. Jesus's service flowed from his loving obedience and loyalty to the Father. St. Paul thus described Jesus as one who "emptied himself, taking the form of a slave" (Phil 2:7). He came to serve God by serving *us*. We, in turn, are to serve God and Christ by serving *one another*.

In his influential study of early Christianity, sociologist Rodney Stark described as "entirely new" the Christian belief that "*because* God loves humanity, Christians may not please God unless they *love one another*." Even "more revolutionary," he argued, was the early Christian insistence that charity must extend "beyond the boundaries of family and tribe."[3] Historians, though, challenge Stark's claim that these ideas were totally unprecedented at the time just prior to the life of Jesus. Jesus's forbears believed that we best show fidelity to God by humbly caring for one another. They trusted a God who "heals the broken hearted and binds up their

---

[2] *Faith in History and Society* (New York: Crossroad, 1980), 71. On service in the New Testament, see John N. Collins, *Diakonia: Re-interpreting the Ancient Sources* (New York: Oxford, 1990).

[3] Rodney Stark, *The Rise of Christianity* (San Francisco: Harper, 1997), 212.

wounds" (Ps 147:3) and who wants his people to offer food to the hungry and satisfy the needs of the afflicted (see Is 58:10). They saw that compassion and justice must extend beyond the "boundaries of family and tribe." In any case, the Jewish and Christian traditions clearly mark service to one another as an essential part of what it means to love God.

Audience

This book is written primarily to Christians who want to think about the religious and moral meaning of service, particularly as it bears on their own lives. I have come to take seriously the themes in this book as a result of trying to live a Christian life, particularly in the context of teaching theology, advising students, and participating in various service and immersion programs run by Boston College. I have also been informed by my experience with the Catholic Worker community in Los Angeles, where for a few years I spent some Saturday mornings with high school students I was teaching. More recently, I have learned a great deal about the meaning of service from my friends in the lay Dominican community in the state prison in Norfolk, Massachusetts.

I write as one who is struggling to be an active and committed Christian. What German theologian Karl Rahner once wrote of himself is true of all Christians: "I have still to become a Christian."[4] I was raised in a Catholic extended family and continue to participate in the Catholic community as an adult. Throughout this book I use *we* to speak about things as they seem to me as a committed Catholic Christian. I certainly don't presume to speak for all Catholics, let alone all Christians. Yet I hope that what is written here resonates with the experience of a broad array of Christians who want to connect their experience of service to important questions about the meaning of their lives and their religious identity as Christians.

Focusing on a Christian audience has both advantages and disadvantages. As our society becomes more pluralistic, many authors (including Christians) promote compassion and justice by appealing to humanistic arguments that can convince secular as well as religious readers about the value of service. They argue on secular grounds that we ought to be more civically engaged, socially aware, and committed to the well-being of the marginalized. This is a laudable enterprise, and it has been done well by humanitarians like Robert Coles, Jonathon Kozol, and Martha Nussbaum, among others.

---

[4] Hugo Rahner and Karl Rahner, *Prayers for Meditation*, trans. R. Brennan (Freiburg: Herder, 1962), 22.

It is also obvious that people who consider themselves nonreligious are as capable of engaging in generous service as anyone else. Human motivations are complex and often opaque to us. Yet I believe that all forms of service involve some kind of an implicit act of faith—a giving of oneself in trust—to what is ultimately good. I share Dorothy Day's conviction that God is present and working, albeit often in an unknown way, "wherever there is truth, justice, love."[5] Her own experience of agnostics and atheists who were selflessly dedicated to social justice helped her to acknowledge that, "those who do not believe in God—they believe in love."[6] I have nothing but respect, admiration, and gratitude for such people—they put most Christians to shame—but they are not the audience for this book.

Something is lost if we avoid religion. From a Christian standpoint a secularized approach to ethics and the social order loses some of the richness and complexity communicated in religious symbols, stories, and practices. Concepts like autonomy, rights, and procedural justice have a proper role to play in public conversation, but to Christians they do not have the motivational power and moral depth of, say, Jesus's parable of the Good Samaritan, the healing of Lazarus, or the Sermon on the Mount (Mt 5—7).

Christianity offers powerful resources for helping us think about how faith illuminates and shapes our understanding of service. The gospel offers something that cannot be found elsewhere—a community inspired by the Spirit and modeled on a particular person, Jesus of Nazareth. Reflection on what religious realities like faith, community, and Spirit mean is especially needed today because many Christians engaged in service find it increasingly hard to see how these religious realities have any connection to real life. Rather than proposing a secular way of thinking about service that tries to speak to the widest possible audience, then, I focus on what faith and the other Christian virtues bring to the table. I hope to help people of faith think more deeply about service in light of the resources provided by the Bible, the wisdom of the Christian tradition, and the contemporary church.

While I write primarily for Christians engaged in service, I have in mind a wide range of readers. The intended audience includes (1) deeply pious believers who are well versed in Christian belief, (2) those who are churchgoing but not devout, (3) those who go to church without much satisfaction, (4) disgruntled Christians who have one foot out the door, and (5) those who were raised by churchgoing parents but now describe themselves as former Christians. Many people today practice compassion

---

[5] Ibid., 340.

[6] *The Duty of Delight: The Diaries of Dorothy Day*, ed. Robert Ellsberg (Milwaukee: Marquette University Press, 2008), 294.

and social service but do so from outside the church. They act on their own, with neither a theological framework nor the support and guidance of a community. The disadvantage of my approach is that it will not appeal to people who do not already consider themselves to be (at least in some sense) Christian. Atheists or agnostics might read this book if they are interested in how Christians think about the moral life or social ethics, but they will probably have a hard time taking its message to heart.

This book is meant to be useful, but it is not to be thought of as a contribution to Christian self-help literature. It does not encourage its readers to unleash their potential, or to take control of their lives, or to find their authentic selves. These are all good goals, but Christian service goes beyond them. Service in the Christian sense is not an ingredient one can just add to life to increase one's happiness; it is an integral dimension of any full human life. Life, like all goods, is a *gift* of a good and loving God. We enjoy it best when we share it with others. Life includes our particular talents, personalities, friendships, communities, and concrete opportunities. The more thankful we are, the more we want to share our gifts with one another. This is the essential source of Christian service.

A friend of mine, the late William B. Neenan, SJ, liked to use a baseball analogy: "Just because you're on third base doesn't mean you hit a triple." You might have reached first base on a walk or been hit by a pitch and then advanced by batters behind you. Or you might have been inserted into the game as a pinch runner. Bill used this metaphor to suggest to college students that just because they are at a good university and have a promising future doesn't mean they earned their place all by themselves. The same goes for their parents, peers, and friends. While they deserve credit for working hard, they did not create the conditions that enabled their hard work to be rewarded. Privilege, properly understood, inspires gratitude and a sense of responsibility rather than self-congratulation and a sense of entitlement.

Bill's point also has theological significance. His deep sense of the giftedness of our lives, talents, friendships, and opportunities reflected a faith steeped in the spiritual tradition of St. Ignatius, the founder of the Society of Jesus (Jesuits). Bill understood every human life as permeated with the kind of divine love Christians call grace, which theologian Karl Rahner described as "the real, fundamental reality of Christianity."[7] Grace—God's free and forgiving presence in each of our lives—is the ultimate origin of whatever service we perform for one another. Serving others does not earn

---

[7] Rahner, "Theology and Anthropology," *Theological Investigations*, vol. 9, trans. Graham Harrison (New York: Seabury, n.d.), 41.

us grace, but it does manifest in concrete ways something of what grace means.

Service thus lies at the very heart of the Christian life. To the extent that we follow Christ, we will want to serve one another. "True faith in the incarnate Son of God," as Pope Francis puts it in *Evangelii Gaudium (The Joy of the Gospel)*, "is inseparable from self-giving, from membership in the community, from service, from reconciliation with others" (no. 88). If service is "faith active in love" (Gal 5:6), and if love is shown in service, then service lies at the core of any life truly shaped by faith. Christians, then, should not think of service as a part-time, extracurricular commitment for volunteers when they have nothing more important to do. It is not something we do when we are either too young or too old to have a "real" job. It is not just an implication or application of the Christian message at particular times and places. Nor is it just the specialization of certain experts in organizations like the Sisters of Mercy, the Society of St. Vincent de Paul, or the Salvation Army (as good as they are). Service is a steady aspect of *any* life grounded in authentic love.

Agenda

This book provides tools to help us think and talk about the Christian meaning of service. It might help to note three goals this book is *not* trying to accomplish. First, it does not intend to provide a comprehensive theology of service. It merely seeks to note some of the key scriptural and theological underpinnings of service in the Christian tradition. It aims to uncover key features of the theological and moral meaning of Christian service.

Second, this book does not discuss how a Christian account of service compares or contrasts with how service is understood in other religions. Christianity places a strong emphasis on service, but so do many other religious traditions. Each has its own distinctive approach to the meaning, exercise, and proper goals of service. Hindus, for example, provide extensive reflection on fulfillment of the dharma, or religious duty, to promote the well-being of human beings. Buddhist service is generated by compassion for all sentient beings.[8] The Qur'an teaches Muslims that "you have been raised to serve others; you enjoin what is good and forbid evil and believe in Allah" (3.111). Given the increasingly pluralistic nature of our society and the globalization of world religions, some readers will find this book's Christian focus to be too parochial. Yet while there is no question that we

---

[8] See, for example, John Makransky, *Awakening through Love: Unveiling Your Deepest Goodness* (Somerville, MA: Wisdom Publications, 2007).

need to think about how cooperation among different religions can promote service, justice, and peace, I am not one of those equipped to do so.

Finally, this book tries neither to talk people into becoming Christian nor to engage in an "apologetics" that refutes the objections of skeptics. The philosopher Ludwig Wittgenstein once wrote to a friend: "If you and I are to live religious lives it mustn't be that we talk a lot about religion, but that our manner of life is different. It is my belief that only if you try to be helpful to other people will you in the end find your way to God."[9] Wittgenstein suggested that the best response to the critics of Christianity lies in service. People are most likely to see truth of Christianity in the actions of those who exemplify its meaning in the way they lead their lives. Few people come to a deeper understanding of Christian life through debates, which often go to the quicker but not necessarily deeper minds. As our exemplars will show, Christians at their best manifest the beauty, truth, and goodness of the gospel in concrete ways. This is why the final model concerns serving others by witnessing to one's Christian faith.

Organization

This book contains two parts. The first part discusses six people whose lives displayed a particularly compelling kind of service to others: Dorothy Stang, SND (stewardship), Dorothy Day (hospitality), Mother Teresa (compassion), Martin Luther King, Jr. (advocacy), Oscar Romero (solidarity), and Pierre Claverie, OP (witness). These figures show what it means to serve others in very distinctive and concrete ways.

The second part of the book examines six corresponding models of service: stewardship, hospitality, compassion, advocacy, solidarity, and witness. This part of the book is meant to provide a kind of conceptual "map" of different ways of serving one another. Distinct "places" are occupied by different models of service, but we should not view them as separate from one another or only linked by various "roads." One can't be in Oakland and San Francisco at the same time, but one can, for example, serve simultaneously as both witness and advocate. A model is a symbolic or conceptual representation of some reality that allows us to understand some of its key features. It describes a pattern of organization in certain experienced realities without claiming to offer an exhaustive explanation of them. Each model has its own distinct identity, strengths, and weaknesses. Each chapter examines a particular model of service in terms of five key topics: its biblical roots, its connection to one important Christian theme,

---

[9] Cited in Norman Malcolm, *Wittgenstein: A Religious Point of View?* (London: Routledge, 2002), 11.

its dependence on a particular moral virtue, ways in which we can grow in that form of service, and the temptations that are characteristically associated with it.

Examining these models can help us come to a better understanding of the ways in which we serve others now and how we might grow in service in the future. This book offers a language and a framework for stimulating further reflection and conversation. Its goal is to facilitate critical appropriation of the virtues that are required if we are to serve one another "in truth and in deed" (1 Jn 3:18). It is best read in a quiet, thoughtful frame of mind in which the reader brings his or her own life to the text. I hope to show that service in an integral dimension to every Christian life rather than just a minor, self-contained, and optional part of the lives of some particularly intense believers.

Whatever our particular backgrounds and convictions, engaging in authentic service is, at its best, a process of engaging in the self-transcending love that Jesus embodied. It is self-transcending in the sense that the more we freely and truly care for others, the more we are drawn beyond our habitual self-centeredness and the narrow world in which it encases us. Christ is the incarnation of self-transcending love, and the church is called to follow him in serving the world as the body of Christ.

This agenda can be daunting. Dorothy Day worried when young people asked, "What can one person do? What is the sense of our small effort?" We need to see, Day countered, that "we must lay one brick at a time, take one step at a time; we can be responsible only for the one action of the present moment." We can do so desiring an "increase of love in our hearts that will vitalize and transform these actions, and know that God will take them and multiply them, as Jesus multiplied the loaves and fishes."[10] Our actions—both positive and negative—can have ripple effects of which we are completely unaware. "Each one of our thoughts, words and deeds is like that. No one has a right to sit down and feel hopeless. There is too much work to do."

Day's image of "one step at a time," however, should not be taken to suggest that everyone grows in service by proceeding through the same predetermined stages. We might study math or science this way, but everyone's path in service is different. While we can grow in how we serve others, there is no universal and uniform sequence for doing so. We are all capable of growing within the particular contexts of our lives, but these contexts vary widely in both the limitations and opportunities they present to us. Each of us has an individual personality, talents, weaknesses, and strengths. Some journeys have a similar cast to them, but none are identical.

---

[10] Dorothy Day, *Loaves and Fishes* (Maryknoll, NY: Orbis Books, 1997), 210.

When reading a book like this one, readers have to discern what is and is not useful for them. In the end, we only really understand what we are talking about when we can put our insights into practice. Though good intentions and practical plans are important, it is often the case that practice comes first and understanding second. We know we have "gotten it" when our actions match our insights and when our insights are grounded in our lived experience.

Day's image of one step at a time resonates with the tone of a well-known prayer called "Prophets of a Future Not Our Own." While usually attributed to Oscar Romero, it was actually written in November 1979 by the late Bishop Kenneth Untener of Saginaw as part of a homily given at a mass for deceased priests.[11] It captures well the faith, humility, and hope that are part of any appropriate understanding of Christian service:

> It helps, now and then, to step back and take a long view.
> The kingdom is not only beyond our efforts, it is even
>   beyond our vision.
> We accomplish in our lifetime only a tiny fraction of the
>   magnificent enterprise that is God's work.
> Nothing we do is complete, which is a way of saying that
>   the kingdom always lies beyond us.
> No statement says all that could be said.
> No prayer fully expresses our faith.
> No confession brings perfection.
> No pastoral visit brings wholeness.
> No program accomplishes the church's mission.
> No set of goals and objectives includes everything.
> This is what we are about.
> We plant the seeds that one day will grow.
> We water seeds already planted, knowing that they hold
>   future promise.
> We lay foundations that will need further development.
> We provide yeast that produces far beyond our capabilities.
> We cannot do everything, and there is a sense of liberation
>   in realizing that.
> This enables us to do something, and to do it very well.
> It may be incomplete, but it is a beginning, a step along
>   the way, an opportunity for the Lord's grace to enter
>   and do the rest.

---

[11] See Bishop Thomas Gumbleton, "The Peace Pulpit," *National Catholic Reporter*, March 28, 2004.

> We may never see the end results, but that is the difference
>   between the master builder and the worker.
> We are workers, not master builders; ministers, not mes-
>   siahs.
> We are prophets of a future not our own.
> Amen.

This prayer suggests that all of us can make some positive difference in our communities, even if we are merely "ministers, not messiahs." We can all "plant seeds that one day will grow." We can water the seeds of others, because our mentors, families, and friends have watered the seeds planted in our own spirits. "Above all," said the French Jesuit Pierre Teilhard de Chardin, we must "trust in the slow work of God."[12] Our own garden must be cultivated. So we must allow God, working through our friends and communities, to strengthen our roots and prune our branches so that our actions can bear fruit.

---

[12] *Hearts on Fire: Praying with Jesuits*, ed. William Harter, SJ (Chicago: Loyola Press, 2005), 102.

Part 1

Exemplars

Part 1 focuses on six exemplars, or role models, of Christian service: Mother Teresa of Calcutta; Martin Luther King, Jr.; Dorothy Day; Sister Dorothy Stang of Brazil (originally Ohio); Oscar Romero of El Salvador; and Pierre Claverie of Algeria. Each of these people is widely recognized as an icon of service. Particular life stories flesh out ideals and aspirations that can otherwise sound abstract.

Each of these exemplars acted in ways that say something significant about the Christian meaning of service. All were touched by powerful, concrete experiences that decisively shaped the rest of their lives. Their deepest convictions did not come from reading books but from encountering reality in the lives of particular human beings. Mother Teresa discovered a very sick person lying on the street, waiting to die. King never forgot hearing his father called "boy" by racist authority figures. And Romero was permanently marked by his moment of gazing upon the corpse of his close friend Rutilio Grande after he and two friends were ambushed by a death squad on a lonely road in rural El Salvador.

But experience is not enough. It has to be followed by critical reflection, concrete action, and specific commitments. Dorothy Stang, for example, was initially moved to serve as a religious sister by her personal piety, but her encounter with marginalized communities in the southwestern United States gave her an expanded sense of who God is, where God can be found, and where God was calling her to serve. As a young woman, Dorothy Day burned with a sense of justice for people who had been treated as if they did not matter. As she matured, she came to feel divine grace gradually pulling her into the Christian life. Her willingness to respond wholeheartedly defined the rest of her life.

We can learn from exemplars by not only paying attention to what they accomplished, but also by coming to see (inasmuch as we can) the shape of their inner lives—*why* they did what they did. We are fortunate to know something about these exemplars' inner lives from their letters, speeches, journal entries, or other writings. Each acted out of a love for the marginalized that was strengthened by faith in Christ and membership in particular Christian communities.

3

Exemplars can help us think about whether our actions match what we profess. Recall Jesus's admonition, "You will know them by their fruits" (Mt 7:20). If we really want to know what we believe in our depths, what our heart is set upon, we need to look at our actions. "I have long since come to believe," Dorothy Day wrote, "that people never mean half of what they say, and that it is best to disregard their talk and judge only their actions."[1] None of us will ever be entirely successful in living up to the ideals we profess, but we can make incremental progress if we take concrete steps to do so. Moral exemplars can help us see how much of our personal growth and resiliency depends upon other people, especially friends. Exemplars show us something about what it might look like to reduce the gap between our convictions and our daily actions.

These exemplars present a number of challenges to us that are worth taking seriously, especially regarding the quality of our service to one another: The challenge of *believing* calls us to steadfast trust in God and fidelity to Christ and his church. The challenge of *willing* involves consistently desiring and choosing what is good. The challenge of *feeling* rightly calls us to develop appropriate emotional responses to good or evil in our lives. The challenge of *thinking* calls us to reflect clearly and critically. The challenge of *doing* involves practicing what we believe in concrete actions. All of these challenges are part of what it means to "love, not in word or speech, but in truth and action" (1 Jn 3:18).

Not everyone viewed the individuals praised in this book as exemplary human beings. Brazilian landowners dismissed Dorothy Stang as a preachy do-gooder and troublemaker from the North; atheist Christopher Hitchens assailed Mother Teresa as a "fanatic, a fundamentalist, and a fraud;"[2] and the Kennedys regarded Martin Luther King, Jr., as naive and sanctimonious.[3] Despite disapproval or opposition, though, our exemplars maintained the courage of their convictions.

We can be misled about exemplars in a few ways. First, we should be careful not to regard them as solitary moral heroes. Poet and activist Daniel Berrigan, SJ, liked to say, "We don't need heroes. We need communities."[4] Social change is accomplished by people working together, Berrigan insisted, not by heroic individuals acting alone. Our exemplars were all deeply engaged in collective action in service of the marginalized. They

---

[1] Dorothy Day, *The Long Loneliness* (New York: Image, 1959), 104.

[2] Christopher Hitchens, "Mommie Dearest," *Slate,* October 2003.

[3] See Marshall Frady, *Martin Luther King, Jr.: A Life* (New York: Penguin, 2002), 78–80, 83, and David J. Garrow, *Bearing the Cross: Martin Luther King, Jr., and the Southern Christian Leadership Conference* (New York: HarperCollins, 1999), 170.

[4] Cited in Rosalie G. Riegle, *Doing Time for Peace* (Nashville, TN: Vanderbilt University Press, 2013), 322.

were able to do what they did because of support from friends, communities, and institutions.

Second, these exemplars did not seek only to live authentically as unique individuals. They didn't think of themselves as choosing their own values or making decisions simply to be true to their own unique selves. Rather than carving out their own autonomous path in the world, they all slowly discovered their true selves as they came to trust more completely in God.

Third, these exemplars should not be taken as one-dimensional figures. If we think of Dorothy Day merely as a holy lady who helped homeless people, we misunderstand what she stood for. This is why she said, "Don't call me a saint, I don't want to be dismissed that easily." Or if we are only familiar with Martin Luther King, Jr.'s "I Have a Dream" speech, we will not know that he had self-doubts, made mistakes, and sometimes failed to accomplish his goals. Unless we are aware of the full range of the difficulties these exemplars had to face, we will not appreciate their strengths and accomplishments. We should thus not put them on a pedestal. They all made mistakes, and they all had weaknesses, blind spots, and moral flaws. Day could be impatient; Stang could be extremely stubborn; and King confessed, "I am a sinner like all God's children."[5]

We should admire exemplars, but in healthy and realistic ways. In a number of places St. Paul makes it clear that Christians are not just to admire Jesus but also to imitate him (1 Thes 1:6; Rom 15:2–3; 1 Cor 11; Eph 5:1–2). Danish philosopher Søren Kierkegaard drew an important distinction between admiration and imitation: "What, then, is the difference between an admirer and an imitator?," he asked. "An imitator is or strives to be what he admires, and an admirer keeps himself personally detached, consciously or unconsciously does not discover that what is admired involves a claim upon him, to be or at least to strive to be what is admired."[6] Kierkegaard criticized the stance of those who admire the greatness of Christ in a way that allows them to hold him at arm's length. *Admiring* in this sense involves keeping a distance from the personal challenge that Christ presents to each of us. No moral exemplar has the status of Christ, of course, but we may still be tempted to admire them from a detached distance.

To imitate is to observe a pattern of behavior and then to try to apply that pattern to one's own action. We can learn from exemplars by imitating them, at least in the sense of putting into practice some of the lessons they learned from their experience. We can reflect on how their values, insights, and virtues might apply to our own lives. As intensely social beings we are

---

[5] King, *Autobiography of Martin Luther King, Jr.*, ed. Clayborne Carson (New York: Warner, 1998), 358–59.

[6] Kierkegaard, *Practice in Christianity in the Essential Kierkegaard*, ed. Edna Hong and Howard Hong (Princeton, NJ: Princeton University Press, 2000), 383–84.

pervasive imitators. Psychologist Michael Tomasello calls children "imitation machines."[7] Instead of constantly having to invent ways to achieve our goals, we grow up observing other people and imitating them (most of the time without thinking about it). This is how we first learn a language and develop social skills and moral character.

Neuroscientists have discovered mirror neurons that equip us to translate behavior that we observe into similar actions of our own. Imitation is not simply replication, which is to copy what someone else has done with perfect fidelity. In genetics, for example, a "replicator" is information that has been copied. Imitation, in contrast, is always selective. When we imitate a pattern of action we have observed, we have to adapt that pattern to our own particular capabilities and circumstances. Successful imitation is flexible, selective, and appropriate. For example, a Little League baseball player will watch David Ortiz swing his bat in a game and then try to swing the same way. The Little Leaguer who is 5'2" and 110 pounds will not swing the bat exactly like the 6'4", 230 pound Ortiz. The All Star has mastered the fundamentals of the baseball swing; he provides the Little Leaguer with a template that can make him a much better batter.

In service, too, we can learn by selectively imitating, but not replicating, the acts and attitudes of exemplars. Selective imitation often has a creative, improvisational character. Consider the case of "Jane," a student volunteering at a soup kitchen. During one of her shifts, she is confronted by a drunk and unruly guest. She might think to herself, "What would Dorothy Day do in this situation?" This question can be helpful if it calls to mind Day's commitment to speaking with respect and kindness to every guest, no matter how troubled or difficult. This reminds Jane to stay calm and speak compassionately to the guest standing in front of her. If he relaxes and regains self-control, everything is fine. But if the guest gets more worked up, Jane has to go a step further and ask herself, "What would Day do *now*?" Most likely she will think, "I have no idea." She has to learn to think on her feet about what action would be most fitting in this particular situation. Good choices rely not only on imitation but also on what philosophers call "practical wisdom." Jane has good will toward this guest, but good will is not enough. She has to decide what to do next. If she isn't sure what to do, one hopes she will get help from more experienced coworkers.

Exemplars can be relevant to our lives in some but not all respects. Attending to the selective nature of imitation can help us avoid thinking that only radicals—people willing to give 100 percent to the most demanding

---

[7] Tomasello, *The Cultural Origins of Human Cognition* (Cambridge, MA: Harvard University Press, 1999), 159.

causes—can perform real service. While all six of our exemplars led "extreme" lives, it is also possible to serve others in less dramatic ways. Service is not all or nothing. We should not think we are all supposed to give up everything and spend the rest of our lives working at a shelter in Calcutta. Some people are called to such a life, but most of us are not. Instead of engaging in the futile attempt to become a very minor version of Mother Teresa or Martin Luther King, Jr., we are called to serve others within the parameters of our particular talents, needs, limits, and opportunities. Service flows from a goodness that is much broader than heroism.

Each of us, in other words, has to "personalize" what we learn from these exemplars. We need to think about how what they did and said might lead us to take a step forward in our life journey. Each of us can take away different insights from these exemplars. A person volunteering in a shelter for battered women might find Dorothy Day to be a relevant exemplar because she tried to help women who were abused. Another who is serving in a community organization that focuses on racial discrimination might find King's words to be most illuminating.

We have most to learn from these exemplars when it comes to the shape of our interior life and our moral character, the cluster of traits, desires, and motivations that shape the tone of our choices and actions. For all their biographical diversity, the exemplars display a remarkable consistency in their abiding appreciation for the virtues of justice and mercy, faith and hope, courage and self-control. Even when they did not live up to these standards on one occasion or another, they continued to recognize their importance. This is true of all the virtues seen in the six models of service presented in Part 2. We become more effective in service if we learn to take care of what has been entrusted to us (stewardship), to be open and generous to guests (hospitality), to be merciful to those who suffer (compassion), to stand up for causes we care about (advocacy), to be loyal to our communities (solidarity), and to speak and act truthfully (witness). We might not need the courage of Oscar Romero, but we all need the courage to take a stand when faced with prejudice, small-mindedness, and indifference to human suffering. We do not all need the compassion of Mother Teresa, but we do need to show compassion toward our friends, neighbors, and colleagues. This is true of all the other virtues as well.

We do not, of course, need larger-than-life figures to teach us these lessons. If we pay attention, we see exemplars of service in our daily lives. Think of a mother who helps her fallen child get up, dust herself off, and move on; or a driver who waits patiently for the elderly lady to climb up the stairs of his bus; or a neighbor who stays out in a blizzard to shovel the snow out of a sick friend's driveway. We all know dedicated parents, selfless teachers, and families who care for severely disabled children or elderly relatives. Such people offer us concrete examples of what it means to lead good lives in the service of one another. The key point is to pay attention to what we see and to act accordingly. In Christian terms, "not everyone who says to me, 'Lord, Lord,' will enter the kingdom of heaven, but only the one who does the will of my Father in heaven" (Mt 7:21).

1

Dorothy Stang, SND

Dorothy Stang (1931–2005) spent over three decades working for social justice and sustainable agriculture in Brazil. She was born in Dayton, Ohio, on July 7, 1931, and raised as the fourth of nine children on a family farm. Her parents worked hard to share their Catholic faith with their children. At the age of seventeen she entered the Congregation of the Sisters of Notre Dame de Namur and she made her profession of final vows in 1956. She was assigned to teach in Catholic elementary schools from 1951 to 1966, first in the Chicago area and then in Glendale, Arizona.

Teaching in Arizona brought her into the lives of Mexican migrant workers and the Navajo people. In 1966, this deeply formative engagement with the marginalized led her to Brazil. She started in the city of Coroatá in the poor state of Maranhão, but she was always willing to go where she was most needed. When the Transamazon Highway opened in 1972, she accompanied people migrating to a remote and inaccessible forest so that they could get land to raise crops and feed their families.

Context

Before going further into her story, we need to note two important features of the Brazilian context within which Stang worked. First, Brazil is marked by great poverty and economic inequality. Economic development has propelled this country into the ranks of middle-income countries, but its rural poor suffer from conditions of deprivation as bad as those found in the poorest countries in Latin America.[1] Brazil is marked by significant inequality. In the 1980s, Brazil had the second highest level of inequality in the world. In 1989, the richest 20 percent of the Brazilian population had 30 times more income than the bottom 20 percent. In 2003, two years before Stang died, 21 percent of the population was living on less than $2 a day.

---

[1] See International Fund for Agricultural Development (IFAD), "Rural Poverty in Brazil," http://www.ifad.org.

By 2004, Brazil had improved slightly to become the tenth most unequal country in the world.[2] Brazil is now the world's sixth largest economy. For a variety of reasons—including economic growth, better welfare services, and the rise of a better skilled work-force—Brazilian society has become more prosperous and poverty is declining.[3] At the same time, more than 8 percent of the population lives on less than $1.25 per day. The north and northeast regions of Brazil (where Stang lived) are much poorer than the south and southeast. On the Gini index, Brazil is the seventeenth most unequal society of the 136 countries measured.[4]

Poverty in Brazil is marked by four factors: rural underdevelopment (particularly in sanitation, education, healthcare, and infrastructure), lack of access to quality education, a regressive tax system (the rich pay lower percentages of their income in taxes than do the poor), and highly concentrated land ownership.[5] The thirty-seven largest Brazilian landowners own more land than the 2.5 million smallest landowners. This concentration of economic power typically translates into legal and political power as well.

Second, Brazil—most notably the Amazon basin—is undergoing massive ecological degradation. The Amazon's 2.6 million square miles of rainforest constitutes slightly more than half of all the rainforests on the planet.[6] It is known as the "lungs of the world" because it produces 20 percent of the planet's oxygen. It also holds 20 percent of the planet's fresh water and 30 percent of its biodiversity (that is, 30 percent of the world's known species). Twenty-five percent of the world's pharmaceutical products come from its plants.

Human activity is rapidly reducing the size of the rainforest. Wild land is being converted to grow soybeans for animal feed, sugarcane for ethanol, and grass to feed cattle. A full quarter of the rainforest has already disappeared. Between May 2000 and August 2005, the Amazon rainforest lost an area of land larger than Greece.[7] Scientists predict that it will be reduced by 40 percent in the next two decades. This destruction will have a very negative effect on global biodiversity, pharmaceutical resources, and global oxygen levels.

---

[2] See World Bank, Brazil Overview, 2012, at http://www.worldbank.org.

[3] World Bank, "Brazil, Argentina and Mexico, Leading the Fight against Inequality," January 25, 2013, http://www.worldbank.org.

[4] Inequality ranked according the Gini index is available at https://www.cia.gov.

[5] See Fabiana Frayssinet, "Brazil: Agribusiness Driving Land Concentration," Inter Press Service News Agency, October 5, 2009.

[6] See "Rainforest Facts," at http://www.rain-tree.com.

[7] http://rainforests.mongabay.com/amazon/amazon_destruction.html.

Competition among groups wanting to exploit the Amazon wilderness has led to an overwhelmingly high level of land theft, illegal logging and mining, government corruption, and death-squad activities. It is important, however, not to blame what is happening to the Amazon exclusively on the predatory behavior of a small group of ruthless landowners bent on getting rich at all costs. Their actions are rewarded by market forces of globalization that make export-driven agribusiness profitable and give large-scale producers a competitive edge over family farms.

In 1964, the first of a series of generals (assisted by the United States ambassador) engineered a coup d'état against a democratically elected government. Generals ruled the country with brutal force until 1985. During this period the state murdered over 450 people and imprisoned, tortured, and exiled thousands more.[8] The generals were supported by authoritarian elites who used harsh and violent methods to repress those they regarded as subversives. In 1979, the Brazilian government passed an unrestricted amnesty law that absolved anyone who committed politically motivated crimes, including torture, murder, and forced disappearances, during the dictatorship. After democracy was reestablished in 1985, powerful ranchers and landowners continued to smear activists like Dorothy Stang as communists and troublemakers.

Another important factor in Stang's context is the set of reforms within the Catholic Church initiated by the Second Vatican Council (1962–65). The Sisters of Notre Dame de Namur sought to be true to the council's vision of the church as the people of God, called to transform the world. The council understood the church as a pilgrim people moving through time as a community charged with the mission of being a sacrament of divine love in the world. To live up to this mission, the council taught, the church must work in solidarity with the marginalized to overcome structures that leave so many people living in subhuman conditions.

Vatican II thus inspired many Latin Americans to support popular grass-roots movements for social justice. Local activists brought people together in base ecclesial communities for prayer, reflection, and action, a movement that continues today. A friend of mine, Fr. Julinao Almeda, is from a little diocese in the State of Espírito Santo (this diocese has forty-two parishes, which is small by Brazilian standards). Each parish is organized into more than one thousand base communities that often play a central role in the lives of their members. The Latin American Bishops Conference (CELAM) at Aparecida described the parish in its "Concluding Document" as "a community of communities" (no. 179).

---

[8] See Archdiocese of São Paulo, *Torture in Brazil: A Shocking Report on the Pervasive Use of Torture by Brazilian Military Governments, 1964–1979,* trans. Jaime Wright (New York: Vintage Books, 1986).

These communities provide a supportive context within which participants reflect on the relevance of the gospel to the particular circumstances
of their lives and communities. They take inspiration from the biblical encouragement to seek the reign of God, care for one another, and put one's
resources at the disposal of the marginalized.

Early Work in Brazil

Dorothy Stang served primarily as an educator. She sought to help people
in poor communities develop their abilities and take charge of their lives.
She saw religious education in particular as transformative. Focused on
more than teaching people to recite parts of the catechism and avoid mortal
sin, she was convinced that the gospel has liberative significance for every
person's life. The message of universal human dignity underscores the right
of every person to have access to the goods necessary for leading a decent
life. This conviction carries important practical implications. Because communities with high rates of illiteracy need schools and competent teachers,
Stang joined other activists in lobbying the government to fund the building of schools. She also encouraged workers to unionize, fought for more
effective and enforceable land reform, and helped sex workers find better
ways to make a living.

Pastoral and political concerns often go hand in hand. One of Stang's
friends observed, "I don't deny that she was a bit of a [Good] Samaritan, but
deep down she was more of a prophet."[9] Her struggle for social justice was
based on her immersion in the lives of ordinary people. She recognized that
effective long-lasting social advocacy has to be based in strong friendships,
mutual understanding, and earned trust forged among those who share a
common life. Stang did not think of herself as the leader of "her" people;
she thought of herself as "part of them."[10]

Stang was immersed in the lives of the people she served. She was not
a commuter for social justice. In the 1970s, she lived in the rural town of
Jacundá. A visitor described the way she lived:

> She was living in a beat-up wooden building belonging to the farm
> workers' union. Two rooms, and the roof leaking like a sieve. Dorothy
> had all her things piled up on a shelf covered with plastic—papers,
> files, boxes of documents, a couple of changes of clothes. And there
> wasn't a morsel of food in the house. I looked in the kitchen and all

---

[9] Bishop Erwin Kräutler, quoted in Binka Le Breton, *The Greatest Gift: The Courageous Life and Martyrdom of Sister Dorothy Stang* (New York: Doubleday, 2007), 106.
[10] Ibid., 161.

I could find was half a dozen cans, the ones you used for storing rice and beans. Well, they were all empty except one, and that had a bare handful of manioc flour.

One of the settlers, Zé Piao, had been killed and we'd gone there to show our support. We arrived there covered in dust, took a shower, hung our hammocks—I remember we had to move them several times on account of the leaking roof—and made some tea. Then Dorothy sent us all to different houses to get something to eat. Simple food—rice and beans, squash and a bit of dried meat. The families shared what little they had. That's solidarity for you.[11]

Stang embodied solidarity with the poor, a commitment made possible by friendship and faith. Her companionship with marginalized people was the basis of her advocacy for their rights and hospitality to strangers. This is how she described her household: "We receive warmly whoever comes and attend to whatever need they bring with them. Sometimes they come from our rural area to sit down at our community table, sometimes we put them up in hammocks so they can stay the night. We stay in their houses, so it's natural that they come to ours."[12] She extended this policy even to people who "gave her trouble." Stang "never rejected anyone," her friend said, "because she always said there was room for everyone, no matter who they were."[13]

In the 1980s, Stang moved to the county of Altamira to work with the impoverished Xingu people. She lived in a mud house in the town of Nazaré. Children there had very little chance to get a basic education, so she poured her energy into lobbying the government to supply the funds needed to build schools and train teachers. She founded the Centro de Nazaré Training Center for teachers. When she arrived, the town had seven schools; by the time she was done, there were twenty-three.[14] She started the first trading post in that town, obtained jobs for people, fought for their land rights, and helped to set up a fruit-processing factory.

Stang was especially dedicated to the well-being of women. She established a women's association to promote family health. Women, her bishop Dom Erwin Kräutler noted, "were considered inferior. And if they were black or Indian . . . she really had compassion for them—she helped them realize their worth."[15] One of her friends said: "She fought for us tooth and

---

[11] In ibid., 95–96.

[12] In ibid., 183.

[13] Ibid., 167.

[14] See Roseanne Murphy, *Martyr of the Amazon: The Life of Sister Dorothy Stang* (Maryknoll, NY: Orbis Books, 2007), 103.

[15] Breton, *The Greatest Gift*, 114.

nail—went on a hunger strike, slept on the sidewalk in Brasília, never gave up. If it hadn't been for her, we'd have nothing. She was always looking out for us. And what she left us was the heritage of knowing how to work together and share things."[16] Stang did not just take over—her compassion led her to participate in a community in which people could work together.

This is not to suggest that Stang was perfect. Like everyone else, she had her flaws and made her share of mistakes. Once she made up her mind about what needed to be done, she could be difficult, forceful, and blunt. Those who admired her thought she was principled or strong willed, but her critics called her stubborn and fanatical in her partisanship. She could be "hard to take," said a friend: "That obstinacy of hers—it was as if hers were the only people who mattered, and everyone was expected to pitch in and help."[17]

Faith is shaped by concrete social circumstances. Stang's spirituality and social context reinforced one another. Her spirituality was shaped by lifelong immersion in the world of the poor, and her social engagement, in turn, deepened her religious commitment. At the core of everything was prayer shaped by the practice of love.

In Brazil, Stang was exposed to the creative springs of liberation theology, the attempt to reflect on faith in light of the experience of the poor. She came to believe that liberation theology helps Christians come to a deeper understanding of their place in the world and the social and political dimensions of the gospel. What is called the see-judge-act method of social action came out of the work of Joseph Cardijn, who worked with young women to form the Young Christian Worker (YCW) movement. He developed the see-judge-act method as a way of engaging people in three realities: the reality of life, human needs, and the struggle to live that is so difficult for the marginalized; the reality of faith and promise of hope in the reign of God; and the reality of action in the world that allows faith to inspire a change in our reality. The see-judge-act method has been useful to many Christian activists in Europe, Latin America, and elsewhere. It has been adapted to help ordinary Christians practice common prayer and reflection about how scripture speaks to their own concrete circumstances.[18] "Seeing" and "judging" together ought to lead us to "act" in concrete ways to better our communities. This approach supported Stang's commitment to cultivate local leadership, strengthen unions, build schools, promote literacy, train

---

[16] Ibid.

[17] Ibid., 168.

[18] See "Structures of Hope in a Fractured World: The Ministry of the International Catholic Youth Movements," in *Ministries in the Church*, ed. Susan A Ross, Diego Irarrázaval, and P. D. Murray, 76–84. *Concilium* 2010/1 (London: SCM Press, 2010).

teachers, and form women's associations. She saw all of these institutions as helping people to become the agents of social change.

The theology of liberation also encouraged prophetic advocacy. Since the 1960s, the Brazilian government had taken steps to promote economic growth in the Amazon basin. It gave incentives for people to migrate from poorer areas of Brazil to the forest by granting ownership of land to settlers who cleared a plot and lived on it for a year and a day. The government granted 250 acre plots of land to settlers who wanted to live within thirty miles of the main highway and 600 acre plots to settlers willing to live in more remote locations. Hoping this program would give small farmers an opportunity to improve their lives, the government built highways, sponsored colonization programs, assigned lower tax rates for income derived from agriculture and pastureland, and offered generous subsidies to businesses willing to invest in the region. In the struggle over land reform, however, the government was generally well intentioned but weak—especially in comparison to wealthy landowners and business interests.

Stang worked with the Brazilian Catholic bishops' Pastoral Land Commission, a body dedicated to land reform and defending the rights of rural workers. She assisted communities of settlers to obtain plots of land and establish farming cooperatives. Powerful people tried to repress this movement with whatever means they could—including violence. Stang responded to this repression by throwing all her energy into securing protection for the settlers. She traveled around gathering documents from various government offices to prove that particular settlers had legal title to their land. She met with journalists to let them know about the landowners' illegal attempts to push settlers off their own property, lobbied federal ministers and other politicians to enforce the law, and informed prosecutors and police officers of illegal activities. Unfortunately, those efforts often went for naught. And when they were successful, her critics became even more adamantly opposed to her work.

The Turn to Creation Spirituality

In 1991, after working in Brazil for twenty-five years, Stang took a well-deserved sabbatical at Holy Names University in Oakland, California. She became immersed in a new theological movement called creation spirituality, a version of "green" theology that stresses the sacramental character of nature and the mystical love of creation.

Creation spirituality enriched her religious vision in a number of ways. First, it helped her come to a more keen appreciation of God as the originator and sustainer of all life and as immanent within nature, including the teeming life of the Amazon. Living in the Amazon had helped her cultivate a deep sense of our embeddedness in the natural world. Creation spirituality, one of Stang's biographers explains, offers a "way of valuing the feminine that brings Western thought in line with indigenous ways of valuing Mother Earth, revisiting biblical concepts of stewardship in terms of conservation rather than domination."[19] A widely viewed photograph shows her wearing a tee-shirt carrying the Portuguese inscription *A Morte da floresta é o fim da nossa vida* (The death of the forest is the end of our life).

This theological awakening helped Stang see that the widely-practiced "slash and burn" agricultural method is unsustainable.[20] Assuming that the forest is a place to be subdued and exploited for their survival, settlers would move to a plot of land, use it up, and then move to another site. Roughly one-third of rainforest destruction in the Amazon has been caused by subsistence farming, so Stang wanted to get the farmers to think about practicing more eco-friendly and sustainable methods of farming.

Second, this period of study reinforced Stang's strong sense of the inter-connection of social justice and ecology. She had experienced firsthand the destructive effects of the assumption that God loves the rich more than the poor and light-skinned more than dark-skinned people. This hierarchical, Eurocentric prejudice made it easy for people to tolerate both the systematic domination of the poor and the exploitation of nature, especially for the benefit of the affluent.

Third, creation spirituality also led Stang to connect social justice and ecology with the inherent dignity of women. Feminist Christian theologians hold that the core of Christian faith affirms that God loves women and men with complete equality and that all are invited to friendship with God. This move was supported by reading scripture with an eye to its use of feminine as well as masculine imagery for God. The Old Testament, for example, speaks of God's caring for Israel like the caring of a mother who gives birth (Dt 32:18; Is 46:3–4), nurses her infant (Num 11:12; Is 49:14–15), and comforts her children (Is 66:12–13). God is likened to a mother who calls, teaches, heals, protects, and feeds her young (Hos 11:1–4). The New Testament also ascribes conventionally feminine roles to the Holy Spirit: life-giving, consoling, comforting, and inspiring (Jn 3:5; 1 Jn 4:7; 5:1). This view allowed Stang to counter the culturally dominant assumption that men are closer than women to God. If God loves men and women equally, feminists point out, then God wills justice to them equally.

Stang knew that it would not be possible to keep the Amazon completely free of all settlement, but when she returned to her community she dedicated

---

[19] Breton, *The Greatest Gift*, 129.
[20] See ibid., 171–72.

herself to work for the equitable and sustainable use of the land and forest. She learned with settlers how to develop small-scale family farms, responsible forest harvesting, and local consumption. She saw that people in small rural communities needed to obtain the knowledge, skills, and other resources that would lead them to a more sustainable way of making their living. She also sought to get the government to enforce existing environmental regulations that would help both settlers and the rainforest.

In 1992, Stang attended the United Nations Conference on Environment and Development in Rio de Janeiro. The Earth Summit helped her appreciate the extent and depth of environmental degradation as a global problem. At the end of the Earth Summit, Boutros Boutros-Ghali, the secretary-general of the United Nations, made a statement that could have been made by Stang herself: "The Spirit of Rio must create a new mode of civic conduct. It is not enough for man to love his neighbor; he must also learn to love his world."[21] Stang exemplified this model of "civic conduct."

After Rio

After the Earth Summit, Stang returned to the Amazon energized about the possibilities for sustainable agriculture and forestry practices. She successfully lobbied the Brazilian government to create preserves in the rainforest where peasants could harvest products (like rubber, nuts, and wood) without burning down the forest. She also worked tirelessly to promote an alternative model of development in which farmers would be grouped around small communities dispersed throughout the rainforest. The model she promoted assigned 20 percent of the land to small farmers and kept 80 percent as forest preserve. Sustainable methods of cultivation allowed farmers to feed their families while preserving the health of the land. Stang had a strong interest in agroforestry, that is, planting crops in the forest rather than on cleared land. To prevent any takeover by big landowners, any farmer who wanted to move out of his settlement could sell his plot only to the local community association.

These activities did nothing to endear Stang to ranchers, wealthy landowners, and commercial farmers, who wanted to expand their vast tracts of undeveloped land. They accused her of violating their property rights, encouraging the landless to invade their property, and even arming peasants and inciting them to violence. None of these claims was true, but that didn't stop the flow of nasty rumors and false accusations.

---

[21] Boutros Boutros-Ghali, "Extracts from Closing UNCED Statements, in an UNCED Summary, Final Meeting and Round Up of Conference," June 14, 1992, UN Document ENV/DEV/RIO/29, 1.

Powerful men did everything they could—including legal maneuvers, intimidation, threats, and outright violence—to drive out settlers and to discourage future settlement. They hired thugs to force settlers from plots of land they had cleared with their own blood, sweat, and tears. Fearing for their lives, some peasants cut their losses and fled. Others refused to give in. Landowners and ranchers were incensed that they could be thwarted by an elderly religious sister that they called "that old woman."

Efforts to intimidate Stang did not work. She did not look for opposition, but she didn't shy away from it either. To protect families from illegal evictions, she alerted government officials to the campaign of violence and called on the police to protect them. She denounced specific illegal loggers and land grabbers by name, and they hated her for it. Stang was committed to staying with the people, no matter what. Her tough single-mindedness was rooted in her deep Christian confidence that God is on the side of the poor. In 2003, she wrote a personal letter that captured something of what she had found out from her life among the poor of Brazil:

> I have learned that faith sustains you. And I have also learned that three things are difficult. 1) as a woman to be taken seriously in the struggle for land reform, 2) to stay faithful to believing that these small groups of poor farmers will prevail in organizing and carrying their own agenda forward, and 3) to have the courage to give your life in the struggle for change.[22]

In 2004, the Pastoral Land Commission listed the names of 160 people marked for assassination in Brazil; forty of them were in the state of Pará where Stang was working. The list gave a price for each target. The second-highest price on the entire list—fifty thousand reais (about twenty-five thousand dollars)—was offered to anyone who would kill Stang.

In response to repeated death threats, Stang's friends urged her to return to the United States once and for all. Now in her early seventies, she could have settled into a comfortable retirement with her religious community. Yet she refused to do so. As she explained in a letter to a friend: "I don't want to flee, nor do I want to abandon the battle of these farmers who live without any protection in the forest. They have the sacrosanct right to aspire to a better life on land where they can live and work with dignity while respecting the environment." In one of the last conversations she had before she was killed, Stang made an impassioned plea to a friend: "Felício, don't ever give up, do you hear me? You have to keep up the fight. You mustn't

---

[22] In Le Breton, *The Greatest Gift*, 189.

give up and you mustn't abandon our people, do you understand? You must keep on fighting because God is with you."[23]

Powerful ranchers in the area of Pará were enraged by Stang's advocacy for peasant farmers and sustainable agricultural methods. In the end, she was murdered because of her work in the Sustainable Development project at Boa Esperança, a village near Anapu, where she lived. A section of the reserve, called Lot 55, was the center of a long and violent struggle between a farmer, Luis Moraes de Brito, and a wealthy rancher named Vitalmiro Bastos de Moura (called Bida).[24] The Institute for Land Reform granted title to a plot of land to Luis, but Bida said that the land was his. The farmer had lived on the land for four years, but Bida had fast-growing grass seed planted on Luis's land, his crops destroyed, and his home burned to the ground.

On February 12, 2005, Stang was on the way to meet local settlers in Anapu to talk about Lot 55 when she was intercepted by two assailants who were looking to cash in on the bounty put on her head by Bida and some friends. They had had enough of this "old woman." The assassins stopped her and asked if she had a weapon. Armed only with the word of God she began to read the beatitudes aloud to the men. They listened for a moment, and then shot her six times and left her body on the road.

The two men who shot Stang were convicted and sentenced to lengthy prison terms. A court also convicted Bida for hiring them. Pará is known for its rich timberlands—but also for its land fraud, corruption, and lawlessness. It is a place where anyone who resists illegal logging and land grabs can be killed with impunity. Since 1985, when the Pastoral Land Commission began compiling records, more than eight hundred rural workers or family members have been killed in Pará. Only three people have ever spent time in prison for these crimes. After a lengthy appeals process in which he tried every legal maneuver possible, on September 19, 2013, Bida was finally convicted for plotting Stang's murder and sentenced to thirty years in prison.

Calling for justice after Bida was initially let off, Bishop Erwin Kräutler summed up the reason why Stand was killed:

Our martyr Dorothy Stang was killed because she believed in a different dream for the Amazon, because she defended sustainable development projects and fought for the 'asentiamento' (settlement) of simple

---

[23] Ibid., 17.
[24] See Michele Murdock, *A Journey of Courage: The Amazing Story of Dorothy Stang* (Cincinnati, OH: Sisters of Notre Dame de Namur, 2009), 109ff.

people in need of farm land to live. She rejected the idea of the infinite growth of ranches that to expand don't accept any contrary voices.[25]

Kräutler is one of three Brazilian bishops who received death threats for denouncing land and environmental crimes and defending rural farmworkers against criminal ranching, logging, and mining interests.

Conclusion

Dorothy Stang represents a form of service that concentrates on compassion and justice for the marginalized. She sought to help people speak from their experience and assume responsibility for their own lives, personally and collectively. She also understood the centrality of stewardship for the land both for its value to human communities and for its own sake as an integral part of God's creation. Christian faith led her to become a servant of the marginalized but also of land, water, plants, and animals. She showed what it means to be a good steward of our resources and of one another.

---

[25] "Sr. Dorothy Stang: Bishops Outraged at Acquittal of Rancher," http://www.archive.xaviermissionaries.org.

2

Dorothy Day

Dorothy Day (1897–1980) is one of the most distinctive twentieth-century exemplars of the Christian ethic of hospitality. Born in Brooklyn in 1897, she grew up in a working-class family and developed a passion for justice early in her life. She always seemed to have a special sensitivity to the plight of people whose lives have not gone well.

As a young woman she saw journalism as a vehicle for promoting justice for workers, immigrants, and the unemployed. She fell in love with another journalist, became pregnant, had an abortion, and the man she loved abandoned her. She then rebounded into another relationship and got married, but that relationship ended in divorce within a year. Day then met Forster Batterham, a botanist, religious skeptic, and anarchist. She fell in love with him, and they entered into a common-law marriage.

Conversion

As a child Day experienced religious longings. She occasionally read the Bible and was intrigued by people who prayed. She was never an active member in any congregation, but from time to time she was drawn to religion. When she became pregnant with Tamar, she experienced a vague desire for a deeper connection to God. Many years later, Day wrote in her diary: "It is joy that brought me to the faith, joy at the birth of my child 35 years ago, and that joy is constantly renewed as I daily receive our Lord at Mass."[1] Always drawn to Catholicism, she began reading Catholic spiritual literature, praying, and going to church. She decided her child would be baptized a Catholic. She did not want her daughter to fall into the same chaos that had troubled her: "I knew that I was not going to have her floundering through many years as I had done, doubting and hesitating,

---

[1] Dorothy Day, *The Duty of Delight: The Diaries of Dorothy Day*, ed. Robert Ellsberg (Milwaukee: Marquette University Press, 2008), 319.

undisciplined and amoral. I felt it was the greatest thing I could do for a child. For myself, I prayed for the gift of faith. I was sure, yet not sure. I postponed the day of decision."[2]

Tamar Teresa was born on March 3, 1926. She was soon baptized. After months of uncertainty, restlessness, and vacillation, Day herself was baptized on December 28, 1926. This was a costly decision, as Batterham disapproved of both religion and marriage as an institution. She continued for years to love her "dearest, sweetest" Forster and hoped that he would eventually change his mind and marry her. He never did.

Atheist friends could not understand Day's conversion to Catholicism. They could not comprehend how someone with her passion for the oppressed could become a Roman Catholic, which they considered to be a staunchly conservative church infected with clericalism and opposed to social justice. She shared their hatred of injustice, hypocrisy, and the exploitation of the poor, but she saw the institutional dimension of the church as a necessary and divinely instituted part of the community of those who seek to follow Christ.

Before her conversion Day had the image of Catholics as willing to go to church and pray for the poor, but then walking past them on the street as if they didn't matter. She came to see that many of these poor were themselves Catholics who found something in the church that helped them.

Day believed that Jesus founded a community and called the apostles, its first bishops, to be its leaders. She was attracted to Catholicism in part because she experienced it as "the church of the immigrants, the church of the poor."[3] The wealth of the church was one of the "stumbling blocks" to her conversion. She eventually came to see the church as a mysterious mixture of holiness and sinfulness. In fact, she wondered if the church's survival of the frailties, ignorance, sins, and crimes of its leaders wasn't actually an indication of its divine institution. Day reminded her readers that Christ warned that the church's greatest enemies would come from within.

The Catholic Worker and Houses of Hospitality

Christian life strengthened rather than weakened Day's commitment to fairness and justice for all. In 1932, she traveled to Washington, DC, to report on the Hunger March for several Catholic magazines. She was deeply moved by the seemingly endless parade of people who had been beaten down by economic hard times but was dismayed that there were no Catholic

---

[2] Dorothy Day, *From Union Square to Rome,* 2nd ed. (Maryknoll, NY: Orbis Books, 2006), 127.

[3] Dorothy Day, *The Long Loneliness* (New York: Image, 1959), 150.

leaders in the march. The next day she went to the National Shrine of the Immaculate Conception and prayed for guidance for "something to do in the social order besides reporting conditions. I wanted to change them, not just report them, but I had lost faith in revolution, I wanted to love my enemy, whether capitalist or communist."[4]

When she returned to Manhattan, Day was introduced to Peter Maurin. Maurin wanted to meet Day because he liked some of her writings and had been encouraged by a friend to speak with her. As soon as they met, they knew they were kindred spirits. Maurin was an itinerant worker who embraced a style of Christianity based on voluntary poverty, manual labor, direct service to the poor, and community living. He became the mentor who helped Day fulfill her desire to "do something in the social order." She gained more notoriety but always insisted that Maurin was her most important teacher. "Without him," she explained, "I would never have been able to find a way of working that would have satisfied my conscience. Peter's arrival changed everything, I finally found a purpose in my life and the teacher I needed."[5] That purpose was to promote Catholic social teachings, peace, and the works of mercy.

Day and Maurin cofounded *The Catholic Worker* newspaper to inform readers about the social mission of the church and its deep connection to the gospel. Day used her skills as a journalist to express Maurin's vision. The first issue of the paper was written to show that the Catholic Church has a social program. Day wrote:

> For those who are sitting on park benches in the warm
>   spring sunlight.
> For those who are huddling in shelters trying to escape
>   the rain.
> For those who are walking the streets in the all but futile
>   search for work.
> For those who think that there is no hope for the future,
>   no recognition of their plight—this little paper is
>   addressed.[6]

Day and Maurin were convinced that effective compassion requires both intelligent analysis and practical action. Maurin posed a rhetorical question: "You know what's wrong with the world? People who act don't think, and people who think, don't act." Day and Maurin built reflection

---

[4] Dorothy Day, "Peter Maurin, 1877–1977," *Catholic Worker,* 1977.

[5] Cited in Robert Coles, *Dorothy Day: A Radical Devotion* (San Francisco: Harper and Row, 1989), 73.

[6] Dorothy Day, "To Our Readers," *Catholic Worker*, May 1933.

into their weekly practice of "clarification of thought," as well as in retreats, workshops, "days of recollection," and spiritual reading.[7]

Recovering the ancient practice of Christian hospitality, Day and Maurin advocated direct, interpersonal care; they disdained the modern assumption that the poor ought to be bureaucratically "managed" by "experts." Christians need to imitate Jesus's direct personal care for the wounded stranger. Because Jesus taught the works of mercy, not the delegation of love to others, each of us must respond directly to the destitute. The Christian sense of hospitality, moreover, can never be satisfied with giving food, drink, and shelter to nameless strangers. Each person must be cared for as a brother or sister in Christ. Indeed, we are to see Christ in our neighbor.

The Catholic Worker ethos of hospitality got started in a simple way. One day some homeless men who had read *The Catholic Worker* decided to see if its editors would live up to what their editorials professed. When they showed up at Day's apartment, she gave them food and a place to stay, and then found an apartment to rent for them. Maurin suggested they provide soup and bread for hungry guests. This first step led to the founding of the first House of Hospitality, a welcoming place not only for food and lodging but for friendship, prayer, reflection, and conversation. The Catholic Worker house on Mott Street in Manhattan was the beginning of a movement that by 1941 included thirty houses across the country. Today there are over one hundred Catholic Worker communities throughout the world.

Catholic Worker communities speak of visitors as guests, not clients. Day took time to listen to impaired guests while "important" people waited their turn. She did not set limits on how long guests could take shelter at a House of Hospitality: "We let them stay forever. . . . They live with us, they die with us, and we give them a Christian burial. We pray for them after they are dead. Once they are taken in, they become members of the family. Or rather they always were members of the family. They are our brothers and sisters in Christ."[8]

Because every person is created in the image of God and thrives in friendship, Day and Maurin wanted to build communities in which members could use their talents and recognize their own dignity. Small communities provide an example of a social order in which no one is shut out or left to die for lack of the basic necessities. Catholic Worker hospitality also addresses spiritual needs. Though it might seem worlds away, Maurin

---

[7] See Mark and Louise Zwick, *The Catholic Worker Movement: Intellectual and Spiritual Origins* (Mahwah, NJ: Paulist Press, 2005), 27.

[8] Quoted in Jim Forest, *All Is Grace: A Biography of Dorothy Day* (Maryknoll, NY: Orbis Books, 2011), 336.

found in the Benedictine monastic tradition an especially helpful guide to the meaning of the Christian life as centered on hospitality, prayer, art, manual labor, and life on the land. The monks understood that a rich interior life is the basis of true hospitality.

Day and Maurin also believed that Jesus made it clear that his followers were not to resort to violence even for the sake of achieving good ends. In the 1930s, Day wrote against the church's support of the fascist Francisco Franco during the civil war in Spain; in the 1940s, convinced that modern warfare cannot be just, she objected to American participation in World War II; in the 1950s, she defied air-raid drills in preparation for nuclear war and rejected the Korean War; in the 1960s and early 1970s, she denounced the war in Vietnam and encouraged young people to refuse military conscription. In 1965, Day was asked by a Catholic pacifist to explain her position. She wrote: "I can write no other than this: unless we use the weapons of the spirit, denying ourselves and taking up our cross and following Jesus, dying with Him and rising with Him, men will go on fighting, and often from the highest motives, believing that they are fighting defensive wars for justice and in self-defense against present or future aggression."[9] She continued her opposition to war of any kind until her death.

Poverty and Possessions

Houses of Hospitality are based on an ideal of voluntary poverty, which Day described as the movement's "most fundamental and necessary plank." She chose to embrace the conditions of the people she served—living in their neighborhood, wearing donated clothing, eating the same food and drinking the same coffee that Houses of Hospitality served to their guests. She did not romanticize deprivation. Here is how she described her neighborhood in the lower East Side of Manhattan: "We live on a waterfront—class war, race war. Mental cases abound, drugged youth haunt our streets and doorstep. Not a week passes when there have not been knives drawn, fists upraised, and the naked face of hate shown and the silence of bitterness and despair shattered by the crash of breaking crockery or glass, a chair overthrown."[10]

Poverty seems like an odd ideal. For one thing, if you want to help people you need possessions. You can't show hospitality if you don't have resources to share with your guests. The poor themselves, moreover, want

⁹ Day, "On Pilgrimage," *Catholic Worker*, July-August 1965.
¹⁰ "Spring Appeal—March/April 1971," *Catholic Worker*, March–April 1971, 2.

to get out of poverty if they can. Idealizing poverty seems to be the prerogative of a few comfortable, middle-class people.

The Christian tradition distinguishes a variety of senses of *poverty*: (1) material poverty refers to not having access to some or all of the goods needed to lead a dignified human life; (2) spiritual poverty is a form of immaturity, worldliness, or excessive material attachments; (3) the religious vow of poverty is a commitment to a way of life centered in a religious community and the imitation of Christ; (4) material simplicity is living with necessities and few if any luxuries, for example, with inexpensive clothing, no expensive vacations, and modest housing; (5) the gospel virtue of being "poor in spirit" is humble dependence on God; and, finally, (6) evangelical poverty is simplicity of life for the sake of discipleship.

Serious deprivation—not only material but also social and other forms— harms people. "In what does poverty consist?" asked Day. "In toilets out of commission in town, in dishwashers who wipe their noses on the dish towels, people who are mental cases."[11] Poverty is nothing to be ashamed of, Day insisted; indeed, the shame belongs to people who have no compassion for those who suffer because of poverty.

The second form of poverty, spiritual impairment, involves a deprivation in our relationship with God, our neighbor, and ourselves. The most obvious manifestation of spiritual poverty is the crass consumerism of people searching for happiness in shopping. But there is a much broader sense in which to be human is to fail to love with all our heart, all our soul, and all our mind (Mt 22:37). What Day said about herself is true of all of us: "I really only love God as much as I love the person I love the least."[12]

The third form of poverty, the religious vow, is admirable when pursued in balanced and healthy ways. It can, for example, help people get beyond their own desires for status or to prove their worth by what they own. This kind of poverty can enable members of a community to feel more connected to one another. Some religious orders define poverty as lack of individual ownership, but others are more demanding in their insistence on living with material simplicity. Priests and sisters who run schools and universities have different needs than those who serve the poor in homeless shelters or refugee camps.

The fourth form of poverty, material simplicity, is an integral part of the lives of some exemplars of service (for example, Dorothy Stang) but not others (for example, Martin Luther King, Jr.). Material simplicity is "doing without" for the sake of diminishing one's wants and sharing in the lot of

---

[11] Day, *The Duty of Delight*, 315.

[12] Day, "On Pilgrimage," *Catholic Worker,* December 1948.

those who are poor. Dorothy Day wrote in her diary about the need to cultivate "the austerity, the detachment, the self-discipline, the interior poverty we so lack. It is our greatest message. To be poor with the poor."[13]

The fifth way of talking about poverty, to be "poor in spirit," is a central part of every truly Christian life. Indeed, it is part of any human life that is led realistically. To be human is to be dependent. We can acquire as many possessions as we want, but they will not take away the essential poverty of the human condition. Any fulfillment granted to us comes not from filling up our emptiness with possessions, but from letting go of things so that we can truly love one another. To be "poor in spirit" is the most liberating, healthy, and life-affirming state one can attain. It is a metaphor for the virtue of humility, a stance of openness to the will of God, a keen sense of our dependence on divine providence, and a freedom from possessiveness that frees us to love our neighbor. This is the spiritual core of Day's commitment to voluntary poverty.

Finally, evangelical poverty embraces material simplicity to pursue a style of life that resonates with that of Jesus. This is the goal of the religious vow in some orders, but some lay Christians also seek it because they want to live a gospel-centered life. Detachment from possessions goes along with stripping ourselves of everything that gets in the way of loving God and our neighbor.

These six categories of poverty can be combined in various ways. The Catholic Worker movement is committed to material simplicity so that its members can become poor in spirit and lead gospel-centered lives. Its members also want to overcome the barrier between rich and poor that is created by money, possessions, comfort, and power. "If we are not among its victims, its reality fades from us," Day observed.[14] Voluntary poverty is both a context for developing freedom from attachment and freedom for love of neighbor: "Once we begin not to worry about what kind of house we are living in, what kind of clothes we are wearing, once we give up the stupid recreation of this world—we have the time, which is priceless, to remember that we are our brother's keeper and that we must . . . build a better world."[15] If we trust God to provide what we truly need, then we can spend our energy on our neighbor. Finally, Day also believed that voluntary poverty is a helpful means for our ongoing growth in Christ—a stripping of the old self to make room for the new self transformed by grace.

---

[13] Day, *The Duty of Delight,* 142–43.

[14] Day, "Poverty and Precarity," *Catholic Worker*, May 1952.

[15] Cited in William Miller, *A Harsh and Dreadful Love* (New York: Liveright, 1973), 97.

The Catholic Church

All of our exemplars share the conviction that we find Christ in the poor. Day credited the Catholic Church—its prayer and worship, teachings and doctrinal authority, spiritual tradition, piety, and devotion to saints—for keeping her on the right path and providing her with nourishment for the journey. Religious practices helped her grow into Christianity by offering sacraments and community, teachings that informed her conscience, exemplars in the lives of the saints, and spiritual structure to her daily life.

Day believed that everything she did in the social order was made possible by grace. She worked hard to live as much as possible in tune with God. She went to weekly confession, attended daily mass, made an examination of conscience every day, took spiritual direction from various priests, recited the Rosary, went on retreats, and at times wrote as well as prayed in the presence of the Eucharist.

Readers today often resonate with Day's spiritual quest, compassion for the outcasts of society, moral integrity, and commitment to social justice. But they are often taken aback, if not chagrined, by the strong Christ-centered nature of her faith and especially by her attachment to the church and sacraments. Day was uncompromising on this point: "Without the sacraments of the church, I certainly do not think that I could go on."[16] As noted above, before her conversion, Day herself was suspicious of Catholicism because of the wealth of the church, the privilege and aloofness of its clergy, and the apparent lack of social conscience in so many ordinary Catholics. She had not known any Catholics who cared about social injustice.

Day's conversion led her to a more complex view of the church. Her ethic of service came to be based on a deep acknowledgment of Jesus Christ as the incarnation of God in the world, the "Word made flesh" (Jn 1:14). Because Jesus was fully human as well as fully divine, Day believed, everything human can be a context within which we find God; we express our love for God in caring for our neighbor. Jesus's passion and death on the cross reveal a God who embraces our frailty, weakness, and suffering.

This view of Christ led Day to see the church as the tangible (if imperfect) body of Christ in the world. Her ethic of hospitality was integrally connected to her loyalty to the community he founded. She did not believe that the latter can be peeled off from the former. Day was not blindly loyal to the church, and she did not ignore its failings and hypocrisy. She liked to quote theologian Romano Guardini, who described the church as the "cross on which Christ is crucified."[17]

---

[16] Day, *The Duty of Delight*, xxi.
[17] Cited in Coles, *Dorothy Day*, 66.

In fact, the more Day came to love the church, the more acutely she was pained by its shortcomings and sins. The church's power, she thought, either attracted the wrong kind of leaders or made them blind and greedy. "I never expected much out of bishops," she confessed in a letter. "I never expected leadership from them. It is the saints that keep appearing all through history who keep things going. What I do expect is the bread of life and down through the ages there is that continuity."[18] Thus to be a Christian, she wrote, is to live in a state of "permanent dissatisfaction with the church."[19] Yet she was not cynical about the institution. She believed that "no matter how corrupt the Church may become, it carries within it the seeds of its own regeneration."[20]

Works of Mercy

Catholic Worker communities engage in corporal works of mercy, like feeding the hungry, giving drink to the thirsty, clothing the naked, and sheltering the homeless, as well as spiritual works of mercy, like counseling the doubtful, bearing wrongs patiently, forgiving offenses, and comforting the afflicted. The last is particularly important. As the old saying goes, hospitality wants to comfort the afflicted, and prophets want to afflict the comfortable. Both are necessary.

Some pious outsiders, moved by a more otherworldly spirituality, accused Day and Maurin of being misguided in their focus on the materially and socially destitute rather than on "sinners," the spiritually impoverished. Day and Maurin modeled Catholic Worker hospitality on the acts and teachings of Jesus, who loved and cared for people regardless of their propriety. Houses of Hospitality adopted the advice of St. Benedict to his monks: "All are to be received as Christ."[21] Like Benedict, Day took Jesus's words literally—"I was a stranger and you took me in" (Mt 25:35). One can be a stranger in many ways—by being poor, or dark skinned, or an immigrant, or unemployed, or addicted to drugs or alcohol, or suffering serious mental illness. Day and Maurin focused on hospitality for those who were rejected because of their "strangeness" to mainstream American society. Houses of Hospitality offer a countercultural vision in which all are welcomed to sit

---

[18] Day, letter to Gordon Zahn, October 29, 1968, cited in *All the Way to Heaven: The Selected Letters of Dorothy Day*, ed. Robert Ellsberg (Milwaukee: Marquette University Press, 2010), 351.

[19] Day, *The Long Loneliness*, 150.

[20] Day, letter to Karl Meyer, August 3, 1971, in Ellsberg, *All the Way to Heaven*, 382.

[21] Rule of Saint Benedict, no. 53.

together, break bread, and talk. The vision is based on a love that invites people to enter into conversation, companionship, and community and resonates with the image of the reign of God as a banquet (Lk 13:20; Mt 22).

Day accented the welcome implied in Jesus's "you took me in." We are not only to receive the stranger as Christ, she said, but even to *see* Christ in the stranger. This happens only when we approach the other with love. The "all" includes those who are different, "weird," or truly strange. Christ, she knew, often comes in the guise of one who is radically other.

Day's Christ-centered spirituality thus did not lead her to downplay the suffering brought by either physical deprivation or psychological distress. Catholic Worker houses do not make hungry people listen to an evangelizing sermon before they get a hot meal. They neither try to reform their guests nor offer a "quick fix" to people with particularly complicated lives. Their commitment to compassion for everyone generates a nonviolent refusal to coerce anyone, even for his or her own good. It also rules out any false spiritualization of material poverty as some kind of blessing for the poor.

In a society obsessed with merit and competition, it is hard to understand why someone ought to extend hospitality to "drunkards and good-for-nothings" and to the "undeserving" as well as the "deserving" poor. Day and Maurin insisted that the scope of Christian hospitality is displayed in Jesus's willingness to eat with anyone. All are welcome to Catholic Worker soup kitchens, medical clinics, and drop-in centers. True hospitality has a generosity and warmth that treats people in a way that is dignified and offers a witness to a love that is not confined to the likeminded and the familiar.

Christian hospitality thus strikes a countercultural note in individualistic societies that encourage welcoming only those who have something to give us in return for what we do for them. Day's willingness to welcome outcasts simply reflected Jesus's injunction, "I was a stranger and you welcomed me."

Friendly critics inside Houses of Hospitality lamented Day's lack of organization. She and Maurin were not planners who looked far into the future. In making big decisions they prayed for guidance from God and went with their hearts. By all accounts Day was not a natural administrator. She did not provide sets of rules or bylaws for Houses of Hospitality. Yet she did learn how to keep the lights on, the newspaper printed, and the doors open.

Conclusion

Day's hospitality was sustainable because it was based on trust in divine providence more than on human ingenuity or modern confidence in the inevitability of progress. Her own faith was built up by her involvement in Christ-centered communities that enabled her to act with hospitality. She was not a social worker who happened to pray and go to mass. "If I have achieved anything in my life," she once said, "it is because I have not been embarrassed to talk about God."[22] Day's spiritual life gave her the strength to persevere in her many commitments—works of mercy, journalism, and civil disobedience. While she was committed to the marginalized before she converted to Christianity, her slow-but-sure assimilation of the Christian message reshaped everything in her life and made her an exemplar of Christian hospitality.

---

[22] Jim Forest, "Servant of God Dorothy Day," http://www.catholicworker.org website.

3

Mother Teresa

Mother Teresa of Calcutta (1910–97) is probably the most widely known twentieth-century exemplar of Christian compassion. Agnes Gonxha Bojaxhiu was born on August 26, 1910, in Skopje, present-day Macedonia. She was raised in a devout Catholic family that regularly took food to the poor and invited the needy to dine in their home. Her father died suddenly when she was seven years old, and her mother managed to raise Agnes and two siblings through frugality, hard work, and prayer. At the age of twelve Agnes told her mother than she wanted to become a missionary. Six years later she joined an Irish missionary order, the Sisters of Loreto.

After studying English with her religious community in Ireland, Agnes traveled to Darjeeling, India, in 1929, to study Bengali and to teach at St. Theresa's School. She professed her first vows to be a sister in 1931 and took as her adopted religious name Sister Mary Teresa, from St. Thérèse of Lisieux, the patron saint of missionaries. Teresa then moved to Calcutta, where she taught at Saint Mary's School for the next twenty years. In 1937 she took her permanent vows to religious life. Six years later she committed herself even more strongly to respond to God's loving will "without reserve" by taking a private vow "to give God anything that he may ask, 'not to refuse him anything.'"[1]

Living in Calcutta had a powerful impact on Teresa. Every Sunday she visited families in the slums: "I cannot help them, because I do not have anything, but I go to give them joy."[2] While she enjoyed teaching, she became increasingly troubled by the suffering of people trapped in backbreaking poverty. She witnessed a horrendous famine in 1942–43 that killed at least two million Bengalis. She was in Calcutta three years later when Hindu-Muslim riots killed five thousand people and left a hundred thousand homeless; August 16, 1946, is still known in India as the day of the Great Calcutta Killings. Violence spread like wildfire to many other locations

---

[1] Mother Teresa, *Come Be My Light* (New York: Image, 2009), 28.

[2] Ibid., 47.

in that country and became a significant factor in the 1947 separation of Muslim Pakistan and Bangladesh from the Republic of India.

In September 1946, Mother Teresa took a train from Calcutta to Darjeeling for her annual eight-day retreat. During this journey she had a powerful religious experience that she later referred to as the "call within my vocation." She felt called to "give up even Loreto where I was very happy and to go out into the streets to serve the poorest of the poor."[3] She left her convent, moved into a pilgrim hostel in a Calcutta slum, and began to wear the simple sandals worn by ordinary people in India.

The Missionaries of Charity

After taking a brief nursing course run by the American Medical Missionaries, Mother Teresa began her work with the unwanted, the unloved, the uncared for. She begged for food and supplies to give to the poor. She began educating small children who did not go to school. She started visiting poor families in their homes, tending to sick children, and caring for destitute people who were very sick or dying on the streets of Calcutta, where life expectancy was around twenty-seven years. Conditions were so bad that carts had to be wheeled around the city every day to pick up the corpses of people who had died overnight.

These activities all flowed from Teresa's commitment to "all those people who feel unwanted, unloved, uncared for throughout society, people that have become a burden to the society and are shunned by everyone."[4] She wrote of the kind of challenge she faced:

> One day, in a heap of rubbish, I found a woman who was half dead. Her body had been bitten by rats and by ants. I took her to a hospital, but they had told me that they didn't want her because they couldn't do anything for her. I protested and said that I wouldn't leave unless they hospitalized her. They had a long meeting and finally granted my request. That woman was saved.[5]

Mother Teresa's work soon inspired some former students to join her. In 1950, the Vatican gave her permission to start a new religious order, the Missionaries of Charity, that would be dedicated to caring for the most neglected

---

[3] Ibid., 39–40.

[4] Mother Teresa, Nobel lecture, December 11, 1979.

[5] Mother Teresa, *One Heart Full of Love* (Ann Arbor, MI: Servant Publications, 1984), 74.

and vulnerable people. These included lepers, street children, former sex workers, refugees, and victims of natural disasters. In addition to the three traditional religious vows—poverty, chastity and obedience—members of her order take a special fourth vow: wholehearted and free service to the poorest of the poor. Unlike Stang and Day, Mother Teresa focused on the immediate needs of the most desperately poor people but did not feel called to promote grassroots organizing, the unionization of workers, or large scale social changes.

Mother Teresa organized her order in a way that would allow Indian sisters to exemplify the teaching of Jesus in specifically Indian terms. The sisters' livelihood comes from the sale of handicraft items and charitable donations. They interpret the vow of poverty as requiring them to live on a very simple diet and refrain completely from tobacco and alcohol. They do not own radios, televisions, or other possessions that most people take for granted. They are normally allowed to own only three saris, one pair of sandals, a plate and metal spoon, one canvas bag, and a few religious items; sisters who live in a cold climate can also own an overcoat.

Mother was a gifted administrator, a woman of deep prayer, and a charismatic leader. After establishing the Missionaries of Charity in Calcutta, she founded other communities elsewhere in India and throughout the world, including Venezuela, Italy, and Tanzania. The sisters' unflinching love of outcasts inspired more young women to join what grew into an international movement. Today the order has grown to include about forty-five hundred sisters present in over five hundred missions in 133 countries. In response to requests, Mother Teresa also founded branches of the Missionaries of Charity for priests and laypeople (co-workers), respectively.

In 1965, Mother Teresa founded Nirmal Hriday (place for the pure of heart), a hospice where the terminally ill could die with dignity. The Missionaries of Charity also run centers for blind or otherwise disabled people, soup kitchens, orphanages, schools for street children, residences for abandoned elderly people, and hospices for the terminally ill. At the very least, Mother Teresa insisted, people should be allowed to die in the presence of love.

The Missionaries of Charity are admired throughout the world by people of many different religious and ethical convictions. Mother Teresa was awarded the Nobel Peace Prize in 1979. She accepted the award "for the glory of God and in the name of the poor,"[6] but she declined the celebratory banquet and requested that the Nobel Committee donate its cost—nearly $200,000—to the poor.

---

[6] "Biography of Mother Teresa of Calcutta (1910–1997)," http://www.vatican.va.

These accolades should not give us the impression that Mother Teresa never made mistakes. Some of those who knew her appreciated her dedication but also criticized some of her decisions and policies. Her fellow sisters sometimes found her to be uncompromising. Her extreme frugality at times led her to deny expensive medicines to sick people who would have probably benefited from them. Her hospices did not always conform to modern healthcare standards of cleanliness and pain management. She has also been criticized for naively accepting donations from shady sources like the corrupt Haitian dictator Jean-Claude "Baby Doc" Duvalier.

Christ-Centered Compassion

Mother Teresa's ethic of service was centered in her Christian belief that every person is precious because we are created in the image of God. She shared this conviction with all of our other exemplars. While we are *created in* the image of God, Jesus *is* the image of God (see Col 1:15) who showed us what it means to serve. To be Christian is to serve Christ in whatever context we live. Mother Teresa described herself: "By blood, I am Albanian. By citizenship, an Indian. By faith, I am a Catholic nun. As to my calling, I belong to the world. As to my heart, I belong entirely to the Heart of Jesus."[7] Humility made her suspicious of ambition and fame. "Don't look for big things," she insisted, "just do small things with great love. . . . The smaller the thing, the greater must be our love."[8]

This great love was developed in the midst of a very difficult spiritual journey. Mother Teresa endured many years of a painful "darkness" caused by a recurring sense of God's absence. This great "dryness" had the effect of heightening her spiritual thirst. Though she often felt abandoned by God, Mother Teresa remained steadfast in her faith and love.

When Mother Teresa died in September 1997, she was given an official state funeral by the government of India. The tomb of this Mother of the Poor was placed in her order's headquarters, and it soon became a pilgrimage site for people inspired by her life, work, and love. Mother's holiness convinced Pope John Paul II to waive the normal five-year waiting period for her beatification (one step before canonization, the official recognition of sanctity). At the beatification ceremony in 2003, the pope called "Blessed Teresa of Calcutta" an "icon of the Good Samaritan" and someone who went everywhere "to serve Christ in the poorest of the poor."[9]

---

[7] Ibid.

[8] Cited in *Come Be My Light*, 34.

[9] Beatification of Blessed Teresa of Calcutta, Homily of His Holiness Pope John Paul II, World Mission Sunday, October 19, 2003.

He praised her consistent willingness to bear witness to the intrinsic value of all human life.

Mother Teresa's piety was centered on the cross as the most powerful revelation of God's love for us. She took Jesus's words on the cross, "I thirst" (Jn 19:28), as pointing to God's urgent longing for each person's heart. Jesus showed how much God wants our friendship. She founded the Missionaries of Charity to "satiate the thirst of Jesus Christ on the Cross for Love and Souls."[10]

Mother Teresa believed that prayer and worship, particularly the Eucharist, are essential for nurturing both love of God and availability to the neighbor. She used to hand out her business card with the following saying:

> The fruit of Silence is Prayer
> The fruit of Prayer is Faith
> The fruit of Faith is Love
> The fruit of Love is Service
> The fruit of Service is Peace.[11]

Mother Teresa did not first find Christ in private prayer and then go out to share Christ with the world. Like Day, she sought and found Christ *in* the world, especially in those who were rejected, disfigured, or troubled. She found Christ in everyone, not just in the "deserving" or "virtuous" poor. Because Jesus is "hidden under the distressing disguise of the poorest of the poor," she believed, those who care for society's "rejects" grow closer to the rejected Christ. This piety led her to see that "in touching the broken bodies of the poor she was touching the body of Christ." She went so far as to say that "we are touching Christ's body in the poor."[12] To love the poor is to love Christ.

If compassion addresses whatever harms human beings, then how we conceive of compassion will be formed by what we think is most significant about human beings. Mother Teresa believed that we are made for love and that the greatest kind of human suffering involves isolation, rejection, or abandonment. The Missionaries of Charity are thus dedicated not only to meeting the physical needs of the "poorest of the poor" but also showing them that they matter. The order is premised on the insight that people can only know that Christ loves them when they experience the love of other people in concrete ways. The purpose of the Missionaries of Charity is

---

[10] *Come Be My Light*, 40.

[11] Cited in Raghu Rai and Navin Chawla, *Faith and Compassion: The Life and Work of Mother Teresa* (Rockport, MA: Element, 1996), 19.

[12] Mother Teresa, *A Gift for God: Prayers and Meditations* (San Francisco: Harper, 1996), 39.

thus: "to carry Christ into the homes and streets of the slums, among the sick, dying, the beggars and the little street children."[13] The sisters do this not by extending abstract good wishes to the poor but by living in close proximity to them and sharing their lives.

Mother Teresa was thus deeply impressed with the evil of social exclusion. Exposure to cultures all over the world led her to believe that "the poverty of the West is so much more difficult to remove [than poverty in India]." She explained in her Nobel lecture:

> When I pick up a person from the street, hungry, I give him a plate of rice, a piece of bread. . . . I have removed that hunger. But a person that is shut out, that feels unwanted, unloved, terrified, the person that has been thrown out from society—that poverty is so hurtable and so much, and I find that very difficult.

This emphasis on social exclusion afflicts more affluent societies as much or perhaps even more than the people of less developed countries.

Ultimately, Mother thought, the greatest human suffering is spiritual. Western societies pride themselves on their material development, but they suffer from spiritual poverty. A few years ago I was with a group of Boston College students in a home for the elderly run by the Missionaries of Charity in Kingston, Jamaica. As I was speaking with the community's mother superior about their work, I noticed on the wall a large map of the world that was dotted with hundreds of small pins. Sister told me that each pin represents one of their communities. I told her that I understood why the Missionaries of Charity would have so many communities in India and Africa but was puzzled that a religious order dedicated to the poorest of the poor would establish houses in a wealthy country like the United States. She pointed out that "there are many forms of poverty."

All of us need physical security, bodily health, and strong social connections, but also salvation and holiness. Mother Teresa's desire to help people grow closer to God, however, did not lead her to ignore ordinary human material and emotional needs. These are complementary rather than competing goals. She thus saw that we do best to reject two opposite extremes: the dualistic assumption that only our spiritual needs count, and the materialistic assumption that only "this-worldly" needs are real. Because all activity in this world has both spiritual and bodily dimensions, compassion has spiritual as well as bodily significance.

We cannot love God without loving our neighbor, but Mother Teresa was convinced that the reverse is also true: we cannot fully love our neighbor

---

[13] Ibid., 43.

without loving God. Because the neighbor is the presence of Christ in our midst, whenever we love the neighbor, we also love Christ—even if we are not aware of doing so and do not profess Christian belief. The love of God is primarily displayed in how we treat our neighbor.

Conclusion

The Missionaries of Charity imposes forms of renunciation on its members that can seem harsh to outsiders. Mother Teresa intended to form communities that are both self-denying and joyful. She was an ascetic—she practiced fasting and other disciplines of self-denial—because she believed that denying herself would purify her love for God and neighbor. She renounced material possessions for the sake of Christ and in order to be available to the destitute. Her order continues to attract people who want to do the same. At one point a journalist who saw Mother Teresa tending to the sores of a leper said to her, "I wouldn't do what you do for a million dollars." She responded, "Neither would I."[14] At the same time, Mother Teresa often spoke gratefully of the joy that blessed her life—the happiness she found in visiting destitute families in the slums of Calcutta, in leading the Missionaries of Charity, and in caring for the dying.

It sounds strange to hear that someone would find joy in the slums. We usually associate joy with weddings, baptisms, and graduations. It was not the slums that gave her joy but the goodness of the people who live in them. Mother Teresa learned to take joy in people wherever they were situated—poor or rich, sick or healthy, young or old, brown or white. Her Christian spirituality and ethic of compassion enabled her to see the dignity of people while also sorrowing at their suffering. To grow in love is to develop a greater capacity for both sadness and joy.

---

[14] Cited in Robert P. Waznak, "On Mother Teresa and Lady Di," *America Magazine*, October 4, 1997.

4

Martin Luther King, Jr.

We now turn to Martin Luther King, Jr. (1929–68) as a paradigm of advocacy. King was born on January 15, 1929, to a middle-class family in Atlanta, Georgia. As a young boy growing up in the racially segregated South, he often felt the pain of racial discrimination. He noticed that while he was enrolled at a school composed entirely of African American students, his white playmate was sent to an all-white school. Young Martin was rudely confronted with the "race problem" when his friend's parents decided their son could no longer play with him simply because they were white, and he was "colored."[1] King knew from a young age that something was deeply wrong with American society.

King majored in sociology at Morehouse College, studied for the ministry at Crozer Theological Seminary, and then received the PhD in theology from Boston University. In 1953, he married Coretta Scott. Toward the end of his doctoral studies they decided that King would follow in the footsteps of his father in the ministry rather than pursue a comfortable academic career in the North. In 1954, he accepted the call to serve the congregation of the Dexter Avenue Baptist Church in Montgomery, Alabama, where his congregation suffered from an entrenched system of racial segregation. He emerged as the leader of the Montgomery Improvement Association (MIA) and rose to become the national leader of the civil rights movement. After the Montgomery campaign he moved to Atlanta to serve as both president of the Southern Christian Leadership Conference (SCLC) and co-pastor, with his father, of the Ebenezer Baptist Church. A library of books has been written on King's work. This chapter focuses on five trademark episodes.

Advocacy in Montgomery

While serving as the new pastor at the Dexter Avenue Baptist Church in 1955, King participated in discussions with other leaders of the black community

---

[1] See Stephen B. Oates, *Let the Trumpet Sound: The Life of Martin Luther King, Jr.* (New York: New American Library, 1982), 8.

to consider ways to challenge Montgomery's racially segregated public transportation system. Union organizer E. D. Nixon was looking for a legal case that would present a court challenge to local Jim Crow laws. On December 1, with Nixon's support, Rosa Parks refused to give her seat on a bus to a white passenger, and she was arrested. Parks was deeply committed to racial justice and was steeped in the principles of civil disobedience. Nixon believed her case would provide the basis for a strong legal challenge to the segregated system. Once Parks was arrested, local organizers began the process that led to a city-wide boycott of the segregated public transportation system.

King was new to the city and not beholden to any of its entrenched interests, so local leaders asked him to lead the newly founded MIA. He agreed to serve. Organizers did not initially aim at the full racial integration of city buses. They only demanded that the bus company hire some black drivers and allow passengers to sit on a first-come, first-served basis. If all the seats were taken, they did not want black passengers in the back half of the bus to be required to give up their seats to white passengers. As modest as it was, this goal was unacceptable to whites who were offended at the prospect of having to stand in the presence of seated black passengers.

Outraged by decades of humiliation and encouraged by their preachers, the black community mobilized a well-organized boycott that brought financial pressure on the city government and some downtown businesses. Many protesters rode in car pools or black-owned cabs instead of buses; some white women drove black domestic workers; and others just walked to work.

Civil rights advocates in Montgomery had been engaged in discussions about how to challenge segregation long before King moved there. This involvement in the church brought him into the movement. Local preachers and other leaders shared a commitment to challenging the system, but they differed over the best strategy for doing so. Some favored taking a juridical path to desegregation, but others pushed the more confrontational approach of a broad-based boycott. After dialogue and analysis, King sided with the latter. His skills at oratory, organization, and negotiation contributed significantly to the final success of the campaign.

King's distinctive contribution to the MIA came from his adaptation of Gandhi's nonviolent principles to the struggle. He convinced organizers to train participants to adopt six convictions: to act nonviolently even when they are afraid; to seek not to defeat the opponent but rather to "win his friendship and understanding"; to direct their effort against "forces of evil" rather than "against persons who happen to be doing the evil"; to be willing to accept suffering without retaliation; to avoid not only physical violence but also "internal violence of spirit"; and to trust that "the universe is on the side of justice."[2] King believed these tenets were based on the gospel and already proven to be socially effective by Gandhi. Boycotters conducted themselves with dignity and remained calm even when harassed, insulted, and taunted by angry whites. Many protestors made significant personal sacrifices that ranged from sore feet to losing their jobs. King was arrested, spat upon, received death threats, and had his home bombed.

The boycott pushed King to leave his "comfort zone" out of concern for people who were oppressed. As leader, his actions came under public scrutiny from the press. For the first time in his life, he knew what it was like to be the object of suspicion and hostility from large numbers of people. The police harassed him, and anonymous enemies threatened not only him but also his wife and young daughter, Yolanda.

Around midnight on January 27, 1956, King, who had just been released from jail, was sitting at home when he received a particularly disturbing phone call. He felt utterly alone, but then he felt drawn to pray for God's help: "I discovered then that religion had to become real to me, and I had to know God for myself." He bent down over his cup of coffee and said:

> "Lord, I'm down here trying to do what is right. I think I'm right. I think the cause that we represent is right. But Lord, I must confess that I'm weak now. I'm faltering. I'm losing my courage. And I can't let the people see me right now because if they see me weak and losing my courage, they will begin to get weak."[3]

King was convinced that God was telling him to stand up for righteousness, justice, and truth. He felt that Jesus was encouraging him to fight on and assuring him that he would always be with him. The spiritual encounter in his kitchen that night left King with a new and much-needed sense of interior peace and confidence. A deeper sense of God's spiritual companionship encouraged him to continue to work as an advocate for racial justice even under highly dangerous conditions.

Personal experience in Montgomery expanded King's empathy for working-class and poor people who had to struggle to pay their bills. Because of his middle-class upbringing and professional status, a commentator notes, King generally "didn't ride buses. He never had to ride buses; he

---

[2] See King, "Pilgrimage to Nonviolence," in *A Testament of Hope: The Essential Writings and Speeches of Martin Luther King, Jr.*, ed. James M. Washington (San Francisco: Harper, 2003), 35–40.

[3] King, *Stride toward Freedom: The Montgomery Story* (New York: Harper, 1958), 134–35.

didn't come from that kind of background. But he cared about people who did . . . for people who were less well-off."[4] King may not have ordinarily used public transportation, but a variety of personal experiences of being discriminated against led him to identify with the plight of people who were treated as, at best, second-class citizens. Ugly expressions of racial hatred added fuel to his burning desire for justice. They led him to want to use his education, his social position as pastor, and his speaking skills as an advocate for racial justice.

In June 1956, a Federal District Court in Alabama ruled that legally mandated racial segregation in Montgomery deprived people of the equal protection guaranteed by the 14th Amendment. The city repealed its ordinance mandating segregation on buses. On December 20, 1956, after 382 days, the boycott ended.

Montgomery bus segregation was emblematic of systematic discrimination not only in public transportation systems throughout the southern states but throughout the country's socioeconomic and political-legal institutions. Anyone who had not absorbed racist ideology would see legally mandated segregation as unjust. The leaders of the movement were able to coordinate the resources of the churches and grassroots organizations to do something about it. Christian convictions gave them the hope and courage needed to persevere despite fierce resistance.

Soon after the Montgomery campaign King became one of the cofounders and the first president of the Southern Christian Leadership Conference. The heart and soul of the SCLC comprised southern black ministers committed to racial justice. Even though it adopted a policy of nonviolence, SCLC's attempt to mobilize large numbers of ordinary people elicited suspicion from conservative blacks, hostility from most southern whites, and lethal violence from white extremists.

The African American community was divided over what to do about pervasive racial injustice. The 1954 *Brown v. Board of Education* decision showed what could be done for the cause of racial justice through legal channels, and some civil rights leaders preferred to pursue racial equality through the courts. Ministers committed to a purely spiritual mission criticized King for meddling in politics, disrupting law and order, and using Christianity to pursue his own selfish political goals. From the left, more militant civil rights groups like the Student Nonviolent Coordinating Committee (SNCC) and the Congress of Racial Equality (CORE) rejected what they took to be King's willingness to allow the white power structure to

---

[4] Shirley Terry, "Martin Luther King's Defining Moment: A Kitchen in Montgomery, Alabama, Past Midnight," http://www.americandetours.com.

dictate the pace, content, and purpose of social change for African Americans. They saw King as a weak advocate pushing a compromise agenda that kept white people comfortable. King had to learn how to advocate in a way that would be pragmatic and effective as well as prophetic and morally ambitious.

From Birmingham to Memphis

A second emblematic moment of advocacy took place in Birmingham, Alabama. In the spring of 1963, local leaders asked King and SCLC to help organize a campaign to desegregate the downtown shopping district. SCLC enlisted black churches and local community organizations to mobilize the people to boycott the stores, publicize their grievances, and conduct mass marches to pursue social change.

After weeks of marching by adults, SCLC decided to put more pressure on the city government by allowing elementary and high school students to participate in the nonviolent marches. Thousands of children began to walk in a calm, orderly manner throughout the business district. The sight of young people marching was disturbing to many observers. Some local civic and religious leaders accused King of using children as pawns in his game of racial politics. He responded that since children and their families are victimized by racial injustice, they have a right to advocate for justice by marching.

Birmingham police responded to this initiative by harassing, intimidating, and jailing protesters of all ages. As in Montgomery, King advocated nonviolent direct action through his inspiring speeches and by participating in the marches himself. Arrested and placed in solitary confinement in the city jail, he was sharply criticized by some local religious leaders for stirring up trouble and advised to stop the campaign and leave Birmingham for good.

In response, King wrote "Letter from a Birmingham Jail" to provide a clear and passionate moral justification for this campaign. He argued that we are all bound together in one human family that transcends racial, ethnic, and political borders, and that "injustice anywhere is a threat to justice everywhere."[5] He insisted that one cannot claim to be Christian and then passively stand on the sidelines and tolerate pervasive racial oppression. Talk of Christian love without concrete action is mere sentimentality. People who benefit from an unjust social system and do not try to change it, King argued, are guilty of moral complicity. The law of the land must be judged

---

[5] *A Testament of Hope*, 290.

according to the higher standards of the moral law. This also goes for the churches. As he was fond of pointing out in his sermons, "eleven o'clock on Sunday morning . . . is the most segregated hour of America."[6]

Public Safety Commissioner "Bull" Connor ordered his men to escalate their use of force to suppress the marches. The result was mayhem. Television stations broadcasted scenes of graphic police brutality around the country and the world. They showed shocking images of young children being blasted by water from high-pressure hoses and chased through downtown streets by policemen and snarling German shepherds. The mass media helped ordinary Americans see the brutality of racial hatred with their own eyes. The city council was incapable of doing anything, and local business owners came under more and more pressure to come to terms with movement leaders. After intense negotiations with SCLC, they agreed to desegregate their stores.

A third important moment in King's work as an advocate is seen in the famous March on Washington in August 1963. SCLC and a number of other important civil rights groups organized a large-scale popular protest in the nation's capital to dramatize the need for racial justice and to pressure the federal government to pass civil rights legislation, especially regarding school segregation and employment discrimination. Many observers worried that the march might degenerate into a riot, but the organizers made sure that the entire event proceeded nonviolently.

An impressive array of major civil rights leaders addressed about a quarter of a million people gathered in front of the Lincoln Memorial. King's famous "I Have a Dream" speech creatively blended biblical prophetic justice with American ideals of fairness and equality of opportunity. He provided an attractive moral vision of a harmonious American society based on fairness and racial equality. The march was considered a great success. Though President Kennedy was assassinated three months later, the march helped President Johnson accomplish the passage of the Civil Rights Act of 1964.

A fourth moment in King's work as an advocate took place on April 4, 1967, at the Riverside Church in Manhattan, where he delivered a powerful speech that strongly condemned the US government's pursuit of the war in Vietnam. After the 1965 campaign in Selma, Alabama, King focused on mobilizing a broad coalition of minorities and liberal activists to use newly won civil rights to promote substantive socioeconomic justice. He criticized the American effort in the war in Vietnam for consuming the nation's economic surplus, exploiting young African American males, and destroying the poor people of a distant country. Up to 1967, King felt

---

[6] Ibid., 101, 107–8, 270.

torn between his pragmatic commitment to advancing civil rights and his increasing sense of the injustice of the war. By April of that year, though, he had come to realize that "a time comes when silence is betrayal," as the Clergy and Laity Concerned about Vietnam had stated.

King's landmark speech, entitled "A Time to Break Silence," described the US government as "the greatest purveyor of violence in the world today" and boldly denounced American intervention as a twentieth-century version of colonialism.[7] Desiring to "give a voice to the voiceless in Vietnam,"[8] King maintained that compassion requires Americans to look at the war from the point of view of ordinary Vietnamese people. King's formative experience with the disenfranchised of his own African American community led him to empathize with the beleaguered ordinary citizens of Vietnam. He pointed out that they were the ones, more than anyone else, whose lives were being taken, villages leveled, fields burned, and way of life destroyed. While poor people in both countries suffer, the rich in both countries prosper. Why, he asked, should poor American draftees die alongside poor Vietnamese soldiers to protect the privileges of rich Vietnamese?

King came to see that the civil rights movement and the antiwar effort both have their roots in compassion and justice. Those who advocate for civil rights are only being consistent in working to end the war. He urged his listeners to commit themselves to getting the US government to end the bombing of North Vietnam, to declare a ceasefire and begin peace negotiations, to curtail any other military buildup in Southeast Asia, and to set a date for the exit of US and all other foreign troops from Vietnam. He also encouraged potential draftees to engage in conscientious objection.

Dorothy Day probably appreciated King's speech, but it received strong negative reaction from others. Many of his civil rights colleagues, influential members of the press, and the Johnson administration were outraged. King publicly contradicted the president and other powerful political figures who, up to that point, had been his strongest allies. Opponents accused King of disloyalty, political naiveté, meddling in foreign policy, and playing into the hands of communists. He was even accused of being a traitor to his country.

King, though, was convinced that opposition to the war was a natural extension of his commitment to nonviolence. Consistency required him to denounce the violence of war as well as the violence of poverty. His public advocacy thus expanded from an initial focus on ending racial discrimination and domestic civil rights to a wider campaign against economic inequality, social injustice, and militarism. King knew that advocacy for peace would cost him access to the corridors of power and influence on policymakers in civil rights matters.

---

[7] Ibid., 233.
[8] Ibid., 238.

Instead of trying to control the future of Vietnam, King argued that we ought to concentrate on reducing the glaring inequality between rich and poor in our own country. "A nation that continues year after year to spend more money on military defense than on programs of social uplift," he insisted, "is approaching spiritual death."[9] An honest look at how our society distributes jobs, income, and wealth, he believed, cannot help but recognize that poverty afflicts whites as well as blacks and reflects the injustice of our larger socio-economic and political-legal institutions. The suffering of poor people can be reduced only if these structures are transformed. Individual acts of charity are not enough: "True compassion is more than flinging a coin to a beggar. . . . It comes to see that an edifice which produces beggars needs restructuring."[10]

A fifth exemplary moment of King's advocacy comes from a speech he gave the night before he was assassinated. On April 3, 1968, he addressed striking sanitation workers in Memphis who were demanding more just wages and working conditions. What has come to be known as his "I See the Promised Land" speech encouraged workers and their allies to remain firm in their demand for equal pay and other forms of economic justice.[11] We must, King said, be willing to assume responsibility for one another.

Reflecting on the parable of the Good Samaritan, he asked his audience to imagine the Levite asking himself, "If I stop to help this man, what will happen to me?" In contrast, King suggested, we can imagine the Good Samaritan coming by, and, reversing the question, asking himself: "If I do not stop to help this man, what will happen to him?" King then suggested that his listeners apply this story to their own situation in Memphis. "The question is not, 'If I stop to help this man in need, what will happen to me?' The question is, 'If I do not stop to help the sanitation workers, what will happen to them?'"[12] Stopping to help did not mean only individual caregiving in the manner of Mother Teresa, but also changing unjust social and economic institutions. To this end, he urged his listeners to promote black economic empowerment in their own communities by patronizing black financial institutions, insurance companies, and other businesses.

King as Advocate

King's advocacy has to be placed in the context of Christianity that was often interpreted in the South (and elsewhere) in ways that effectively told the oppressed to be submissive, obedient, and politically passive. Heaven—"a

---

[9] Ibid., 241.
[10] Ibid.
[11] Ibid., 279–86.
[12] Ibid., 284–85.

future good over yonder"—awaits those who accept their allotted place in this life. King pushed for a complete rejection of this ideology. His social activism was rooted in a Christian vision of every human person as created in the image of God and called to live with dignity as a full and active agent within a "beloved community." Far from blessing the status quo, he understood that Christianity carries radical social demands. Christians must be on the side of the disenfranchised and underprivileged. King went so far as to describe the civil rights movement as a struggle to redeem the soul of America.

Rather than the bastion of order and otherworldly tranquility, the church is called to the prophetic task of denouncing injustice and "rocking the boat" for the sake of justice. Any church that is vitally engaged in the life of its congregants has to be on the side of the living God, who is working to promote a forgiven, healed, and reconciled society grounded in justice and equal rights.

In recent years, King's legacy has been interpreted in ways that downplay his commitment to achieving deep structural socioeconomic change in the United States—to change not only racial attitudes but also racist institutions like courts and businesses.

Unfortunately, King's role as an iconic public figure has come at the expense of his message. His message has been domesticated and reduced to endorsement of a noncontroversial "service." Doing so ignores his prophetic insistence on justice, equality, and equal opportunity. King's image has been crafted to mute determination to build African American self-determination and collective agency. As one observer puts it, "The celebration of the iconic King encourages rituals and rhetoric without righteousness, and expressions of concern and good will without the pursuit of justice and the actualization of the beloved community."[13]

The King Holiday and Service Act of 1994 encourages individual acts of charity and righteousness rather than collective action in the pursuit of justice. President Clinton noted how the passage of this bill led individuals to set aside a "day of service" to engage in activities like renovating schools, donating blood, and organizing food drives "to make their contribution to Dr. King's legacy of service."[14] This stylized public image of King honors his nonviolence but not his civil disobedience, his compassion but not his prophetic advocacy, and his stirring oratory but not his drive to mobilize the disenfranchised to demand social justice.

It is important to note that King's advocacy was not that of a solitary moral hero who singlehandedly achieved the civil rights victories of the

---

[13] Ibid., 256.
[14] Ibid., 253.

1950s and 1960s. His success was based on the work of countless numbers of collaborators and supporters. Indeed, civil rights activist Ella Baker went so far as to say that "the movement made Martin rather than Martin making the movement."[15]

Speeches accomplish nothing by themselves. Prophetic oratory can move people deeply, but they must be followed by organization, energy, and concrete action. King was able to galvanize people because of preparatory work already done by thousands of people at local levels in parishes and grassroots organizations. He learned a great deal from civil rights forbears (for example, A. Philip Randolph and Bayard Rustin), worked in collaboration with other talented leaders (for example, James Lawson and Ralph Abernathy), and had the invaluable help of his own assistants (for example, John Lewis and Andrew Young), who knew how to write grants, lobby politicians, raise funds, recruit volunteers and staff members, organize meetings, and draft practical plans of action. Unfortunately, the SCLC was at times significantly limited by insufficient collaboration. Other civil rights organizations at times accused it of undermining local organizations, leadership, and initiatives by grabbing the limelight and treating King as a messianic figure.

King had his share of setbacks, missteps, and failures. Some of these were organizational and strategic. Some community organizers criticized King for being a dreamer who failed to do the nitty-gritty work of constructing a powerful, disciplined, stable organization with strong connections to local communities. This weakness appeared in different ways in the disappointments of Albany, Georgia; St. Augustine, Florida; and Chicago, Illinois.

Some of King's mistakes came from personal weaknesses. He could act with great courage in the face of daunting challenges, and he could calm traumatized congregations. Yet as a student he developed the habit of copying the work of other authors without proper attribution. As an adult he did not always treat women well. His behavior reflected the sexism, patriarchal privilege, and the sexual double standard seen in many quarters of American society at that time. Activists from SNCC sharply criticized the dominance of male preachers within the SCLC and their hierarchical exercise of power within the organization. Michael Eric Dyson reminds us that "King's views on women were shaped by ideas and practices common in the thirties, forties, and fifties, when the religious, academic or social subcultures that nurtured King rarely challenged traditional gender roles

---

[15] Ella Baker interview by John Britton, June 19, 1968, Washington, DC, tape 203, transcript, Civil Rights Documentation Project, Manuscript Division, Moorland-Springarn Research Center, Howard University, Washington, DC, 41, 44.

and values that enhanced men's lives while curtailing the social [and religious] possibilities of women."[16] Figures can be exemplary in one domain of life while failing to be so in others. We can learn from King, and even be inspired by him, while acknowledging the complexity of his character and its reflection of his own context.

Conclusion

King constitutes an exemplar of advocacy on behalf of people oppressed by racial discrimination, economic injustice, and violence. He was great, says historian Manning Marable, because he "personified [his people's] own best hopes, their desire for human equality, their love of God, [and] their will to resist."[17] He spoke up for people who had been unable to speak on their own behalf, but also participated in a collective effort to enable millions of African Americans to express their own frustrations and aspirations in public, nonviolent, and collective ways.

---

[16] Michael Eric Dyson, *I May Not Get There with You: The True Martin Luther King, Jr.* (New York: Touchstone Books, 2000), 198.

[17] Marable, "King's Last Years, 1963–1968: From Civil Rights to Social Transformation," in *Fulfill the Dream: A Tribute to Dr. Martin Luther King, Jr.*, ed. Howard Richards and Cassie Schwerner (Richmond, IN: Earlham College, 1988), 20.

5

Oscar Romero

A dramatic exemplar of Christian solidarity with the poor is found in Oscar Romero, the archbishop of San Salvador from 1977 to 1980. Solidarity refers to support for a cause based on identification with a community or ideal. Romero discovered the meaning of solidarity through growing close to people who had been the victims of economic injustice and state terror. He made enemies among those who resented both his public denunciation of human rights abuses and his insistence on transformation of the economic, political, legal, and military institutions of El Salvador. He was assassinated March 24, 1980.

Romero's Context

In the 1970s and 1980s, El Salvador had the highest levels of inequality in Central America. The average daily wage of both poor urban workers and landless campesinos was about US$2.80, well below what a wage earner would need to obtain the necessary "basic basket" of subsistence goods at that time.

In the late 1970s, a growing insurgent movement triggered harsh and violent repression by the military of anyone who wanted to change the status quo. The countryside became more and more dangerous. Soldiers and armed militia detained, tortured, and "disappeared" students, journalists, and labor organizers. People migrated to the capital, San Salvador, for greater security. Because of a severe shortage of housing, many displaced people were forced to settle in either tenements in the center or shantytowns on the periphery of the city. They often went without adequate food, running water, electricity, sanitation, and healthcare. By 1980, 643,000 of the capital's 858,00 residents inhabited slum housing.[1] The wealthy, meanwhile, lived in large houses protected by armed guards, German shepherds, and razor wire.

---

[1] See El Salvador, Country Studies of the Library of Congress, at http://countrystudies .us/el-salvador/34.htm.

At this time economic and social elites controlled the state, organized fraudulent presidential elections (notably in 1972 and 1977), and directed military and paramilitary forces to repress popular movements by kidnapping, torture, rape, and murder. In 1978, government forces killed 687 citizens; in 1979, the number rose to 1,796.[2] The increase in violence and severe deprivation in El Salvador bred popular unrest. Associations of teachers, laborers, campesinos, students, and religious believers began to demand their rights more and more insistently. They wanted access to due process, freedom of the press, and fair elections, among other rights. They also insisted on ending police and military repression.

Romero's Transformation

Oscar Romero was born in 1917 in the small Salvadoran town of Ciudad Barrios in the province of San Miguel. After completing his theological education and ordination to the priesthood, he served for twenty-two years as a parish priest in the diocese of San Miguel.

As a pastor, Romero was known for being conscientious, self-disciplined, and kind to people of all social classes. He was attentive to the material as well as the spiritual needs of his parishioners. As Salvadoran activist and attorney Rubén Zamora explains, "He gave shelter to drunken people on the street and asked the wealthy for money, which he would redistribute to the hungry." At the same time he did not pay much attention to—or at least say anything public about—the rampant economic injustice that was crushing the people of his country. Early in his work as a priest, Zamora said, Romero had "only an 'external' relationship to poverty."[3]

In 1970, Romero was appointed auxiliary bishop of the archdiocese of San Salvador, where he served under the leadership of the more progressive Archbishop Luis Chavez y Gonzales. Chavez had been a participant in Vatican II and had a strong commitment to the church's mission of social justice. He had the diplomatic and pastoral skills to be able to support peasant cooperatives while also maintaining cordial relationships with government officials and members of the economic oligarchy. As the situation in El Salvador became more polarized, this balancing act would become untenable.

In December 1975, Romero became the bishop of the diocese of Santiago de Maria. There he came into more direct contact with people

---

[2] See William Stanley, *The Protection Racket State: Elite Politics, Military Extortion, and Civil War in El Salvador* (Philadelphia: Temple University Press, 1996), 1–2, 222.

[3] Rubén Zamora, "The Empowering Spirit of Archbishop Romero: A Personal Testimony," http://kellogg.nd.edu/romero.

subjected to dehumanizing conditions. Every harvest season thousands of migrant workers came to his diocese to labor on coffee plantations. They toiled long hours doing backbreaking labor, survived on meager amounts of food, and often had to sleep on the ground. When Romero saw what some of these laborers were going through, he invited them to take up residency in his seminary buildings.

In addition to the exploitation of workers, Romero saw firsthand what the military did to those whom it considered to be subversive or even sympathetic to subversives. In July 1975, National Guard troops entered the hamlet of Tres Calles. Guardsmen went from house to house looking for people who had earlier engaged in an action that blocked the national highway to protest the rise in prices of basic staples. The troops did not find the demonstrators, but they shot six of their relatives to death and then mutilated their bodies.[4]

When Romero learned of the massacre, he went to the village to console the families of the victims. This was one of many such attacks conducted by the Salvadoran military on civilians, but it was the first whose bloody results he encountered personally. Shaken and angered by the horror, he condemned the murders in his funeral homily. He went personally to the local superior of the National Guard to denounce the violence and wrote a private letter of protest to the president of the Republic, but he did not denounce the murders in any public way.

A series of personal encounters led Romero to begin to understand the root causes of so much violence. Personal contact led Romero to raise questions about Salvadoran institutions. He came to realize that the problem was a matter not only of the sins and vices of individuals, but of systematic and structural forms of injustice. Seeing the institutional roots of poverty also led him to ask religious questions. Romero began to wonder, Zamora explains, "how the owners of the coffee *fincas* [plantations]—Christian families who would go to church in Sundays and partake of the Eucharist—could treat their workers in such a manner."[5] Rather than challenging the abusive exercise of power, traditional priests all too often focused on the next life and allowed their powerful parishioners full autonomy in the "temporal realm." Extended contact with poor people led Romero to begin to identify with their plight. He came to see Salvadoran society from their point of view—the beginning of his preferential option for the poor. Solidarity with the poor convinced him that charity is no substitute for social justice.

---

[4] See James R. Brockman, *Romero: A Life* (Maryknoll, NY: Orbis Books, 1998), 54.

[5] Zamora, "The Empowering Spirit of Archbishop Romero."

On February 23, 1977, Romero was installed as the fourth archbishop of San Salvador. Rumors at the time suggested that Salvadoran elites approved his appointment because they considered him a safe choice to replace his more liberal predecessor. As a matter of fact, some members of the oligarchy objected to his selection because he had already spoken publicly about the rights of the poor.

Though holding an exalted position, the archbishop signaled his commitment to live humbly right away. Rather than taking up residence in the archbishop's mansion, he chose to live in a small room behind the chapel of a hospital that provided medical care to people suffering from cancer. The sisters who worked there eventually convinced him to move into a small house they had built for him on the hospital grounds.

Less than a month after Romero was installed as archbishop, on March 12, 1977, a death squad ambushed and killed his good friend Rutilio Grande, SJ, along with his two traveling companions, fifteen-year-old Nelson Rutilio Lemus and seventy-two-year-old Manual Solorzano.[6] Grande had been an advocate of grassroots efforts to promote social justice, as well as an outspoken critic of the government's violent repression of popular organizations. He facilitated the formation of base Christian communities of campesinos who wanted to engage in reflection, prayer, and conversation to understand of the connection between their Christian faith and their own dignity, human rights, and social responsibility.

We get a taste of Grande's passion for justice from a sermon he gave after the government expelled Colombian priest Mario Bernal Londono from El Salvador:

> I am fully aware that very soon the Bible and the Gospels will not be allowed to cross the border. All that will reach us will be the covers, since all the pages are subversive—against sin, it is said. So that if Jesus crosses the border at Chalatenango, they will not allow him to enter. They would accuse him, the man-God . . . of being an agitator, of being a Jewish foreigner, who confuses the people with exotic and foreign ideas, anti-democratic ideas, and i.e., against the minorities. Ideas against God, because this is a clan of Cain's. Brothers, they would undoubtedly crucify him again. And they have said so.[7]

---

[6] See Thomas M. Kelly, *When the Gospel Grows Feet: Rutilio Grande, SJ, and the Church of El Salvador* (Collegeville, MN: Michael Glazier, 2013).

[7] Cited in "Report on the Situation of Human Rights in El Salvador, Chapter II: Right to Life," Organization of American States' Inter-American Commission on Human Rights (translated from Spanish), Case 2338, November 17, 1978.

As we have seen, Romero had been slowly moving toward greater engagement with the suffering of the poor even before he had become archbishop. The shock of Grande's assassination jolted him into acknowledging the severity of the crisis in his country. For a long time Romero had assumed a kind of individualistic virtue ethic according to which the situation of the poor would improve if only members of the Salvadoran elite deepened their personal faith and charity. Grande's murder jolted Romero into a more realistic and prophetic way of viewing Salvadoran society, the church, and his own role as archbishop. He made a decision to shift the direction of his life: "When I looked at Rutilio lying there dead I thought, 'If they have killed him for doing what he did, then I too have to walk the same path.'"[8]

Solidarity with Christ implies real, concrete solidarity with the poor in whom Christ is present. The Sunday after Rutilio and his companions were murdered, the archbishop decided there would only be one mass in the entire archdiocese. Many people were confused, and some of his brother bishops were angry, but the mass at the Cathedral was attended by thousands of people and over one hundred priests. It made a strong statement: the church is one people, one body of Christ, united in its grief, anger, and desire for justice and peace.

Romero's transformation was not, in a strict sense, a conversion, at least if taken to mean a decisive movement from unbelief to belief or from membership in one religious community to another. His commitment to become more truly aware of "the world of the poor" led to a powerful spiritual, moral, and social self-understanding. It entailed a more "horizontal" spiritual path in which he found God's presence in the poor. "It is the poor who tell us what the world is, and what the church's service to the world should be."[9] This movement carried important implications for the church. One story gives a glimpse of his new openness. At one point he came upon a group of campesinos involved in a deep conversation about how a passage from the Gospel of John bears on their own community. After a time they noticed that the archbishop's "eyes were 'brimming with tears.'" When they asked him what was the matter, he said, "I thought I knew the Gospel, but I'm learning to read it another way."[10]

---

[8] Cited in Michael J. Campbell-Johnston, SJ, "Martyrdom and Resurrection in Latin America Today: Archbishop Oscar Romero," in *Truth and Memory: The Church and Human Rights in El Salvador and Guatemala*, ed. Michael A. Hayes and David Tombs (Herefordshire, UK: Gracewing Publishing, 2001), 48.

[9] Archbishop Oscar Romero, *Voice of the Voiceless* (Maryknoll, NY: Orbis Books, 1985), 69, 179.

[10] Maria Lopez Vigil, *Monseñor Romero: Memories in Mosaic* (Maryknoll, NY: Orbis Books, 2013), 192.

Justice

Romero moved from being a giver of charity to a vocal advocate for justice. He came to see that without a complementary commitment to social justice, the virtues of faith, hope, and charity can be reduced to individualistic, otherworldly piety that looks the other way when confronted with structural evil.

Christian service is often associated with a stance of political and social neutrality that stands above partisanship. "It is very easy to be servants of the word," Romero noted, "without disturbing the world."[11] The "spiritualized word" does not bother anyone because it does not enter into real life, especially not those forced to live on the margins of society. As he came closer to seeing himself as one of the poor, he tried to see all of Salvadoran society—not just its religion but also its political system, economic practices, and security apparatus—from "below," from the point of view of those oppressed by them. One cannot effectively and honestly proclaim the good news in El Salvador, he saw, without also denouncing systematic oppression. Christian service requires not impartiality but rather special attention to those who suffer the most.

Solidarity with the poor does not reject wealthy people. Romero always insisted that justice aims at the common good of all society, not just the good of the poor. But the preferential option for the poor suggests that we build up the common good by giving attention to the weakest and most vulnerable sectors of society. If we are physically ill, we administer medicine to the part of our body that most needs our attention. The whole body benefits when the sick part is healed. If a whole society is suffering, similarly, we ought to focus on the part whose suffering is the greatest. Doing so promotes the good of society overall as well as the good of the part that is hurting the most. To those who are privileged, of course, this shift of priorities can seem like rejection.

The option for the poor is not an endorsement of class warfare. As Romero explained in a homily:

> When we say "for the poor," we do not take sides with one social class. What we do is invite all social classes, rich and poor without distinction, to take seriously the cause of the poor as though it were their own. The cause of the poor is the cause of Jesus Christ— "whatever you did to one of these poor ones: the neglected, the blind, the lame, the deaf, the mute, you did to me."[12]

---

[11] Romero, Homily, December 10, 1977, in *The Violence of Love*, ed. James R. Brockman, SJ (Maryknoll, NY: Orbis Books, 2004), 18.

[12] Homily, September 9, 1979, in Brockman, *The Violence of Love,* 162–63.

Openness to the poor led Romero to concrete friendships—what he called an "apostolate of companionship."[13] His main goal was to listen. He patiently welcomed hundreds of campesinos who traveled from all over the country to bear witness to the violence that was being inflicted on them. They told the archbishop about the disease and malnutrition of their children and the abduction, torture, and murder of their neighbors, coworkers, and family members. Their witness deepened his solidarity.

Romero's transformation was dramatic, but it did not happen as a kind of "road to Damascus" event. It was a slow and painful process that he never considered completed. Solidarity with the poor led him to delay or give up fulfilling obligations that often occupy bishops—fundraising, construction projects, promoting vocations, maintaining good relations with powerful donors, and the like. Romero's critics said he was wasting his time hanging out in the slums, but it was here that his friends lived, and it is here that the church is incarnated in the poor. He showed courage in dealing with the misunderstanding of his friends as well as the hostility of his opponents. He had to face new challenges and severe trials. Love of those who suffer, of course, itself brings suffering.

Evolving priorities led Romero to new friendships and unexpected joy, but also led some old friends to feel abandoned or judged.

Persecution

In a radio address shortly after the murder of another priest, Rafael Palacios, Romero shocked many listeners with the following observation: "It would be sad, if in a country where murder is being committed so horribly, we were not to find priests also among the victims. They are the testimony of a Church that is incarnated in the problems of its people."[14] In response to the increasingly violent persecution of pastoral agents, Romero made this shocking announcement on the radio:

> "I am glad, brothers and sisters, that our church is persecuted precisely for its preferential option for the poor and for trying to become incarnate in the interest of the poor and for saying to all the people, to rulers, to the rich and powerful: unless you become poor, unless you have a concern for the poverty of our people as though they were your own family, you will not be able to save society."[15]

---

[13] Romero, *Voice of the Voiceless*, 155.

[14] Homily, June 21, 1979, cited in Scott Wright, *Oscar Romero and the Communion of Saints* (Maryknoll, NY: Orbis Books, 2010), 97.

[15] Homily, July 15, 1979, cited in Michael Campbell-Johnson, "Be a Patriot: Kill a Priest," *The Tablet*, November 25, 1989.

Romero was persecuted not only for vigorously defending the poor, but also for insisting that members of the Salvadoran elite could be truly Christian only if they entered into solidarity with the poor. This suggested, outrageously to some listeners, that the marginalized have an intrinsic dignity that is equal to that of the upper class. This message offended people who were raised with the assumption that they were superior to the poor. Salvadoran elites assumed that Catholicism legitimated their power, privilege, and right to rule. Their piety assured them that God made some people poor to attain salvation by exercising the virtues of humility and obedience and other people rich so that they could gain salvation by exercising charity and prudence.

One can see why Salvadoran elites felt betrayed by Romero. He was trying to turn everything upside down. Instead of the upper class leading an obedient lower class, Romero proposed that all people have a right to a say in how their communities are structured. Whereas, modern charity for the poor assumes paternalism, solidarity with the poor insists on partnership and shared responsibility.

Romero's opponents accused him of being a communist, but he was in fact just applying standard Catholic social teachings to the context of his own country. He spelled out what they needed to do: allow workers to unionize, repeal unjust laws, grant amnesty to the unjustly imprisoned, stop abusing human rights, account for the disappeared, and allow exiles to return to the country.[16] Romero thought of himself as inviting members of the elite to renew their relationship to Christ by exercising compassion for the marginalized and working as their advocates.

Passionate love for the poor emboldened Romero to undertake the role of being a voice for the voiceless through preaching, radio broadcasts, pastoral letters, and lobbying government authorities. He publicly condemned the use of kidnapping, torture, and murder by agents of the state and their right-wing conspirators. He denounced structural injustice embedded in El Salvador's biased judiciary, corrupt electoral politics, and oppressive economic system. He also condemned guerrillas for their atrocities, particularly their assassination of right-wing political figures.

Romero did not just condemn violations of human rights. He also offered a positive vision of Salvadoran society marked by justice and peace. Because poor people are moral agents in their own right, they must be given an opportunity to advance through hard work. To this end he advocated land reform and broad-based citizen participation in the political process.

---

[16] Brockman, *The Violence of Love*, 76–77.

Though temperamentally cautious, Romero did not allow anxiety, fear, or social rejection to change his course. He learned that solidarity with the poor necessarily involves vulnerability. During the last year of his life he was subjected to a stream of death threats. Friends asked him to get bodyguards, but he refused special protection as long as ordinary people had to fear for their lives. To be one with people, he said, is to be vulnerable the way they are vulnerable and to suffer what they suffer.

Romero refused to back down, be silent, or run away. His enemies, like those of Dorothy Stang and Martin Luther King, Jr., accused him of imprudence, arrogance, and self-righteousness. They did not see that the source of his courage was his faith in a God of redemptive suffering who "so loved the world that he gave his only Son" (Jn 3:16). Romero's courage was rooted in his solidarity with the poor and faith in Christ.

Powerful members of the Salvadoran oligarchy used every means at their disposal to isolate, silence, and discredit him. They subjected him to a relentless campaign of persecution. The Salvadoran right had influential allies within the church. The papal nuncio of El Salvador and some cardinals in the Vatican made Pope John Paul II uneasy with Romero's performance in El Salvador. They regarded him as a dupe of the communists, if not outright sympathetic to them.

In early May 1979, the archbishop traveled to Rome to see the pope. He was put off a number of times and had to exert great personal effort to obtain a personal audience. After waiting many days, Romero did get to speak with him on May 7. The pope was unhappy with the lack of unity among the bishops of El Salvador. After hearing Romero's concerns, John Paul II advised him to be both courageous and prudent. Romero was disappointed over how much the pope had been influenced by negative reports of his pastoral activities, but he was pleased at their open and frank discussion.[17] He left Rome knowing that some influential church officials were lobbying the pope to have him replaced.

A second, more supportive meeting with John Paul II took place in January 1980, just three months before Romero was assassinated. The pope greeted the archbishop warmly and cautioned him for the sake of the church not to be too identified with the political left. Romero shared the pope's concern that the church not get coopted by either political side. The archbishop expressed gratitude for the strength and insight that he received from the pope's social teachings. At the conclusion of the meeting he felt confirmed and strengthened: "The pope said that he agreed with everything

---

[17] Oscar Romero, *A Shepherd's Diary*, trans. Irene B. Hodgson (Cincinnati, OH: St. Anthony Messenger Press, 1986), 215.

I was saying and, at the end, he gave me a very fraternal embrace and told me that he prayed every day for El Salvador."[18]

On March 24, 1980, an assassin shot Romero in the heart while he was celebrating mass in the chapel of Divine Providence Hospital. John Paul II publicly acknowledged Romero as a victim of persecution of the church by the political right in El Salvador. On a visit to that country in March 1983, and against the advice of local trip organizers, the pope insisted on praying at Romero's tomb. Later that same day he used the occasion of an open-air mass before 750,000 Salvadorans to describe Romero as a faithful servant of the church who sought to end violence and reestablish peace in that war-torn country. The pope described Romero as a "servant of God" and insisted that no ideological point of view should be allowed to deny his sacrifice for the people of El Salvador. In an interview on his flight to Brazil on May 9, 2007, Pope Benedict XVI, in response to a question about the possibility of Romero's beatification, said that the archbishop was "certainly an important witness of the faith." More recently, Pope Francis has officially categorized him as a martyr and authorized his canonization.

Conclusion

For all his humility, Romero continues to be a towering figure in Salvadoran culture. Believers travel to pray at his tomb in the cathedral, and his image is given a place of prominence in parish churches, painted on murals in public spaces, and pinned to the walls of modest homes in rural hamlets throughout the country. Roughly half the population supports him, but the rest still consider him to have been too "political," a "loose canon," or a naive tool of the communists who got in over his head.

The Catholic Church, though, recognizes Romero as an exemplar of Christian solidarity with the poor. This is a role he was brought into by circumstances not of his own choosing. As a young priest he wanted to be holy but neither a prophet nor a martyr. Powerful face-to-face encounters and the development of deep bonds with poor communities led to a profound expansion of his social concern and commitment to social justice. He shifted from a position of clerical social neutrality to viewing every reality—politics and the economy, church and state—from the point of view of those who are most vulnerable, abused, and excluded from power. This change of heart and mind energized his relentless advocacy for social transformation of the major institutions of Salvadoran society. Romero

---

[18] Ibid., 467.

became a beacon of hope for people on the margins who felt abandoned by everyone else. Though it cost him his life, his support and solidarity have been life giving to millions, not only in El Salvador but throughout Latin America and beyond.

6

Pierre Claverie, OP

A recent exemplar of a witness is found in Pierre Claverie (1938–96), the late bishop of Oran, Algeria, whose narrow, parochial understanding of Eurocentric Christian faith grew into devotion to a loving God who seeks to be engaged with people everywhere. Claverie challenges the prejudice of Christians against Muslims that has become widespread in the North Atlantic societies in our day. The Muslim became, for him, the privileged place for meeting God in the world. Claverie's life showed what the inner unity of all six forms of service—stewardship, hospitality, compassion, advocacy, solidarity, and witness—looks like in one particular cultural setting. Claverie believed the church in Algeria was called to service in the form of Christian-Muslim dialogue, cooperation, and friendship.

Context

Algeria occupies the vast space in North Africa that borders Morocco, Libya, and Mali. Four times the size of France, it is the tenth largest country in the world. Arab conquest in the seventh century led to the virtual elimination of Christianity in this region. Christianity was reintroduced by French colonization in the nineteenth century. Colonial law prohibited missionaries from proselytizing, but it did allow Christians to engage in charitable works like teaching and nursing. Missionaries established schools, infirmaries, and libraries, and they trained staff to run these institutions; they also worked in various kinds of humanitarian efforts like disaster relief.

After a bitter civil war that lasted from 1956 to 1962, Algeria gained its independence from France. Most Christians in Algeria were foreigners, and after the war they resettled in Europe. The population of Christians dropped precipitously from around a million in the early 1960s to under fifty thousand in the late 1980s. Fewer than 2 percent of its current inhabitants are baptized.

By late 1991, the military had taken control of the government. In 1992, the Algerian regime abruptly canceled a general election that it feared would give victory to the opposition party, the Islamic Salvation Front (ISF). When the government banned the ISF and arrested some of its leaders, radical Islamicists took up arms and attacked the government and its supporters. The military retaliated. Human rights groups denounced the military for kidnapping and torture. When the French government supported the ruling regime, jihadists began targeting French and other European citizens. In the mid-1990s, the Armed Islamic Group (GIA) engaged in the indiscriminate killing of civilians, including massacres of entire communities. Violence escalated, and between 1992 and 1998 more than 100,000 people were killed.

Islamistic insurgents killed foreigners to drive out European interests that they thought were propping up an illegitimate government. Strongly associated with colonial and neocolonial enterprises, the church became a special target. Between 1993 and 1996, nineteen priests and nuns were murdered, including seven Trappist monks from the monastery of Notre Dame d'Atlas.

Like Romero, Claverie was repeatedly threatened. Friends asked him to leave the country, but he refused because he was convinced that he had a mission to work in Algeria as a witness to Christian-Muslim solidarity. He was strongly convinced that he had a duty to accompany the Algerian people and to testify to the possibility of friendship between Christian and Muslim Algerians. On August 2, 1996, he and his driver, Mohammed Bouchikhi, were killed by a bomb placed by terrorists at the entrance to his residence.

Claverie's Dual Transformation

Claverie was assassinated at the age of fifty-eight. Born into a French-speaking community of fourth generation settlers (known as *pied-noirs*) in Algeria on May 8, 1938, Claverie came from a warm and loving but not particularly religious family. His Catholic identity was strengthened by his participation in a local Boy Scout troop run by Dominican friars, the congregation he would later join.

Claverie's conscience was awakened during his time as an undergraduate student at the University of Grenoble in France (1957–58), where he went to study math, physics, and chemistry. As Algerian insurgents were fighting against the colonial French government for their independence, French citizens were caught up in an intense debate over the legitimacy of colonialism, the war, and the practice of torture (which the French used extensively in Algeria). While he initially defended the goal of preserving a French Algeria, debates with his friends gradually led him to change his mind.

These debates led Claverie to recognize how little his Franco-centric view took seriously the Algerian people's hopes and desires for their own country. He came to see that the whole colonial system was supported by a subculture, a social order, and an ideology that made it easy to keep within the confines of a culturally homogenous community. A cultural wall kept from view the fact that Europeans had the power to "monopolize three-quarters of Algeria's wealth" and deprive the Arab majority of "their place in the sun."[1]

Growing up, Claverie had neither Arab friends nor Arab classmates. Later, writing about his family, he explained, "We were not racists, only indifferent, ignoring the majority of the people of the country." He later acknowledged, "I was able to live for twenty years in what I now call the 'colonial bubble' without even seeing the others." He had regarded the millions of Arabs surrounding him as merely the landscape or decor of his life. Despite its ostensibly universal message, the church did not challenge this self-enclosed mindset. Though hearing countless talks and sermons on the love of neighbor, Claverie did not recall any acknowledgment of the fact that the "Arabs were also my neighbors."[2]

Claverie's political and social awakening coincided with a spiritual deepening. A decisive moment came on May 12, 1958, as he and some friends were walking on a student pilgrimage in the mountains. The beauty of his surroundings inspired him to see as never before that religion means a lot more than rules and rituals. He came to a sudden appreciation of the importance of a living and personal faith, a faith that is "more present" and "more alive" than what most conventionally religious churchgoers recognize. This eye-opening religious experience led him to want to give faith a much more important role in his life. He wrote to his parents to tell them that he felt called to the priesthood, a decision, he explained, that would enable him to spend his life doing something truly worthwhile. In the priesthood, he wrote, "[I would be able] to give myself entirely to something that I feel is the most beautiful thing in the world; it is to wear myself out for something that would be worth the effort for others as well as for myself."[3]

These two aspects of Claverie's transformation—social and religious—reinforced one another. His Boy Scout troop had been guided by Dominicans, so he decided to apply to join their community. He hoped religious life would give him an opportunity to play some role in taking down the walls separating Europeans from Arabs and Christians from Muslims.

---

[1] Jean-Jacques Pérennès, *A Life Poured Out: Pierre Claverie of Algeria*, trans. Phyllis Jestice and Matthew Sherry (Maryknoll, NY: Orbis Books, 2007), 46.

[2] Ibid., 9–10.

[3] Ibid., 25, 27.

Apostolate of Friendship

Joining the Dominicans in 1958, Claverie went through his early formation process, took vows, and then studied theology at the famous school of
theology at Le Saulchoir, France. While his primary focus was theology, he
also began to learn Arabic and to read the Qur'an. In 1965, he completed
his course of theology and was ordained a priest.

Claverie decided to pursue his ministry in Algeria. When he returned,
his country was independent and most French descendants had left. The
remaining Catholics were a smaller minority than ever. He was sent to
Algiers to head the Diocesan Center for Studies of Language and Pastoral
Care (Les Glycines). This position gave him an opportunity to build a less
narrow-minded Christian approach to Algerian culture than the colonial
mentality would allow. The center was dedicated to promoting "theological
reflection that attempts to integrate the experience of encounter with others
[and] to listen to the Word that God speaks to us here in Algeria and to live
by it."[4] Claverie's approach to theological reflection resonates with aspects
of what we have seen in Stang and Romero.

Back in his own country after years of study abroad, Claverie threw
himself into what he called the adventure of rediscovering the world into
which he had been born but never really embraced. He needed to learn
how to serve both church and society as a leader of a small Christian minority in the midst of millions of Muslim and Arab Algerians. Traditional
Christian missionaries assumed that their task was to save souls by getting
people baptized. As a young priest, Claverie had been enormously taken
with the Sacred Heart sisters who taught him Arabic in Lebanon. "There
is no proselytizing in their attitude," he pointed out, "but rather love and
a truly disinterested service to the people to whom they have been sent."
He adopted this same attitude in his service to Algerians. To this end, he
wanted not just to immerse himself in Algerian culture, but also, he said,
to "Algerianize" himself.[5]

The core of Claverie's rebirth centered on a vision of inclusive solidarity:
"Discovering the Other," he wrote, "listening to the Other, letting oneself
be shaped by the Other, does not mean losing one's identity or rejecting
one's values; it means conceiving of a 'humanity in the plural,' without
exclusion."[6] Three key commitments marked Claverie's service: to meet
others in face-to-face encounters, to pay attention and listen honestly to
what they have to say, and to live in accord with what these encounters
led him to understand. Encounter, attentiveness, and integrity all generate

---

[4] Ibid., 81.
[5] Ibid., 64, 67.
[6] Ibid., 258–59.

a respect for the truth and appreciation for the goodness of humanity in all its personal, social, and religious diversity. Christians can best witness to the inclusivity and universality of divine love, Claverie held, through concrete acts of service, especially by offering hospitality in ways that build relationships and facilitate mutually respectful dialogue with others. This was a courageous set of goals in a context in which opponents demonized one another.

Claverie was known for his attitude of availability. Friends said that when anyone came to visit him, he always acted as if he had nothing else to do but speak with them. Instead of focusing on problems internal to the church, he much preferred to face outward and to "go out to meet others."[7] This drive to meet and talk with others is only truly Christian when it comes from love. For this reason, Claverie thought, it must be respectful and not coercive while also truthful. It must neither ignore the wrongs done in the past by Christians to Muslims nor give up important Christian convictions in order to be accepted by Muslims.

After being ordained a bishop in 1981 and assigned to the diocese, Claverie continued to develop strong friendships with Arabs. While a much-in-demand speaker at academic conferences, he was more interested in building friendships with particular Muslims than in analyzing theories about Christian-Muslim relations.

A stance of dialogic engagement enabled Claverie to act as witness to a number of different constituencies. To the French, he testified to the value of Arab cultures and Islamic religion. He visited France and French-speaking Catholic centers to give talks, attend meetings, and participate in conferences to testify to the concerns of Algerians. To Arabs, Claverie became a witness to the decency and humanity of Christians. Devoted to bridging the gap, he was convinced that we can only witness the truth of the other if we get out of our own closed mindsets and insular social circles and allow others to speak for themselves.

Dialogue is a means of understanding the self as well as the other: "I discover myself in confronting realities outside myself." We are shaken out of own normal way of viewing things when we are confronted by realities that we don't choose and that we don't control. This is not a matter of just reading books or attending lectures, but of immersing oneself in the struggles of flesh and blood people. Claverie did not build friendship with Algerians to convert them to Christianity. He did so out of a deep conviction that grace works in and through concrete human relationships: "friendship comes from God and leads to God."[8] These friendships often began among

---

[7] Ibid., 131.
[8] Ibid., 210, viii.

people who worked together on practical problems faced by poor neighborhoods. He established and ran libraries for students, rehabilitation facilities for people with disabilities, and homes for the aged. Such pragmatic activities provide "platforms of encounter" that can establish a baseline of respect and trust: "When you feel you are all human beings, you can come closer to one another."[9]

Experience taught Claverie that Christians need to learn how to be friends with Muslims in a way that incorporates four conditions: (1) respect for the other person; (2) humility that acknowledges that we don't know everything and that we have something to learn from the other; (3) a commitment to examine our history, culture, and tradition more objectively and honestly; and (4) a willingness to state the full truth of what we believe and not to offer half-truths for the sake of cordiality or consensus building.

Claverie did not believe in dialogue because he was a relativist, but rather because dialogue is the path to truth that we all benefit from walking: "Dialogue is a work to which we must return without pause: it alone lets us disarm the fanaticism, both our own and that of the other."[10] Dialogue need take place neither on neutral territory nor on our own turf. As the process of de-colonization led the Christian community in Algeria to get smaller and smaller, Claverie saw that the church must go out into Algerian society and show the values that Christians and Muslims hold in common. While he endorsed the tolerance, respect for human rights, and procedural fairness advocated by liberal democracies, he also understood Christians and Muslims could be bound together as partners in civil society.

Because Christian missionaries were less needed for education and social services, Claverie came to the church in Algeria simply to be close to the people, especially the poorest Algerians. He believed that in this context the "spirit of the gospel"[11] lies in the formation of friendships with Algerians, showing that the God of Jesus Christ can inspire respectful love rather than a desire to dominate the other.

Witness to Interreligious Solidarity

While in these ways Claverie tried to serve the poorest of Algerians, he also insisted that the church is not a humanitarian agency, but rather a community of Christians called to witness to the unconditional love of

---

[9]   John L. Allen, "Interview with Dominican Fr. Jean-Jacques Pérennès," *National Catholic Reporter*, October 22, 2007.

[10]   Ibid.

[11]   *A Life Poured Out*, 101.

God. He displayed a complex mix of traits; he was prayerful and practical, incremental and prophetic, patient and passionate. His work for peace in polarized circumstances was fraught with social, political, and religious difficulties. Deeply grateful for all that he had received from living as a guest in the house of Islam, the bishop was considered a friend by many Muslims.

Claverie's daily experience of the goodness of ordinary Muslims convinced him of the deeply problematic nature of two extreme but popular positions: Western Islamophobia and Islamic Jihadism. The former leads Christians to lump all Muslims into the same category as fundamentalist extremists. The latter targets all Europeans as neocolonial imperialists. The best of both traditions envision the Almighty as merciful, just, and peaceful.

Commitment to his friends, the process of dialogue, and long-term peace led Claverie to hold out hope for reconciliation. A year before he died he wrote: "Reconciliation is not a simple affair. It comes at a high price. It can also involve, as it did for Jesus, being torn apart between irreconcilable opposites. An Islamist and a *kafir* (infidel) cannot be reconciled. So, then, what's the choice? Well, Jesus does not choose. He says, in effect, 'I love you all,' and he dies."[12]

Disturbed by the rising tide of violence, Claverie felt compelled to publically denounce terror in editorials and media interviews. Toward the end of his life his friends urged him to be quiet or even leave Algeria until things settled down. He responded: "I cannot remain silent. What I can do is be a witness to the truth." He knew he was in danger, but he said, "I cannot abandon Algeria to the Islamists."[13]

In 1994, his friends Brother Henri and Sister Paule-Hélène were helping students in a poor neighborhood of Algiers when they were shot. Their assassinations made Claverie's vulnerability even more obvious, but he refused to give up his mission. In a sermon right after their deaths, Claverie said: "I have struggled for dialogue and friendship between people, cultures and religions. All that probably earns me death, but I am ready to accept that risk."[14] He took reasonable precautions and did not want to be a martyr. Yet he insisted on staying in Algeria to show that Christians can be in solidarity with Muslims.

Three more points are worth making. First, his most important form of witness was the way he lived his life. According to one of his friends, a religious sister from Beirut, "Pierre's importance lay in who he was, and not so

---

[12] Interview of October 26, 2007.

[13] *A Life Poured Out*, 238.

[14] Timothy Radcliffe, OP, "The Promise of Life," February 25, 1998, http://www.dominicans.ca.

much in what he said. It was enough to just look at him." His commitment resonates with Dorothy Day's conviction that the best witness to Christ is presented by those engaged in the concrete practice of love: "[We] hoped in our hearts that our ideals were being expressed in the way we behaved with one another, and with the people we served."[15]

Second, it obviously took enormous courage for Claverie to persevere in this path. It would have been much safer simply to keep at a reserved distance as a minority other in a vast Muslim society. Many Christians are tempted either to believe that the otherness of Islam makes dialogue pointless or to reduce Islam to just another version of monotheism and therefore just a kind of Christianity without the incarnation. Claverie always insisted on respect for the irreducible element of otherness in Islam.

Third, Claverie was a man of community. It is important not to think of him as a moral hero who operated on his own. He was not only a bishop, the "shepherd" of a diocese, but, before that, a Dominican priest formed by his tradition's commitment to a way of life structured by prayer, worship, and study. He was sustained by fellowship with priests, fellow bishops, lay coworkers, and many fellow Algerians, both Muslim and Christian. Fellowship made it possible for Claverie to offer his life for the sake of interreligious solidarity.

Conclusion

Pierre Claverie is an exemplar of what it means to serve others by acting as a witness to the truth affirmed in Christian faith. He testified to divine love in many ways. He sought to get out of the cultural "bubble" of his upbringing and into the world of Arabs and Muslims. He did so through civic engagement, platforms of encounter, and fraternal collaboration with Muslim friends.

In acting as a witness to faith as a small religious minority holding no political or economic power, he performed a service to the church. He helped Christians see that the gospel has nothing to do with holding people of other faiths in contempt. Indeed, he showed that Christians can find God in Muslims. His life testified to the possibility of developing a form of Christianity purified of colonial and neocolonial religious superiority and one that emphasizes instead the common roots of all of the children of Abraham. He showed how cultural initiatives and concrete projects of service can unite Christians and Muslims in mutual esteem, collaboration, and social justice.

---

[15]   Robert Coles, *Lives of Moral Leadership* (New York: Random House, 2000), 145.

In showing the possibility of friendship among people with different religious convictions, Claverie served God by caring for both the church and the world. He trusted that God could and would overcome all the obstacles human beings put in the way of peace:

> When you send forth your spirit, they are created;
> and you renew the face of the ground. (Ps 104:30)

Pierre Claverie's life bore witness to God's love for all of humanity.

Part 2

Models

A model is a symbolic or conceptual representation of some reality that allows us to understand some of its key features. Models can be practically useful when they identify patterns of meaning that are at least implicitly present in our lived experience. The set of models developed in the next six chapters account for six distinctive ways in which we serve one another. Models can help us reflect on our strengths and weaknesses, insights and oversights, achievements and shortcomings. They can help us see where we might be prone to "specialize" in one or two ways of serving but ignore others, for example, to act compassionately and to offer hospitality to visitors, but to shy away from advocacy or solidarity. These models point to the virtues we might cultivate in ourselves if we want to grow in our capacity to care for others.

Each of the following six chapters examines a particular model of service: stewardship, hospitality, compassion, advocacy, solidarity, and witness. The treatment of each model considers five topics: the biblical roots of a particular model of service, theological reflection on a relevant theme, a particular virtue that supports that way of serving, ways in which people grow in that kind of service, and the temptations that typically face people who serve this way.

It is particularly important to make a few points about three critically important topics: the use of the Bible, theological reflection, and the nature of virtue.

The Use of the Bible

The Bible sheds light on the Christian meaning of service. As the word of God, the Bible is the central norm for how we ought to lead our lives. As the author of the Letter to the Hebrews puts it, "The word of God is living and active, sharper than any two-edged sword" (4:12).

Christians regard the Bible as the church's book. It is a sacred record of how God inspired the people of Israel and then the early followers of Jesus to form communities of faith. Just as they had to discover the will of God in their particular contexts, so do we. Jesus showed the disciples what it means to make the love of the Father the center of everything—their actions and attitudes, the life of their communities and their interpretations of scripture and the course of history. The risen Christ shared his Spirit with the disciples to build communities—the church—whose actions would testify to the love of God.

We can only interpret these teachings appropriately if we are formed in communities sustained by his Spirit of Christ. As Martin Luther King, Jr., put it, the church is "a great fellowship of love that provides light and bread for lonely travelers at midnight."[1] Christians are to apply what Jesus taught in ways that are informed by the Spirit that leads them to begin to have the "mind of Christ" (1 Cor 2:16). This approach highlights our responsibility not only to pay attention to what God inspired people to do in the *past*, but also to where the Spirit may be leading us *now* and in the *future*.

Faith calls us to an ongoing relationship with God, not just to repeat traditional formulas and go through the motions in church without thinking about what we are saying or doing. Biblical texts can provide the *form* within which we can expect God to speak to us today. If, for example, we wonder how God is challenging us to deal with a difficult friend or family member, the Bible suggests that whatever we do ought to take the form of patience, humility, and love. The concrete way this form is expressed in our actions—what we say or do—depends on what is appropriate given our particular circumstances. The Bible tells us about the form or shape that Christian service will take, but it does not necessarily dictate specific instructions.

Sound decision making is not just a matter of consulting one's conscience and leaving it at that; friends, community, and conversation play key roles. As Christians, we seek to make decisions that reflect the love of God and love of neighbor. Jesus of Nazareth is *the* icon of such love. Exemplars show us what form Christian service took in their circumstances. But each of us has to figure out what shape it might take in our own particular contexts.

Christians seek to interpret the Bible in ways that are relevant to their lives and communities. We approach particular texts with two broad goals in mind. We want to be (1) faithful to the truth that the text proclaims and, at the same time, (2) open and honest about the truth as it becomes available to us from nonscriptural and nontheological sources like the sciences, literature, and ordinary human experience. Our interpretation of the Bible,

---

[1] Martin Luther King, Jr., *Strength to Love* (Cleveland: William Collins and Word Publishing, 1963), 62.

in short, must be at once "historical, communal, and developmental"—we seek wisdom in a process that is ongoing, challenging, and cumulative.[2]

The Bible offers a rich set of resources for reflecting on service. It speaks in many different ways and to many different kinds of issues, but it converges on some key themes. It offers a "vision of life in society before God" that is intended to shape the way of life of a community in all its dimensions. We see in the broad span of biblical history a growing apprehension of God's love for human beings. God calls us to form communities of love and justice, and to give special attention to the least of our brothers and sisters. The touchstone of whether we are acting in accord with this vision is our treatment of the marginal.[3]

Biblical texts are historically situated expressions of divine revelation, God's self-communication to human beings. This self-communication always takes place in particular cultural contexts and uses the medium of particular human languages and concrete symbols. The Bible speaks metaphorically of God as warrior, potter, shepherd, and king because these images had evocative power in Ancient Near Eastern contexts. Living in the third millennium after Christ, however, we have to figure out how the truth disclosed in these images can become a living truth for us, in terms that bring their deeper meaning home to us.

All generations of Christians, in every culture, function as communities of interpretation that try to identify how biblical texts apply to their own contexts. Christians interpret biblical texts in the context of a living, vital, and creative fidelity. Pierre Claverie distinguished between the experience of God and the reading of scripture:

> The first step toward God is always that of taking stock of what we are called upon to live through in our lives. It is through this that we experience God. God reveals himself to us only to the extent to which we plunge into the realities we have been given to face. . . . He does not reveal himself through books. The Old and New Testaments are nothing other than the record of the experiences of God that men and women have had throughout their lives.[4]

---

[2] Lisa Sowle Cahill, *Women and Sexuality* (New York: Paulist Press, 1992), 16–17.

[3] John R. Donahue, SJ, "The Bible and Catholic Social Teaching: Will This Engagement Lead to Marriage?" in *Modern Catholic Social Teaching: Commentaries and Interpretations*, ed. Kenneth R. Himes, OFM (Washington, DC: Georgetown University Press, 2004), 21.

[4] Cited in Jean-Jacques Pérennès, *A Life Poured Out: Pierre Claverie of Algeria*, trans. Phyllis Jestice and Matthew Sherry (Maryknoll, NY: Orbis Books, 2007), 211.

The meaning of a specific biblical text is thus not restricted to what its author intended to communicate. The second Isaiah, for example, did not have Jesus in mind when he wrote about a suffering servant who would come to redeem Israel (Is 53), but centuries later Christians came to draw see this figure as foreshadowing Jesus (see Acts 8:34–35; Mt 8:17). The wider Christian interpretations of the meaning of particular biblical texts include not only what their sacred writers meant by what they wrote (as best as we can determine now), but also how later generations came to understand what God has communicated to the church through them. The Bible, for example, says nothing about human rights, but in the modern period the church affirms that because all persons are created in the image of God, we ought to respect their rights.

Cultures from different regions of the world, moreover, can shed light on the meaning of a biblical text in ways that had not been seen in other times and places. Christians from African and Latin American cultures today, for example, can help those from Europe and North America come to a better understanding of aspects of what it means to participate in a community, to celebrate the blessings of our lives, and to care for our extended families.

The Bible offers norms, aphorisms, exhortations, and commands that are directly relevant to service. One thinks most immediately of Jesus's command to love our neighbor, but also of his instructions regarding the works of mercy. We are called to imitate the love of God in concrete acts of service. Just as God gathers the outcasts, for example, so should we (Ps 147:2). The Bible also offers support for people whose service has led them to be opposed or rejected. One can easily imagine Oscar Romero, for example, finding strength in this psalm:

> Out of my distress I called on the Lord;
>   the Lord answered me and set me in a broad place.
> With the Lord on my side I do not fear.
>   What can mortals do to me? (Ps 118:5–6)

The analogical use of scripture is especially important when it comes to trying to understand how we ought to serve others in our own contexts. The Bible uses patterns of thought, feeling, and action that engage us at an imaginative and affective level in our relationship to God. It communicates insights that are personally relevant to each of us, but we come to grasp them only after taking the time to reflect carefully about the meaning of a specific passage. It is not enough to ask ourselves, "What did this text mean to Christians in the past?" We also need to ask, "What does God say to me, personally, in this particular story or teaching?" Or "What does God want to tell us, as a community, in this particular story or teaching?"

We can first read these passages with a sympathetic imagination and then reflect on how what they tell us relates to our own experience, both past and present. Absorbing the narrative pattern of the Good Samaritan or the Prodigal Son, for example, can shape our hearts and minds in ways that lead us to act more compassionately whether or not we actually come across a victim lying in a ditch or a son who returns home after a period of self-indulgent thoughtlessness.

The Christian community draws on the Bible in ways that help to form us into people who are more Christlike. We cannot replicate the specific actions of Jesus and his disciples, but we are called to imitate, appropriate, and enact the virtues embodied in their actions and enunciated in their teachings. We are called to act analogously in our own specific contexts.

Consider, for example, the story of Jesus washing the feet of the disciples the evening before his arrest (Jn 13:1–17). This story sheds light on the meaning of Christian service, but it cannot be reduced to ethical imperatives like "be humble" or "sacrifice yourself for others." It provides a holistic pattern in which we can imaginatively participate in Jesus's way of being through serving one another. We make a decision about how to "love one another" (Jn 13:34) by cultivating an informed, intuitive sense of what is needed and helpful at a particular time and place. We can ask: If Jesus acted in this way, how ought I to act to serve and nurture others in analogous ways in my life? If Jesus did this for his friends, what should I do for the people with whom I am surrounded? What does it mean, in my life, to bend down to wash the feet of another person? Dorothy Day believed this passage tells us that we are "to serve others, not to seek power over them."[5]

The Gospels depict the disciples as continuing to participate in Christ by engaging in his mission. The service of the disciples, William Spohn contended, "develops out of participation in the life of Christ as they enter into the same humiliation and exaltation he underwent."[6] Christians do not seek to mimic the life of a holy man who lived a long time ago, but rather to participate in the ongoing Spirit of the risen Christ who dwells among us now. We move from the church's worship of Jesus and from the service of fellow Christians to what it means to be Christlike in our own context.

Theological Reflection

Each of the next six chapters offers a brief theological reflection on a theme as it bears on the Christian meaning of service. The term *theology* comes

---

[5] Dorothy Day, "Obedience," *Catholic Worker*, December 17, 1966.

[6] William Spohn, *What Are They Saying about the Use of Scripture in Ethics?* Rev. 2nd ed. (Mahwah, NJ: Paulist Press, 1995), 96.

from two Greek roots: *logos*, which refers to processes of understanding, reasoning, and reflecting; and *theos*, God, the Lord, the Almighty. *Theology* from the time of St. Anselm has most often been defined as "faith seeking understanding."

This classic formulation, however, is deceptively simple. All three terms have multiple meanings. *Faith* can mean an act of intellectual accent (I believe what you say is true), or an act of trusting someone (I believe in you), or an act of loyalty (I will stand by you). *Understanding* can refer to a cognitive act such as proving the answer to a math problem or an act that is more intuitive, like a person's ability to grasp what a friend is trying to say. *Seeking* can also be understood in different ways, for example, as affective growth, intellectual deepening, or social transformation. These three terms are all related to the most difficult theological term of all: *God.*

In a sense anyone who thinks about matters of faith engages in theology. Those who ask questions—Who or what is God? Can people who accept the Big Bang say that God is "Maker of heaven and earth?" or What does it mean to say that Jesus is both fully human and fully divine?—are practicing theology.

The informal theology we see in religious reflection and dinner-table conversation is different from the academic discipline of theology, but it, too, tries to make sense of religious stories, symbols, and teachings and to explore what they mean for the way we pray and lead our lives. Theologians devote their professional lives to developing skills and knowledge that can help them contribute to the Christian community's reflection on the reality of God and on all things in relation to God. It is a form of service to other Christians and to the church as a whole. Theology is a calling or vocation, not just a career.

Each model of service is grounded in fundamental Christian convictions. This book tries to illustrate the theological basis of Christian service by tying each model to at least one theological theme. Thus, the chapter on stewardship discusses creation, the chapter on hospitality reflects on the covenant, the chapter on compassion focuses on Jesus Christ, the chapter on advocacy turns to the Holy Spirit, the chapter on solidarity examines the church, and the chapter on witness takes up sacraments and sacramentality.

The Nature of Virtue

We are creatures of habit—routine patterns of thinking, feeling, and acting. If we want to serve others, we ought to cultivate the appropriate virtues. The most lasting and reliable forms of service come from people who are virtuous rather than just externally good. The exemplars discussed in this book exhibit a certain set of virtues that enabled them to serve others. The term *virtue* refers to good habits of heart and mind that lead to right acts. The more virtuous we are, the better we serve others. Fully developed virtues give direction and order to our lives, stability of character, and consistency in conduct. Virtues bring balance and accuracy to our thoughts and feelings and lead us to treat others with compassion and justice.

Our routines shape who we become as ethical and spiritual beings. The essential basis of growth in any of our models of service involves building good habits. Human life is structured by habits. The word *habit* is misleading if taken to mean a mindless routine, for example, the habit of coming in the door and throwing your coat on the sofa. Far from mindless, a moral habit is a consistent tendency to reason and make choices in certain characteristic ways. Business people who are just, for example, regularly treat their employees, customers, and competitors respectfully and fairly.

Virtue ethics asks us to reflect on whether the specific habits that give shape to our lives are good for us. Christian virtue ethics suggests we evaluate our habits in terms of the standards given in the Bible, especially in the life and teachings of Jesus.

How do we become more virtuous? There are two features of personal moral progress in Christian ethics. First, Christians believe that living virtuously is made possible by the transforming power of grace, the love of God active in our lives. The love of God works to heal, reorder, and expand how we love. Grace works in and through human experience, relationships, and communities. Grace does not override our power of choice, but it provides us with motivation and direction that we cannot produce on our own.

Second, we learn by doing. Jesuits often say that we ought to pray as though everything depends on God and work as though everything depends on us. The second half of this adage encourages trust, gratitude, and reverence for God. The first accents our responsibility to make good choices and develop good habits.

We cultivate habits by making good choices about how to act. As Aristotle observed: "The things we have to learn before we can do them, we learn by doing them, e.g., men become builders by building and lyre-players by playing the lyre; so too we become just by doing just acts, temperate by doing temperate acts, brave by doing brave acts."[7] We build good habits by repeatedly making the right choices and doing the right acts. We have some choice about which habits we wish to develop.

---

[7] Aristotle, *Nicomachean Ethics*, trans. David Ross (New York: Oxford, 2009), Bk. II, 1103a 32–33, 23.

Christian service is sustained by virtues cultivated in community by members who seek to live in fidelity to Christ. Conversion, Romero said, is the "continued demand upon us to destroy whatever is sin and to bring into being ever more powerfully all that is life, renewal, holiness, and justice."[8] Jesus did not offer any theory of the virtues, but he did encourage people to speak honestly, act compassionately, judge wisely, and live with integrity. The center of Christian life is love of God and love of neighbor, and we can learn to love better by becoming more virtuous. Jesus challenged people to a change of heart. He found people turned in on themselves and invited them instead to turn toward the Father in wonder, gratitude, and love.

Virtues are not just habits that enable us to avoid sin or obey the law. By orienting us to God, our greatest good, and by enabling us to develop truly good friendships, virtues are the path to the greatest form of human fulfillment. As Karl Rahner puts it, "Christianity ultimately . . . announces that the absolute, holy, and living God is the total fulfillment of human existence. Then with that come a joy and a fulfillment of a fundamental kind exceeding everything else."[9]

Christian virtue ethics is not "perfectionistic" in the sense that it is constantly telling us where we fall short of perfection. It points to virtues that we aspire to develop in our lives with the help of grace. Day observed in a letter to a friend: "It is good to urge each other on to virtue, but remember, we are comrades stumbling along, not saints, drifting along in ecstasies." No one should be held to impossible standards. Day noted "The older I get, the more I meet people, the more convinced I am that we must only work on ourselves, to grow in grace. The only thing we can do about people is to love them, to find things to love in them."[10] The more we "find things to love" in one another, the more we transcend the narrowness of our own little worlds.

The center of Christian ethics is the virtue of love *(agape)* or charity *(caritas)*. Some Christian writers avoid the term love because it is all too often used in a hackneyed and sentimental way. It is clear that we should not reduce the Christian use of the term to a warm feeling of attraction to another person. Thomas Aquinas helpfully spoke in terms of the "love of benevolence"[11] and King spoke along similar lines when he advocated "creative and redemptive good will" for others.[12] It is the kind of love that

---

[8] Archbishop Oscar Romero, *Voice of the Voiceless* (Maryknoll, NY: Orbis Books, 1985), 57.

[9] Karl Rahner, *Faith in a Wintry Season* (New York: Crossroad, 1989), 10.

[10] Dorothy Day, *All the Way to Heaven: The Selected Letters of Dorothy Day*, ed. Robert Ellsberg (Milwaukee: Marquette University Press, 2010), 124, 253.

[11] Thomas Aquinas, *Summa Theologiae*, II-II, 27, 2.

[12] King, *Strength to Love*, 50.

sees the goodness in someone who is difficult, annoying, or "rough around the edges." It is a love that embraces not only people who are quiet and well-behaved, but those who are loud and badly in need of a bath; not only the good looking and healthy, but those who are unhealthy and unattractive. It is a love that embraces the "discards," society's "losers," and "hopeless" cases. This "Christ is in our midst," as Jim Forest puts it, is "not in a tidy, well-scrubbed, church-on-Sunday Christ, but a Christ for weekdays, a Christ in patched clothing, a Christ of slums and flop houses, a Christ homeless and jobless, a Christ of soup lines."[13]

Realistic talk of Christian love does not assume that we can just wake up in the morning and decide to start having good will toward others. We can only learn to exercise authentic love by working hard and consistently choosing to act on the right dispositions and attitudes. Cultivating love takes a willingness to engage in self-denial and self-discipline. In Dostoevsky's novel *The Brothers Karamazov*, Zosima, an elderly and holy monk, shares the following wisdom about love: "Brothers, love is a teacher, but one must know how to acquire it, for it is *difficult* to acquire, it is dearly bought, by *long work over a long time*, for one ought to love not for a chance moment but for all time."[14] Anyone can love once in a while, by chance, from a pleasant mood or a momentary surge of positive feelings. Dostoevsky thought only a properly formed character enables one consistently to love the right way.

Virtues are not all or nothing. Character is a "mixed bag," and none of us is either purely virtuous or purely vicious. We can be generous and compassionate in one situation but petty and apathetic in another. Social psychologists tell us we are more likely to be helpful to another person if we are in a good mood, if someone whom we respect is watching us, or if we are not feeling stress from a pressing obligation.

If we have virtues, then, we have them imperfectly. Even the best people can say foolish things, make bad choices, and act selfishly. Conversely, as King pointed out, "An element of goodness may be found even in our worst enemy."[15]

Recognizing the inconsistent and uneven nature of our moral characters, the Christian community provides resources to help us become better human beings. It offers helpful practices (worship and prayer), exemplars, instruction, stories, fellowship, and service programs. The Christian call to conversion involves a lifelong process of transformation under the influence of grace that works primarily in and through our relationships with other

---

[13] Jim Forest, *All Is Grace: A Biography of Dorothy Day* (Maryknoll, NY: Orbis Books, 2011), 127.

[14] Fyodor Dostoevsky, *The Brothers Karamazov*, trans. Richard Pevear and Larissa Volokhonsky (New York: Random House, 1990), 319.

[15] King, *Strength to Love*, 49.

people. Conversion is not a solo commitment. Community enables us to see fellow members leading recognizably Christian lives and to believe in our own capacity to change.

Christian morality challenges us to build on our strengths and work on areas in which we are weaker. It aims to form our character in two ways. First, it seeks to allow our hearts to be shaped by divine grace to love God and love our neighbor with greater simplicity and generosity. Second, it challenges us to build a more consistent character by cultivating particular virtues. Dorothy Day, for example, worked on trying not to be too quick in judging people, and Oscar Romero prayed that God would give him the courage to remain steadfast in the face of persecution.

Christian integrity seeks its center in an ordered love. To the extent that we love God and our neighbor properly, we will also have more consistency in our desires for various goods, beliefs about the world, and the quality of our actions. Speaking of Jesus, King said, "Never in history was there a more sublime example of the consistency of word and deed."[16] The will to integrity drives us to become more integrated people by centering us on the love of God and love of neighbor.

Acting virtuously is also costly. For example, the official who doesn't take a bribe is worse off financially than he or she would otherwise have been. At the same time, he or she is better off *overall* as a human being. Virtues, particularly those central to having a strong character and moral integrity, bring internal rewards like peace of mind and self-respect that cannot be obtained in any other way.

Living virtuously is also rewarding because it enables us to live in right relationship to God, one another, ourselves, and other creatures. It provides the necessary basis of whatever true human fulfillment we can attain in this life. The greatest product of virtue in this life is friendship. Since friendship depends on the virtues, people who live virtuously are capable of the deepest kinds of friendship. Community is friendship writ large.

Acting viciously, however, is costly. The areas in our lives where we are less than virtuous are where we have trouble. Vice not only hurts our relationship with other people, but it also always harms us. We can't be truly happy, for example, if we can't control our tempers when we feel provoked, if we can't moderate our appetites for food or sex, or if we go around betraying confidences and stabbing our friends in the back. If we do not love other people as friends, moreover, we cannot be true friends to ourselves. Virtue is thus not only the basis of service but also of true and appropriate self-love.

We now turn to our six models.

---

[16] Ibid., 37.

7

Stewardship

St. Paul wrote to the Corinthians: "God loves a cheerful giver. And God is able to provide you with every blessing in abundance, so that by always having enough of everything, you may share abundantly in every good work" (1 Cor 9:7–8). We now turn to the first model of service, stewardship, which is based on the fundamental premise that each of us, like all other creatures, belongs to God and not to ourselves. Or, as Abraham Heschel puts it: "Our life is not our own property but a possession of God. And it is this divine ownership that makes life a sacred thing."[1] Created in the image of God, we are responsible for one another, the earth we inhabit, and the creatures that live on it with us. This chapter discusses (1) stewardship in the Bible, (2) theology of creation, (3) the virtue of temperance, (4) growing in stewardship, and (5) temptations of stewardship.

Stewardship in the Bible

The early chapters of the Book of Genesis provide some of the key texts for the Christian ethic of stewardship. In the first story of creation God creates plants and animals and then the narrator proclaims: "And God saw that it was good" (Gen 1:21; 25). Before human beings appear on the scene, God creates all other creatures and declares them "good." Created on the same day as land animals, we too are commanded to "be fruitful and multiply." While we belong to the rest of creation, we alone are created in God's own image and likeness (Gen 1:26). This suggests that we are created to serve as God's representatives on earth.

Ancient Near Eastern accounts of creation tended to depict humanity as created to be the slaves of the gods; humans exist in order to provide food, clothing, and honor to their divine masters. The *Enuma Elish*, for example,

---

[1] Abraham Joshua Heschel, *Moral Grandeur and Spiritual Audacity*, ed. Susanna Heschel (New York: Farrar, Straus, and Giroux, 1996), 328.

depicts a great cosmic order in which mortals must toil on the earth to meet the needs of the gods. Biblical texts, in contrast, refer to humanity in royal terms. We are not God, but we are assigned a unique responsibility to exercise "dominion" in God's place. In Genesis, the Creator says, "Let us make mankind in our image, in our likeness, so that they may rule over the fish in the sea and the birds in the sky, over the livestock and all the wild animals, and over all the creatures that move along the ground" (Gen 1:26). This responsibility to rule means we are deputized to act as guardians, caretakers, or stewards of creation. It also means we are answerable to God for how we treat other creatures.

The second story of creation depicts God telling the first man to "serve and keep"—to "work and take care of"—the earth (Gen 2:15). The English word *keep* is translated from a Hebrew word based on *shamar*, which means to care for, sustain, and protect (see Ps 121). God asks the first man to name the animals to see if they can be suitable companions for him. In this cultural context the power to name gives one a kind of authority over what is named. Animals do not satisfy the man's need for a helper, so God creates the first woman from the "rib" of the man. Her closeness to him leads him to proclaim, "This is now bone of my bone, flesh of my flesh" (Gen 2:23). The accent here falls on companionship rather than, as in the first creation story, on procreation.

The first creation story envisions us as caretakers of creatures on behalf of God. In the second story God gives the first couple responsibility to care for creation as they would a garden. They are entitled to survive and prosper by using the earth and its animals, but they are also expected to take care of other creatures. They are to use the fruits of creation to meet their needs but not recklessly destroy creatures. God's creatures are not theirs to do with as they please. The name Adam is first used in the third chapter of Genesis. It comes from the Hebrew word for "red earth." We share in God's life *(nephesh)* with all other living creatures, but we alone pray and worship God.

As salvation history unfolds in the biblical narrative, Israel, the chosen people, is repeatedly reminded not to forget that God is the real owner of creation: "The earth is the Lord's, and everything in it, the world, and all who live in it" (Ps 24:1). Proper treatment of the land is essential to righteousness. God reminds the Israelites: "The land is mine and you are but aliens and my tenants. Throughout the country that you hold as a possession, you must provide for the redemption of the land" (Lev 25:23–24).

Care of the land went hand in hand with providing for the needy. The law required farmers to leave the corners of their fields unharvested so that something would be left for the poor. It allowed them to harvest their olive trees only once a year (Dt 24:20) and to leave the remaining produce for either the poor or strangers in the land (Lev 19:10; 23:22).

Stewardship is associated with careful planning. Joseph, for example, did not simply tell Pharaoh to trust that God would provide, but rather he told him to store excess grain in years of plenty to be used in the lean years that were to come. If he had not done so, many Egyptians would have starved to death (Gen 41:33–36, 46–49). Stewardship also comes to be associated with the wise use of money. "The plans of the diligent lead to profit," the Book of Proverbs tells us, "as surely as haste leads to poverty" (21:5). The blessings of possessions, property, and wealth help us fulfill our responsibility to one another.

The New Testament builds on this line of thought when it depicts stewardship as an expression of loyalty to God. We are to be stewards of our own talents and abilities, which have been given to us for the benefit of others and to build up our communities (see Rom 12:4–8). Most important, St. Paul wrote, as "servants of Christ" we are called to be "stewards of the mysteries of God" (1 Cor 4:1).

The first Christian communities gathered in Christian homes. This implies that not all Christians were required to leave their homes, families, and possessions to follow the itinerant Jesus (see Acts 1:13; 1 Cor 16:19). Martha and Mary, for example, used their home to host Jesus (see also Lk 10:38).

Stewardship made Christian charity possible. Resources were to be used to help people (see Lk 8:3). Ancient Romans believed that the rich ought to be generous with their resources, particularly in building monuments, bathhouses, and theaters for fellow citizens. Early Christians, on the other hand, were encouraged to use their possessions to help the needy. Jesus told them to store up "treasures in heaven" by giving alms to the poor (Mt 6:19–20).

Christian stewardship combines three traits: gratitude for the blessings God has given, trust in divine providence, and practical intelligence in managing one's resources. If we are properly grateful, we will take care of what we own. If we take care of what we own, we will be better able to take care of others. St. Paul advised the Corinthians to give according to their means (2 Cor 8:11).

Second, stewardship, and indeed the entire Christian life, is based on an abiding trust in divine providence. Faith in Christ was the basis of Dorothy Day's "abandonment to divine providence."[2] This trust shapes a distinctive sense of priorities. Thus Jesus teaches: "Do not fear those who kill the body

---

[2] Day, *All the Way to Heaven: The Selected Letters of Dorothy Day*, ed. Robert Ellsberg (Milwaukee: Marquette University Press, 2010), 246.

but cannot kill the soul; rather fear him who can destroy both soul and body in hell" (Mt 10:28). This is echoed in Jesus's saying that we ought not be anxious about clothing, food, and drink. We ought, instead, to "strive for his kingdom, and these things will be given to you as well" (Lk 12:31). He tells his followers that they can correct their misplaced priorities by selling their possessions and giving alms to the poor so that they will have an "unfailing treasure in heaven" (Lk 12:33).

Trust in divine providence frees one to accept the paradoxical teaching that "those who love their life lose it, and those who hate their life in this world will keep it for eternal life" (Jn 12:25). "Life" here does not refer to social or even biological life but participation in the divine life. Jesus is thus described as "the way, and the truth, and the life" (Jn 14:6).

God always wants what is best for us in this life as well as in the next, but God does not control the world as a puppeteer controls puppets on a stage. The world is pervaded by contingencies that can either help or hurt human beings. We can get terrible diseases or have devastating accidents or be victims of random acts of violence. One twin gets brain cancer, and the other is perfectly healthy.

Faith in divine providence is sometimes conceived as trust that God will always protect us from bad things. This is obviously not the case, as we see in the life of Jesus himself. Christian faith does trust, though, that God will never forsake us. Christian hope expects that when we live completely in the service of Jesus, we will lead the best life possible for us in our concrete circumstances and be blessed with "eternal life."

When bad things happen, victims often say: "Where was God? Why did God let this happen to me?" They might wonder, "Is God punishing me with cancer because I ignored my parents and cheated on my spouse?" Or they might be comforted by saying, "Everything happens for a reason"; they take this to mean that God has a plan whereby a terrible harm will contribute to an even greater good. This move comes from a desire to think that the world is structured by an overarching moral order, but biblical texts like Job and Ecclesiastes remind us that prosperity is not distributed in proportion to virtue nor suffering in proportion to vice. St. Paul did teach that "all things work together for those who love God" (Rom 8:28), but at times we have no idea how. Life is full of contingencies, and these contingencies mean that people can be hurt by bad luck. God does not control the contingencies of the world. Freak accidents happen to people. Trusting in divine providence cannot be a matter of naïvely thinking God is going to surround each of us with a protective shield that wards off all dangers.

A realistic faith affirms that God will not abandon us in the midst of whatever pain and suffering we are forced to absorb. The infant Jesus was called Emmanuel, which means "God with us" (Mt 1:23; see Is 7:14). This kind of trust gave Jesus the strength to endure the passion without falling into discouragement, fear, and desperation. He trusted that, despite all appearances, the Father would not allow death to be the last word. Christians place the meaning of Jesus's passion and death in the context of his resurrection. We see our own death as a gateway to the eternal life shared with the Father, Son, and Spirit.

Stewardship as Christians conceive it is based on trust in divine providence that at the same time both relaxes our attachment to possessions and intensifies our care for what has been entrusted to us so that we can care for one another. We live in a state of permanent vulnerability to harm, albeit with an awareness calmed by faith in divine providence. This realism underscores the importance of stewardship. We are not to be careless with our safety or with the goods that enable us to care for one another. Part of acting as a good steward means comforting and encouraging people when they are struggling without offering shallow platitudes that don't help anyway.

Hope in Christ resists the temptation to feel defeated, bitter, and cynical. Jesus teaches us not to run away from hard times but to face up to them and accept them as the particular path by which we are called to continue to grow in the love of God and neighbor. All of our exemplars would agree with Day when she wrote that suffering endured in faith and hope can "purify our love." This is all part of the process of "putting off the old man and putting on the new."[3]

Divine providence works in and through normal channels of creation, both natural and human. This means good stewards have to know how to exercise practical wisdom. Many animals grow thick winter coats, but we do not. Trusting in divine providence does not mean that we don't buy a winter coat if we need one.

Stewardship is grateful for blessings but does not cling to possessions. Jesus tried to reduce the emphasis people put on external things: "one's life does not consist in the abundance of possessions" (Lk 12:15). Possessions are instruments for helping us meet our needs and those of other people, but they must not be placed at the center of our lives. Jesus did not say that money or other possessions are inherently bad, but he did warn his disciples not to overvalue them at the expense of more important values.

Human worth—our own and that of other people—rests not on our appearance, possessions, or socioeconomic status but on God's unconditional love. This approach to possessions has important ethical implications. If we do not assume that our own worth depends on having expensive clothing or

---

[3] Ibid., 246, 138.

a large house, we are less likely to look down on people who dress simply or live in modest neighborhoods. This also applies to expensive cars, vacations, private schools, and so on.

Theology of Creation

Christians conceive of God as an eternal outpouring of infinitely generous goodness. The world did not have to exist. God was neither compelled to create the world nor did God create it in order to satisfy some otherwise unmet divine need. God creates out of gratuitous love. Each of us is contingent; we live only because of the pure goodness of God.

Second, creation and all creatures are intrinsically good. Particular creatures are good in themselves, not only when they provide practical benefits to human beings. It is good that they exist and flourish. God wants to share this goodness with different creatures according to the kinds of beings they are. Inanimate objects partake of goodness in that they exist as part of the world. Plants manifest their own kind of beauty and goodness in living and growing. Animals manifest God's goodness in whatever particular ways they flourish.

Third, God makes the world simply in order to share the divine goodness with creatures. The Creator brings some creatures into existence—human beings—who are capable of knowing and loving God. To us, he offers friendship.

Fourth, Christians affirm that God the Father creates the universe through the Word and that "all things were made through him" (Jn 1:1, 10). In Jesus of Nazareth we are given the "Word made flesh." He reveals in the most profound way the nature of God as Father. Jesus's life, death, and resurrection show us the self-giving love that lies at the core of both what it means to be God and what it means to be human. To be a fully developed human being is to participate fully in divine love. Jesus Christ reveals the ultimate purpose of creation as the union of humanity with God and, in the Spirit, the risen Christ continues to dwell in human history today.

Created in the Image of God

The belief that we are created in the image of God has three important implications: First of all, we did not have to exist. The fact that our existence is contingent means that we are fundamentally dependent on all that has made it possible for us to be. This dependence stands in some tension with the emphasis we give to independence, personal freedom, and autonomy. We look up to the "self-made man" for working hard to become financially successful, and we place a high value on self-sufficiency. We must not forget that to be human is to be shaped by the natural processes, social networks, and cultural matrices within which we are embedded from the beginning of our existence. God creates us in and through these contexts, and therefore the appropriate human response is an attitude of grateful dependence. Yet, as self-reliant individualists, we would rather help ourselves than be helped by others. But as Karl Barth pointed out, when we insist on being "our *own* helper" in all things, we turn away from the help that God offers to us.[4]

Limitations help us learn to love another. St. Catherine of Siena imagined that God could have given each of us all the goods we needed to be entirely self-sufficient, materially as well as spiritually. But, she thought, God instead chose to make us limited, frail, and dependent on one another and to bestow different gifts to different people so that we would learn both to give and to receive from one another. She imagined God saying, "I wanted to make each of you dependent on the others so that you would be forced to exercise charity in action and will at once."[5]

Second, we are created as embodied beings. God loves the whole person—body and soul—not just part of us. An overly spiritualized view of the person sees the body as insignificant or even bad. A distorted view of the person encourages us to neglect our own bodily needs and those of others. Our exemplars saw that we cannot claim to love others but ignore their pain. In stewardship, we take care of our resources so that we can use them to enhance the lives of other people or other creatures. As created in the image of a God who is Father, Son, and Spirit, we are made for friendship and community.

Third, we are created with an intrinsic dignity simply by virtue of being human, regardless of our particular talents, achievements, and status. Because we are created in the image of God, who loves each one of us, we are called to approach one another with attention, sensitivity, respect, and even a kind of reverence. This implies that we can't use other people as we please or treat them as if they were objects. It also implies that we ought not to allow other people to treat us as a mere thing. We have a right and duty to affirm our self-worth and to treat ourselves with respect.

It is important to note that we all *equally* created in the image of God. As created in the image of God, there is nothing we can do either to earn or to destroy what comes with our human nature. To be created in the image of God implies that it is good that we exist. The problem is that we don't

---

[4] Karl Barth, *Church Dogmatics*, vol. 4.1, ed. G. W. Bromiley and T. F. Torrance, trans. G. W. Bromiley (Edinburgh: T&T Clark, 1956), 459, emphasis added.

[5] Catherine of Siena, *The Dialogue*, trans. Suzanne Noffke, OP (New York: Paulist Press, 1980), 312.

always see it that way. We often have an attitude that says implicitly that we value others because they do things for us, or because they are "good" people, or because they are our friends. We go beyond this attitude when we recognize that it is good that others exist because they are human beings and their very existence is a manifestation of the goodness of God.

Each of us has the same human dignity whether we are upstanding citizens or criminals. This runs contrary to the prevalent assumption that we have to prove our worth and earn the love of others. This worth applies equally to Osama bin Laden and Mother Teresa. When we see the horrible things some people do to others, of course, we can be tempted to call perpetrators "animals" or "monsters." In denying that they are human, we distance ourselves from them ("I would never do that"), make ourselves feel safe ("I am around human beings, and human beings do not do such things"), and give ourselves moral freedom to do what we want with them. It is true that people at their worst—say, one who assaults or murders another person—act in ways that run contrary to both their own human dignity and that of other people. But even vicious people are still human beings who are loved by God. While we have to protect our communities, we must, as stewards, do so in a way that accords with everyone's human dignity.

Stewardship as Exercising Responsibility

Because we are created in the image of God, we are bearers of moral responsibility in two senses. We are responsible to others for our intentions, choices, and actions. We can, of course, refuse to take responsibility for how we choose to lead our lives. We can make choices that slowly make us feel more and more disappointed, bogged down, anxious, or guilty or that allow us to drift into distractions or addictions.

While we are influenced by factors like heredity, upbringing, and social circumstances, they do not completely determine our actions. We are responsible to make good choices in the midst of these conditions. When we make bad choices, they do not have to define the rest of our lives. As responsible, though, we have to "own" them and, if possible, make amends for the harm we have done.

Second, we are responsible for others in the sense that we care about their well-being and want to act in ways that are good for them. Yet while we are capable of taking responsibility for one another, we can also evade, diminish, or deny this responsibility. "It's not my problem" is repeated generation after generation. Or, as Cain put it, "Am I my brother's keeper?" (Gen 4:9). We can evade stewardship by blaming the victim or ignoring friends who need our attention.

Stewardship, is essentially exercising responsibility for goods and people with whom we have been entrusted. Theologian James Gustafson explains that the steward is "caretaker of what he or she does not own."[6] This description accords with Heschel's statement that "our life is not our own property but a possession of God."[7] The word *own* in this sense refers to absolute possession without responsibility to others. The Christian conviction that God is the real owner of everything in creation challenges the centrality our culture gives to personal autonomy, individual liberty, and private property. We assume that we own whatever we acquire through our own efforts without force or fraud (or through receiving gifts from those who legitimately own what they then give to us). Christian faith, in contrast, regards our possessions as a loan given to us for the fulfillment of God's purposes.

Stewardship in the Christian tradition plays a role in friendship, romantic love, marriage, family, and all relationships. There is no more important form of stewardship than parents' care for their children. We are also called to be stewards of one another through productive activity in working. Those who work are in some sense stewards either of the goods they produce or the services they provide to others. Professionals like accountants, lawyers, and dentists, for example, all exercise responsibility on the basis of a special kind of trust that comes with their roles.

Stewardship as Ecological Responsibility

The language of stewardship is used often today in the sphere of ecology, but it has come under criticism. The concept of dominion is used in biblical texts written centuries ago, when most people had to struggle every day to eke out a living. Life was, at best, precarious. Humans had little power to protect themselves from elemental forces of nature like withering heat, pounding wind, and flood waters. There were no antibiotics, fierce animals weren't in a zoo, and the Coast Guard wasn't around to save drowning fishermen.

The exponential increase in human technological power in the last hundred years or so has led to practices that have had a massive and unanticipated negative impact on the planet. Agribusinesses in the upper Midwest, for example, use large amounts of fertilizer (especially nitrogen and phosphorus) on their fields. Some of these chemicals drain into the Mississippi River and then drift down the river and into the Gulf of Mexico. Once in the Gulf, these chemicals combine with treated sewage from American cities

---

[6] James M. Gustafson, *A Sense of the Divine* (Cleveland: Pilgrim Press, 1994), 92.

[7] Heschel, *Moral Grandeur and Spiritual Audacity*, 328.

and have created a "dead zone" in which oxygen is so low that marine life can no longer survive. This effect was not anticipated, but now we have to decide what to do about it.

Relentless destruction of natural habitats has been fueled by irresponsible patterns of consumption. The *Living Planet Report 2014* of the Zoological Society of London finds that since 1970, wildlife species populations have declined by 52 percent and freshwater species by 72 percent. The rapid pace of our use of natural resources puts us in danger of disrupting the ecological balances that have preserved the planet's climate for millions of years. These include the water cycle, ocean biodiversity, the nitrogen cycle, and the habitats of millions of species. By 2030 we will need the equivalent of two of our planets to live at the current rate of global consumption. Rapid depletion of water and land resources has a disproportionate impact on the poor, particularly in the form of higher food prices, floods and droughts, famine, epidemics, forced migration, and violent conflict.

There are a number of ways to conceive of our relationship to the natural world. We mention three: dominion, reverence for nature, and participatory stewardship.

Dominion

Mainstream Christian ethics now refers to dominion in terms of stewardship rather than domination. The churches have sought to correct the radical anthropocentrism—religious as well as secular—that evaluates the worth of species and habitats only in terms of their potential to benefit human beings.

Christian stewardship emphasizes the goodness of creation and insists on a strong sense of ecological responsibility. It suggests that nature has intrinsic rather than purely instrumental worth and aesthetic, moral, and spiritual significance. It calls us to recognize that some indigenous cultures can teach us how better to respect the harmony and integrity of nature. As Pope John Paul II writes in *Ecclesia in Asia*, "It is the Creator's will that man should treat nature not as a ruthless exploiter but as an intelligent and responsible administrator" (no. 41).

Stewardship authorizes us to take from nature in order to meet legitimate human needs, but it also insists that we only function properly as God's delegates when we do so in ways that are ethically responsible. We violate our responsibility when we stand by and let factories poison fish or trucks dump toxic waste onto the vacant lots of our cities. Stewardship thus entails conservation, for example, setting aside forest preserves and wetlands, protecting endangered species, raising standards of fuel efficiency, and restricting the amount of fish that can be harvested from sensitive areas.

Stewardship also seeks to repair ecological damage; for example, it takes measures to restore Amazonian rainforests and to return disturbed tracts of land and waterways to their natural states.

Critics of stewardship, however, reject the ethic of dominion for implying that the human race stands above the rest of the natural world. They point to advances in a wide variety of sciences that have made us increasingly aware of our dependence upon the natural world—the sun, oil, air, water, elements, ecospheres, and the planet as a whole. In the last few decades neuroscience, biological anthropology, and other scientific fields have made more and more apparent our similarities to other species, particularly to other primates. We are part of nature rather than "master" of it. To "subdue" does not seem to accord with our profound dependence on the natural world, the limits of our power and its potentially destructive effects, and our responsibility to care for creatures for their own sakes.

Reverence for Nature

An alternative model of our relation to nature replaces the term *dominion* with *reverence*. The reverence model rejects stewardship/dominion for its human-centered view of nature. Dorothy Stang found in creation spirituality a new way of appreciating the spiritual significance of our integral place within nature. She came to believe deepening our ecological sensitivity brings us closer to God. Her experience in the Amazon led her to see us as part of an interdependent web of nature rather than as at the top of a hierarchy of being. Instead of governing nature, Stang believed that we ought to seek to regain our lost intimacy with the earth and its creatures. In being more spiritually connected to nature, she believed, we come closer to the selves God intends us to be.

The ethic of reverence underscores the intrinsic value of nature and promotes a strong sense of wonder and awe in the presence of its beauty, delicacy, and magnificence. Creation spirituality describes God in female as well as male terms. It promotes spiritual practices that seek to attune us to the presence of God in the natural world as well as in our human communities. Its strong sense of our kinship with other animals encourages us to treat them with care and even, in a sense, to serve them.

The reverence model stands in tension with the Bible, which, unlike some other ancient religions, depicts creation as good but not sacred. The reverence model tends not to distinguish higher and lower forms of life. The chimpanzee, the rat, and the amoeba all stand in the same circle of life. By saying that one is not more valuable than the others, the reverence model can have difficulty making practical moral decisions when the good of some creatures competes with those of others. Consider the example of Rock

Creek Park in Washington, DC. White-tailed deer became so prolific that they were destroying almost all the young native vegetation and preventing the forest from regenerating itself.[8] For the good of the park, authorities had to adopt lethal (sharpshooters) and nonlethal (fertility control by immuno-contraception) methods to reduce the deer population.

We need ways to feed and otherwise take care of our own species as well as others. Farmers have to plow fields, dig irrigation canals, and spread insecticide to stop pests from destroying their crops. We need to eat, so every year farmers grow over 800 million metric tons of corn and fisherman catch 120 million tons of fish. We cannot do whatever we want to other animals, but because we need places to live and to work, loggers harvest trees to sell to contractors so that they can build houses, apartments, and office buildings. This is not to endorse runaway consumption, but simply to observe that an undiscriminating appeal to reverence for nature is not consistent with human civilization on the scale into which it has grown—even as the rate of population slows. The reverence model rightly urges us to cultivate a more robust appreciation of our ties to other species, but its critics wonder whether reverence is the best image for expressing our relation to nature.

Participatory Stewardship

The limitations of the first two models of our relation to the natural world lead to a third, a revised view of stewardship we can call "responsible participation." *Participation* points to both our dependence on the rest of the natural world and our action upon it. As James Gustafson notes, "The human venture is participation."[9] We are participants within the patterns and processes of nature as well as culture and society. We participate well when we respond to the world intelligently and responsibly.

The participation framework forces us to acknowledge that gains in power over nature are also accompanied by tradeoffs and losses. It requires us to assess how potential courses of action are likely to have an impact not only on human communities but also on other animals, their habitats, and larger ecospheres. This implies that at times we need to take measures to restrict human activities for the sake of the well-being of other animals. We are called to care for as well as to be served by nonhuman animals.

The participatory version of stewardship understands ecological responsibility in relation to two key criteria: the common good and integral human development. First, the Christian tradition regards the *common good* as an

---

[8] NPR News, All Things Considered, "Park Service Uses Sharpshooters to Cull Deer in D.C. Park," April 1, 2013.

[9] James M. Gustafson, *Ethics from a Theocentric Perspective*, vol. 2 (Chicago: University of Chicago Press, 1984), 13.

essential criterion of justice. The common good is not the sum total of the particular goods of individuals but the good of a community overall. A painting hanging in a person's bedroom is a private good, but a sculpture in a park is a common good. Justice recognizes the legitimacy of private goods but also promotes a common good that includes the good of rich, middle class, and poor alike. The common good traditionally encompassed villages, guilds, towns, and whole societies. Ecological consciousness has made us recognize that the good of local communities includes urban ecology and surrounding ecospheres. The ecojustice to which Stang was deeply committed sees that the common good includes not only the well-being of human communities but also that of animals, plants, and landscapes. The problem of climate change has turned us even more expansively to the planetary common good.

Stewardship urges us to accept our limits and to exercise self-restraint. It resists "free-market fundamentalists," who think only in terms of the competing preferences of individuals. Rather than assuming that technology and economic growth will automatically provide the answers to most of our problems, participatory stewardship aims at sustainable growth and reasonable consumption.

Second, ecological responsibility also has to be coordinated with a commitment to *integral human development*. The principle of the universal destination of the world's goods holds that all people have a right to conditions that give them an opportunity to lead good lives. This principle resonates with King's conviction that "God intends that all of his children shall have the basic necessities for meaningful, healthful life." A God of love would not want "some to wallow in the soft beds of luxury while others sink in the quicksands of poverty."[10]

Ecological responsibility and economic progress are often put in competition. We are often told that we have to choose between either protecting nature for its own sake or exploiting it for the sake of human progress. Tradeoffs are indeed often unavoidable. Sometimes, as in the case of malaria control, we have to harm some part of nature to protect vulnerable people. At other times, as in the case of rainforest logging, we have to restrict economic development to protect endangered species as well as threatened human communities and their cultures.

Integral human development sees the value of both sets of goods. It recognizes our need for sustainable economic growth, especially when it comes to meeting the needs of the global poor, but it also acknowledges our responsibility to be good stewards of the natural world. Economic

---

[10] Martin Luther King, Jr., *Strength to Love* (Cleveland: William Collins and World Publishing, 1963), 102.

development and ecological responsibility are necessary conditions for the cultural, social, psychological, moral, and spiritual development of our communities. Integral development includes the full range of human goods needed to provide the basics of life for persons, families, and their communities. It aims not only at production of goods and services but also at their equitable distribution. We are becoming increasingly aware that the common good depends on sustainable practices that will allow future generations to flourish.

The Virtue of Temperance

Temperance is the virtue that leads us to respond appropriately to the goods that bring us pleasure. This virtue is also used in a more general sense to talk about the proper ordering of any of our desires. Stewardship requires an appropriate ethic of self-restraint, moderation of desires, and simplicity of lifestyle. Pleasure, satisfaction, and enjoyment are all good, as long as we pursue them the right way.

Temperance might be the least exciting of all the virtues. It has neither the compelling nature of justice nor the heroic appeal of courage nor the warmth of compassion. Yet it is essential to living a good life. People often mistakenly confuse the virtue of temperance with Puritanical repression. At times, of course, we have to forgo certain kinds of pleasures, but the virtue of temperance typically aims at the moderate satisfaction of our desires rather than at their complete negation. We have been created with capacities for enjoying food, drink, dance, sex, music, physical play, and other pleasures. The inability to enjoy them (anhedonia) is a symptom of clinical depression.

It is easy to see someone like Dorothy Stang as an exemplar of stewardship, but it seems like a stretch to describe her as a person of temperance. Only a person of extremes would be willing to go from Dayton, Ohio, to the middle of the Amazonian rainforest and then to stay there when powerful men put a price on her head. She had the uncompromising commitment of a prophet more than the moderation and balance of a temperate person.

Yet passionate conviction and strong personality are not necessarily at odds with the virtue of temperance. In fact, they reinforce each other when rooted in a strong love of what is good. The virtue of temperance has nothing to do with holding wishy-washy views that never offend anyone. Prophets often seem intemperate to their opponents. Jesus's critics thought he was intemperate as well as a friend of dubious characters—"a glutton and a drunkard, a friend of tax collectors and sinners" (Lk 7:34).

The temperate person enjoys pleasures but does not allow them to displace more important goods. Stang thoroughly enjoyed good meals, music, festivals, and holidays. She loved visiting her family, and she appreciated the ordinary comforts that come with middle-class American life. Yet she was willing to give them up for the sake of companionship with settlers in the Amazon because she was convinced that is where God wanted her to be. She went into the jungle because that is where she felt called to serve. She lived in desperately poor circumstances for long stretches of time—without indoor plumbing, windows, a refrigerator, or the air conditioning that would have given her some relief from the blazing heat and withering humidity of the rainforest. Stang came down with malaria more than ten times and also had a terrible bout with Dengue fever. She was willing to live with these hardships not out of a pious attempt to purify her soul, but to be close to her friends.

Temperance is tailored to particular personalities and contexts. What is temperate for one person in one particular time and place may not be so for another person in another time and place. Stang developed a form of temperance that was appropriate for a missionary, religious sister, educator, and community organizer living in the Amazon. In a similar way Day developed a form of temperance suited to her role in Catholic Worker communities. Each of us thus has to ask what form of temperance is appropriate for us within the particular circumstances of our own lives.

We can only be good stewards to the extent that we are temperate people. When we waste our resources, we have less to use on behalf of others. The virtue of temperance helps us avoid two vices that make it especially difficult to function as good stewards: gluttony and greed. Food and drink are good but, like any goods, they can be abused. We can think of gluttony as a vice that has both personal and social dimensions. The word comes from the Latin *gluttire*, which means to swallow or gulp down. Most Christians today don't give much thought to this particular vice; it's hard to see how it could have ever been considered one of the "seven deadly sins."

Widespread patterns of eating in the developed world are connected to both social injustice and ecological destruction in faraway places. The growing demand for beef in both the developed world and in emerging markets offers strong incentives for agribusinesses to continue to convert Amazon rainforest into cattle ranches. Brazil is the largest beef exporter in the world, and its cattle industry is a huge producer of carbon-dioxide emissions.[11] Overconsumption of meat contributes to a host of global problems, including deforestation, air pollution, ozone depletion, and the destruction of the traditional homelands of indigenous people. Many ecological activists

---

[11] "Brazilian Beef: Greater Impact on the Environment Than We Realized," *Science Daily*, March 7, 2011.

argue that norms of justice as well as temperance require us to reduce the amount of meat in our diet.

Social temperance also requires responsible family planning. After returning from a trip to the Philippines during which he met former street children who had been abandoned by their parents, Pope Francis pointed out the imperative of responsible parenthood. To be stewards of the planet we have to responsibly plan the number and spacing of the births of our children. He told a reporter, "Some people think—excuse my expression here—that in order to be good Catholics, we have to be like rabbits."[12] Two hundred thousand babies are born every day. The United Nations predicts that global population growth rates will stabilize by 2050 to produce a world population of 9.6 billion.[13] Many experts consider this number to be well-beyond the sustainable carrying capacity of the planet at our current levels of consumption.[14]

Our large global population is putting enormous strain on energy reserves, biodiversity, and supplies of food and potable water. It also contributes to global inequality, conflict, and violence. Increased population produces even more of the human activities that are now causing climate change, species extinction, and the destruction of habitats from wetlands and woodlands to coral reefs. It also leads to greater levels of overall industrial production, consumption, and pollution. Population growth is especially problematic in countries in which it leads to the increased production, sale, and use of cars and the roads on which they are driven, all of which has hugely negative effects on air pollution, oil consumption, climate change, and habitat destruction.

Reducing the rate of population growth by itself, however, is no silver bullet. Social justice is also decisively important. Population rates tend to decline in regions where infant mortality has been reduced and women have access to higher quality healthcare, higher levels of education, and higher standards of living.

Second, the virtue of temperance also resists greed, the vice that most tempts people in our society. Greed refuses to observe appropriate limits. It violates justice by taking goods that belong to others (or hoarding goods that would enable others to survive). Greed also violates temperance when,

---

[12] Shannon McMahon, "Pope Francis: Stop Breeding Like Rabbits," *Boston Globe*, January 20, 2015.

[13] "World Population Projected to Reach 9.6 Billion by 2050—U.N. Report," *UN News Centre*, June 13, 2013.

[14] See, for example, Alan Weisman, *Countdown: Our Last Best Hope for a Future on Earth?* (Boston: Back Bay Books, 2014). A more optimistic view is provided by Fred Pearce, *The Coming Population Crash: And Our Planet's Surprising Future* (Boston: Beacon Press, 2010).

in an analogous sense, it leads one to be carried away with the pleasure of making money or acquiring possessions. Greed refuses to be constrained by reason or proportioned to the needs of others. Stang, for example, saw how the greed of Brazilian landowners and ranchers led them to steal land from small farmers, defend their claims by fabricating land titles, bribe government officials, tell lies about her and her colleagues, and hire brutes to use violence against settlers.

Well-meaning people today can be tempted to think they have to face a radical choice: either live like Stang and sleep in a hut in a malaria-infested jungle or just have a normal middle-class career and raise a family in sub-urban comfort. The choice, in other words, is between "saving the world" or "selling out." The dichotomy is false. Some of us are called to live like Stang, but most of us are not. It is entirely possible to serve others while also providing a decent standard of living for our families. We can grow as stewards by extending the circle of those for whom we care and increasing the quality of our caregiving for family members and friends. Both commitments involve matters of degree rather than an all-or-nothing choice.

An ethic of sufficiency seeks to promote sustainable patterns of consumption.[15] Christians who do not take up the way of voluntary poverty are still expected to practice restraint in their consumer habits and to share what they have with the underserved. What counts as sufficient for a good human life, of course, varies from one context to another. It includes the minimum requirements for water, food, shelter, and healthcare, but it goes well beyond mere subsistence requirements. It aims at what is sufficient for a good life, not merely survival. This ethic is not purely personal or individual. It implies support for socioeconomic, political, and legal institutions that enable people to develop and exercise their capabilities to provide for themselves.

Growing in Stewardship

We now turn to ways of growing in stewardship. There are countless ways of becoming better stewards in our own particular contexts. Young people learn to become stewards by taking care of friends and younger siblings, and, in different ways, their pets and possessions. Most adults become better stewards primarily by parenting their young children or struggling to care for disabled, very sick, or elderly loved ones. We can grow in stewardship in many other ways as well.

---

[15] On this distinction, see James B. Martin-Schramm and Robert L. Stivers, eds., *Christian Environmental Ethics: A Case Method Approach* (Maryknoll, NY: Orbis Books, 2003).

First, we can grow in stewardship by expanding the range and depth of our love of what is good in all its forms and dimensions—human and nonhuman, natural and cultural, individual persons and wider communities. Learning how to love what is good is the core of virtue and a skill essential to living well. People who love the world the right way are better off than those who do not. They can take pleasure and delight, find comfort and peace, in the concrete goods of their lives. Prayer, sacraments, music, art, worship, and service enable us to become better stewards when they develop our capacities for wonder, awe, gratitude, and reverence.

The Christian tradition conceives of recreation as *re*creation, not just entertainment, distraction, or stimulation. We are "recreated" by engaging in activities that enable us to enjoy the goodness and beauty in life. Sabbath rest structures our week so that we acknowledge and celebrate the goodness of our lives. It helps us to remember that work, while noble, is not the only meaningful human activity, and that money is not an end in itself, but a means to the end of the good life.

Second, we can also grow in stewardship by becoming more informed about specific kinds of challenges faced by people and other creatures for whom we are responsible. Love for creation brings a responsibility to be more curious and to work hard to understand it. It seeks to overcome the ignorance and complacency that facilitate social injustice and environmental destruction.

Climate change is a case in point. The use of fossil fuels has led to the highest levels of carbon dioxide in the atmosphere in three million years. In the United States, support for environmental protection was treated as a nonpartisan matter until the political debate that surrounded the drafting of the Kyoto Protocol in 1998. Since then the topic of climate change has been a major battle in the "culture wars." Some powerful businesses have worked hard to confuse the public about whether human activity is having a negative long-term effect on our climate.

A strong scientific consensus recognizes human-caused climate change as a serious threat to the health of the planet.[16] A majority of Americans believe that scientists are divided over the issue. In a 2009 Pew poll, 84 percent of scientists agreed that global temperatures were rising because of human activity, but only 49 percent of the public thought so. A poll in March 2013 reported that 37 percent of Americans think global warming is a hoax.[17] A 2013 study conducted by faculty at Yale University found that

---

[16] See Joint Science Academies, "Joint Science Academies' Statement: Global Response to Climate Change," 2005. See also IPCC, "2014 Report of the Intergovernmental Panel on Climate Change."

[17] Jim Williams, "Conspiracy Theory Poll Results," Public Policy Polling, publicpolicypolling.com website.

while nearly two in three Americans acknowledge human-caused climate change, this percentage dropped from 70 percent to 63 percent after a particularly cold winter. We cannot be responsible participants in the natural world if we do not acknowledge the damage we are doing to it.

Third, each of us, as individuals, can undertake commitments to become a better steward in some concrete way. On a personal level, for example, we are better stewards when we eat more healthy food, get more regular exercise, or develop a neglected talent. On the interpersonal level, for example, we are better stewards when we eat meals with family members or friends. On the community level, for example, we act as better stewards when we volunteer in a local civic organization or parish or school.

We can also increase our capacity to be good ecological stewards by undertaking concrete commitments to specific causes. A vast range of human activities harm the environment: toxic waste dumps; air pollution; strip mining and mountaintop removal; polluted rivers, lakes, and wetlands; a damaged ozone layer; illegal poaching and fur trade; species extinction; acid rain; and rainforest destruction. None of us can take on all of the causes of ecological destruction, but each of us can undertake specific and proportioned commitments that over time can make some concrete difference somewhere. We can engage in letter writing campaigns to government officials and political representatives, write blogs, carry on one-on-one conversations, circulate and sign petitions, volunteer for NGOs, support boycotts (of ivory, diamonds, baby seal skin products, among others), participate in nonviolent protests, and give financial support to environmental groups like the Sierra Club, World Wildlife Fund, and Greenpeace. There is practically no end to opportunities for getting involved.

We can grow in ecological stewardship by working not just as individuals or small groups but also within institutions dedicated to ecological concerns. Large-scale inequities cannot be addressed sufficiently by changing individual attitudes and lifestyles. To paraphrase King, virtue cannot be legislated, but behavior can be regulated.[18] We can create legally mandated incentives that encourage individuals and communities to act more responsibly and address these issues at a collective level through socioeconomic, legal, and political reforms. We can work for institutional changes through political activism. Small voluntary commitments are not enough. As citizens we have a right to demand that lawmakers, public-policy advocates, and politicians do more to protect our communities and the wider natural world. What specific policies we ought to promote in particular circumstances is, of course, a matter of prudent judgment.

---

[18] King, *Strength to Love*, 34.

Temptations of Stewardship

Every model of service brings with it certain negative possibilities—ways in which people who engage in it typically can go awry. A realistic recognition of temptations can help us resist them.

Temptations always contain some element of what is good; otherwise they would not be able to draw us in. When we give in to temptations, we often engage in self-deception. We make excuses, deflect attention from what we have done, minimize its harm, or blame others. These tactics can even come into play when we are trying to act in admirable ways. If we don't recognize temptations, we are more vulnerable to them.

We can take a brief look at five temptations often faced by stewards: stinginess, domination, workaholism, neglect of loved ones, and neglect of people who fall outside our particular domains of stewardship.

First, people who exercise stewardship can become so protective that they cling to the goods for which they are responsible. We can feel so protective that our sense of responsibility is weakened. Stewardship should not be confused with the hoarding of resources (Mt 6:20; Lk 12:16–21). Christian stewardship is as openhanded as reasonably possible.

Second, people who strive to be good stewards can be tempted to be too controlling of other people, especially when they think it is for their own good. Dorothy Day made this resolution in her diary: "Not to try to make order where people do not want order. Leave them alone but just love them." She later added a note of psychological realism: "We can have no control, no power over others, only over ourselves, and . . . this is a grace, a gift, which we must continually pray for."[19] Rather than "fixing" others, appropriate stewardship seeks to create conditions that enable people to make good choices for their own lives. We can't lead other people's lives for them.

Third, stewards can be tempted to workaholism. We normally think of the workaholic as the driven careerist obsessed with his or her achievements, income, and social status. But some people become workaholics for altruistic reasons. Doctors who focus only on their patients can ignore the needs of their nurses and other colleagues, and pastors can be compassionate to parishioners but impossibly hard on their parish staff. We best resist this temptation by cultivating a wider gratitude for the people around us, a realistic awareness of their limits, and an empathy for the burdens they have to carry.

Fourth, stewards can be tempted to neglect their loved ones. Work can be a channel of stewardship, but devotion to some responsibilities can create an imbalanced neglect of others. Well-intentioned and self-sacrificing idealists

---

[19] Dorothy Day, *The Duty of Delight: The Diaries of Dorothy Day*, ed. Robert Ellsberg (Milwaukee: Marquette University Press, 2008), 294, 505.

can take friends for granted or reduce one's familial role to breadwinning. In a letter to a good friend, Dorothy Day lamented, "how our crowded lives make us neglect those dear to us."[20] To a young man struggling with his parents, she wrote: "When you say you want to love your fellow men you just have to begin at home. . . . It is so easy to love people at a distance—not folks at home. I know how it is. We each of us have been thru it all."[21] Such behavior can afflict the missionary who works so hard that his marriage falls apart or the civil rights lawyer who spends so much time on cases that she never sees her children.

Our responsibility to be good stewards applies in a special way to those closest to us. Loving people in our own family is not as exciting as caring for those who are more remote or in more desperate circumstances. An ethic of service can provide an excuse for staying away from a difficult teenager at home or a troubled friend at work. As Mother Teresa pointed out, "It is easier to give a cup of rice to relieve the hunger of a needy person than to comfort the loneliness and the anguish of someone in your own home who does not feel loved."[22] When a journalist asked her what he could do to advance world peace, she answered: "Go home and love your family."[23] We can resist this temptation by developing a stronger awareness of connections to and responsibilities for the people in our life. We need a clear sense of what the Catholic tradition calls the order of charity—the set of priorities that protect and promote our relationships with our loved ones as well as other kinds of connections and duties.

Finally, stewards can be drawn to the opposite temptation, that is, to focus narrowly on responsibilities to their own community in such a way as to neglect responsibilities to outsiders. An owner of a small business can be very good to his employees and customers but be completely heedless of others.

I am reminded of a time I was invited by the friend of a celebrity to go to dinner at a high-priced restaurant. Fifteen people had drinks, appetizers, entrees, and dessert. It was an incredible feast, and we all had an amazing time. At the end of the meal the manager of the restaurant told the celebrity that the bill for the meal was "on the house." I have no idea what the bill was, but I'm sure the dinner was very expensive.

As we were slowly trickling out of the restaurant, a homeless man came to the entrance and asked the manager if he had any food to spare. The scene immediately reminded me of Luke's story of Lazarus, "who longed

---

[20] Day, *All the Way to Heaven*, 182.

[21] Ibid., 220.

[22] *Mother Teresa: Essential Writings*, ed. Jean Maalouf (Maryknoll, NY: Orbis Books, 2008), 81.

[23] Cited at Mother Teresa of Calcutta Center, motherteresa.org website.

to satisfy his hunger with what fell from the rich man's table" (Lk 16:21). The manager, who had just picked up the entire tab for the party, told him the restaurant had nothing to give him. I suppose the manager was just going by the owner's policy or didn't want to create a precedent. In any case, this story shows how easy it is to be generous to the well-off while brushing off those who are out in the cold.

Parishes and congregations face the same temptation. Pastors need to solicit donations to pay the church's heating bills and get the roof fixed. Sometimes they speak a lot more about the well-being of their parish than about the poor of their neighborhoods. To be faithful to the full message of the gospel, stewardship needs to be complemented by compassion to the "least" of our brothers and sisters, including outsiders.

Conclusion

Stewardship is the model of service that works to take care of what has been entrusted to us. This responsibility comes with our status as created in the image of God. We can only be good stewards if we exercise the virtue of temperance, which enables us to moderate our desires for human goods. We can grow as stewards by working to give appropriate care to the full range of people and goods in our lives rather than just serving some to the neglect of others.

8

Hospitality

"I was a stranger and you welcomed me" (Mt 25:35). Hospitality is the practice of welcoming guests into one's home or community. This chapter examines the moral and spiritual significance of hospitality as a model of Christian service. To do so, it discusses (1) hospitality in the Bible, (2) theological reflection on covenant, (3) the virtue of generosity, (4) growing in hospitality, and (5) temptations of hospitality.

Hospitality in the Bible

Israelites learned about the value of hospitality from their experience. Biblical narratives portray the early ancestors of Israel at various times as nomads, alien workers, and slaves in Egypt. This experience taught them what it is like to be vulnerable while traveling or living in foreign lands. The later covenant with God at Mount Sinai prohibited Israelites from harming the foreigner: "When a stranger sojourns with you in your land, you shall not do him wrong" (Lev 19:33). It insisted that justice applies equally to Israelites and resident aliens in Israel (Lev 24:22).

Ancient Israel distinguished two kinds of strangers: traveling foreigners and resident aliens. The former were people from other lands who for some reason (for example, to conduct trade or to seek refuge in times of war) temporarily visited Israel. Resident aliens, on the other hand, were foreigners who lived among Israelites on a more or less permanent basis. Most resident aliens had to eke out a living as day laborers and were vulnerable to exploitation. They are listed, along with widows, orphans, and the poor, as a class of needy persons (see Ex 22:21–22).

Israelites remembered that God cared for their ancestors in the wilderness and that God, not Israel, is the permanent owner of the land. The Israelites considered themselves to be sojourning on God's land rather than occupying it as its owners (see Lev 25:23). The Israelites knew what it was like to be resident aliens, and they were instructed to be good to strangers in their midst: "You shall treat the stranger who sojourns with you as the native among you, and you shall love him as yourself, for you were strangers in the land of Egypt: I am the Lord your God" (Lev 19:34). Israelites "should see on the face of the resident alien a memory of what they were in Egypt."[1]

Care for resident aliens did not require Israelites to be naive about the fact that the nations across the border were potential or actual enemies. Hence the prayer of the Psalmist: "May all who hate Zion be put to shame and turned backwards" (Ps 129:5). Israel had to survive as a small nation threatened by powerful neighbors—including, successively, the Egyptian, Assyrian, Babylonian, Hellenistic, and Roman empires. The naked aggression, horrifying cruelty, and grinding oppression of these empires led some Israelites to regard them as held in the grip of demonic forces.

The law of Israel was complemented by a culture of hospitality. Hosts were to offer traveling strangers fresh water to drink, an opportunity to take a bath and put on clean clothing, a decent meal, and a place to rest before resuming their journey. Hosts were also expected to supply their guests with provisions for the next leg of their journey and, if needed, to guide them to its next stage.

Hospitality to strangers was provided on request and free of charge. Yet since both host and guest were vulnerable to exploitation, hospitality was not unconditional; it had a definite shape and limits. The stranger was expected to say something about who he is, where he is from, and where he is going and why. The host was expected to offer a decent but not lavish amount of food. Guests were not to move in and treat their host's home as if it were their own. Hosts were not to pry into their guests' affairs, and guests were not to take anything that their hosts had not offered.

New Testament interpretations of hospitality grew of out this tradition. St. Paul urged the Romans to "extend hospitality to strangers" (12:13). Describing hospitality as an expression of love (Rom 12:9–13), he urged the Christian community in Rome to "welcome one another, therefore, just as Christ has welcomed you" (Rom 15:7). He advised them not only to welcome friends but also strangers (Rom 12:13).

The Gospels depict Jesus as an itinerant who had "no place to lay his head" (Lk 9:58; Mt 8:20) and who relied on the kindness of whoever would welcome him (Lk 9:58). Jesus taught hospitality as one of the concrete ways of living higher righteousness: "I was a stranger and you invited me in" (Mt 25:35).

A particularly poignant depiction of hospitality occurs in the thirteenth chapter of the Gospel of John, when Jesus shows his love for the disciples

---

[1] Enrique Nardoni, *Rise Up, O Judge: A Study of Justice in the Biblical World*, trans. Sean Charles Martin (Peabody, MA: Hendrickson, 2004), 81.

by bending down and washing their own feet. The disciples are taken aback when Jesus expressed a desire to do to this because in their culture washing another's feet was considered an act of servitude. Hosts in ancient Palestine would typically greet their guests and then give them water so they could remove their sandals and wash their feet. It is understandable, then, why Peter initially resists Jesus's offer to wash his feet. Jesus, however, insisted: "Unless I wash you, you have no share with me." Peter replies with his typical exuberance: "Lord, not my feet only but also my hands and my head!" (13:8–9).

Jesus's action enables Peter to see in a concrete way the kind of service that characterizes discipleship: "So if I, your Lord and Teacher, have washed your feet, you also ought to wash one another's feet." Jesus makes his point clear: "I have set you an example, that you also should do as I have done to you." This episode is completed with a Johannine beatitude: "If you know these things, blessed are you if you do them." It draws a clear connection between hospitality and faith in Christ and the Father: "Very truly, I tell you, whoever receives one whom I send receives me; and whoever receives me receives him who sent me" (13:14–20).

Receiving hospitality is a way of honoring the host. In some ways it can be harder to receive hospitality than to give it. The giver of hospitality exercises agency, but the recipient has to give up control and allow himself or herself to accept another's generosity. In a broader way, Christian discipleship can be described as a way of learning how to accept God's hospitality. We are welcomed into God's creation and invited to be God's guests.

Jesus rejected the practice of using hospitality to separate insiders from outsiders. He was willing to have his disciples feast when others thought they should be fasting, eat with unwashed hands, pick grain on the Sabbath so they could eat, and dine with people who lived in violation of the law. The religious conventions of his day regarded purity regulations as a way of maintaining Israel's status as a holy nation, set apart from others, and steadfastly loyal to Yahweh. The people took it for granted that one could be religiously contaminated or defiled by eating with those considered unclean—a category that included lepers, the sick, Samaritans, the poor, Gentiles, people who had regular contact with Gentiles, and people with dishonorable occupations like tax collecting and prostitution.

In sharing meals with tax collectors and "sinners," Jesus deliberately extended hospitality to the despised, marginalized, and excluded. His hospitality was not a matter of easy-going friendliness but a vivid and startling depiction of the radically inclusive character of God's love. Jesus offered table fellowship to all, even to his own betrayer, Judas (Mk 14:18–20). Jesus used meals as a way of showing the inclusive nature of the reign of God. He refused to be rigidly bound to regulations that were supposed to protect the religious purity of the righteous.

The open table fellowship displayed by Jesus continues to be counter-cultural in our time. We often use meals as a way of strengthening bonds with friends while keeping others at a distance. In their first weeks of college, many students feel uncomfortable going to dinner because they don't yet have any friends to eat with. Racial boundaries are apparent on many campuses where black students typically eat with other black students, white students eat with other white students, and so on.

Jesus offended "respectable" society not only by welcoming "undesirables," but also by not telling sinners that they must first repent of their sins and make amends before they could join him. Opponents could view his inclusive hospitality as something like an ancient Jewish version of being "soft on crime." Jesus, in fact, never tells anyone to repent before joining him to break bread. This is true not only of those who sinned out of weakness but even those who sinned through their misuse of power over others. Instead of leading with a call to repentance, Jesus led with compassion. His hospitality enabled people to see their need for forgiveness and reconciliation (see Lk 19:1–10).

The Letter to the Hebrews advises: "Do not neglect to show hospitality to strangers, for thereby some have entertained angels unawares" (13:2). This quotation refers to the important episode when Abraham sees three strangers at Mamre and hurries to greet them (Gen 18). He invites them into his tent, gives them water to wash their feet, and feeds them. These strangers turn out to be angels, who tell Abraham that God will soon fulfill his promise to give him a son.

In the New Testament an echo of this story is found in the parable of the Prodigal Son (Lk 15:11–32). This story is one of three in chapter 15 of the Gospel of Luke that depict God's desire to seek out, find, and welcome the lost. In this story the younger of two sons asks for his inheritance and then squanders it in a far-off land. During a famine the younger son has no way to obtain food and decides to return home. He tries to figure out a way to get back into his father's household and formulates a persuasive speech to deliver to his father. As the son approaches home, his father sees him from a distance and rushes to embrace him before the son can utter a word of apology. Rather than demanding repentance, the father greets his son with an outpouring of extravagant affection. "That is the kind of Father we have," observed Day. "No judgment here. Only the madness of love, deep, profound, as profligate in its way as the son's tawdry loves had been profligate."[2]

---

[2] Dorothy Day, *The Duty of Delight: The Diaries of Dorothy Day*, ed. Robert Ellsberg (Milwaukee: Marquette University Press, 2008), 165.

In the second part of the story, the dutiful elder son criticizes his father for welcoming back his irresponsible brother. It turns out that neither of these sons understand their father's unconditional love for them. The younger son did not return home because he missed his family or because he felt guilty about abandoning them but because he was starving. The elder son mistook his relationship to their father as like that of "hired servants." The father, in contrast, makes the goods of the household freely available to both because he loves them, not as payment for the fulfillment of duties. He wants to base his family's relationships on love rather than on a prudently calculated reciprocity. The father sees an "us," but the two sons think only in terms of "I" and "you."

The father shows hospitality to the son who had become alien in both his geography (far away) and diet (eating with pigs). The father bears some interesting similarities to Abraham. Both hurry to greet the new arrival. Both take care of their physical needs, give special attention to food, and do so with lavish generosity. Both issue an invitation to come inside (though the elder son insists on remaining outside while complaining to his father).

The father, though, is much more extravagant than Abraham. It is sometimes harder for us to open our hearts to family members who have betrayed us than it is to welcome strangers into our home. Yet the father doesn't give the slightest hint that he feels anger or even disappointment toward his derelict son. His only hint of disapproval is directed at the elder son's envy and resentment. He tells the elder son he's been included all along—just not on his terms.

The church was able to grow because of the hospitality of early Christians. Before buildings were erected for the purpose of Christian worship, Christians opened their homes for use as house churches in which believers could hear the gospel preached and worship. We can see in the New Testament traces of the challenges these kinds of meetings presented—some members thought they were better than others (1 Cor 11:17–32), a host excluded people who should have been welcomed (3 Jn 9—10), and some communities only extended hospitality in half-hearted ways (1 Pet 4:9).

The Gospel of Luke may place a special emphasis on hospitality. Perhaps it was written to help believers whose communities gathered in house churches. Jesus sends disciples out as itinerant prophets to villages, but not everyone is in a position to lead an itinerant lifestyle. Christians like Martha and Mary learned to extend hospitality as an important form of Christian service.

Some people welcomed Jesus, but others did not. The scribes and Pharisees complained about Jesus's willingness to accept hospitality from "tax collectors and sinners" (Lk 5:30; also 15:32). Levi the tax collector, for example, welcomes Jesus into his home and offers a great feast for him (see Lk 5:29). Similarly, Zacchaeus, a wealthy tax collector, welcomes Jesus into his home—after Jesus announces he is coming to his home—and in doing so is recovered as a "son of Abraham" and incorporated back into the community that had shunned him (Lk 19). A key question for the first Christians was whether they would be welcomed or rejected by the communities they visited. We are told that those who showed kindness to the disciples were at the same time welcoming Jesus, and that those who mistreated the disciples would be taken as also rejecting Jesus (see Mt 25:31–46).

Theological Reflection on Covenant

This chapter connects the practice of hospitality with the theology of the covenant. In the Ancient Near East a covenant was a binding agreement between two parties, typically a treaty between a king and a vassal. The former promised protection from external threats; the latter pledged to be loyal and to provide assistance when needed.

The covenant between God and Israel provides the basic narrative structure of the Old Testament. Covenants provide key landmarks in the history of the people of God. After the flood God enters into a covenant with the human race as represented by Noah. The Book of Genesis, or "origins," focuses on the great patriarchs (Abraham, Isaac, and Jacob) and their families as the founding families of the people of Israel. God chose Abraham to be the father of the chosen people, and Abraham responded with obedient trust. He left his home and traveled to the place where God wanted him to go. He and his descendants struggled to establish themselves as a united family in the land God had given them.

When famine overtook their land, Jacob and his sons were forced to migrate to Egypt. After the death of Jacob's son Joseph, the Hebrews were enslaved by the Egyptians and subjected to cruel oppression. God, however, notices the suffering of the people: "The Lord said, 'I have observed the misery of my people who are in Egypt; I have heard their cry on account of their taskmasters'" (Ex 3:7). God then acts compassionately to deliver them from evil and to bring them to a place of safety where they can flourish: "I know their sufferings, and I have come down to deliver them from the Egyptians, and to bring them up out of that land to a good and broad land, a land flowing with milk and honey" (3:8). All this, the text reiterates, reflects God's compassion and justice: "The cry of the Israelites has now come to me; I have also seen how the Egyptians oppress them" (3:7–9). God brings the Hebrews to Mount Sinai where they enter into a covenant with God, who promises to bless Israel in exchange for Israel's loyalty. The blessings include land, protection from enemies, health, children, and the joy of righteous living. Israel is to show its loyalty to God through faithful worship and living justly.

At the foot of Mount Sinai the people of Israel ratify the treaty by ceremonially splitting an animal in two and sprinkling its blood on the people (an image that later plays a important role in Christian interpretations of both the death of Jesus and the Eucharist). This ceremony was followed by a sacred meal eaten in the presence of God (Ex 24). The people construct an ark to hold the two tablets of the law (Ex 25:10–21). According to 2 Samuel and 1 Kings, the ark was kept in a tent until King David and King Solomon erected the central place of worship, the Jerusalem Temple.

The Sinai covenant slowly enables these people to become one nation and one country. It unites the Twelve Tribes not just by blood or political expediency but by loyalty and obedience to God. This covenant provides the framework for interpreting God's earlier promises to Noah and the patriarchs, guidelines for worship and daily life, and standards by which kings and people are judged by the prophets.[3]

As time goes on, the people of God often fail to live up to the covenant, particularly by practicing idolatry and mistreating the poor. God remains faithful to the covenant with Israel out of "steadfast love" *(hesed)* but also calls Israel to repentance. The prophet Jeremiah expresses God's love for Israel this way: "I have loved you with an everlasting love; therefore I have continued my faithfulness to you" (Jer 31:3).

The story of Israel thus involves an on-again, off-again relationship with God. The people fall into bad ways; they ignore God and violate the covenant; and then, as expected, they are punished. Sometimes their wrongdoing is so outrageously at odds with God's will—particularly in their negligence or exploitation of the poor—that the prophets judge them deserving the harshest of punishments. Yet God is "generous in forgiving" (Is 55:7) and "merciful and gracious, slow to anger, and abounding in steadfast love and faithfulness" (Ex 34:6).

Israel's commitment to the covenant can only be sustained through a process of continual renewal. The prophet Jeremiah contrasted the old law of Mount Sinai written on "tablets of stone" with the "new covenant" that God makes with Israel after the exile in Babylon. The Lord promises: "I will put my law within them, and I will write it on their hearts; and I will be their God, and they shall be my people" (Jer 31:33).

Heart refers to the very core of a person's identity and thought. When people's deepest desires are shaped by love, they want to serve God and live

---

[3] See ibid.

righteously. Fidelity to God is not just a matter of conducting the right kind of religious rituals but of caring for people with justice and compassion. Jeremiah strikes a tone of healing, hope, and consolation: "They shall all know me, from the least of them to the greatest, says the Lord; for I will forgive their iniquity, and remember their sin no more" (Jer 31:34).

Christians regard the New Testament as the new covenant. Jesus is the one whose obedient fidelity fulfills God's promise of salvation, not only to the chosen people but to anyone who believes the good news. In the old covenant the people were made holy by the blood of sacrificial animals; in the new covenant, Christians believe, we are made holy by Jesus's blood.

Paul describes the Lord's supper as a sacred meal that establishes the new covenant: "In the same way he took the cup also, after supper, saying, 'This cup is the new covenant in my blood. Do this, as often as you drink it, in remembrance of me'" (1 Cor 11:25). Paul understood Jesus as offering his own life for the sake of his disciples. When we drink Jesus's blood and eat his body in the Eucharist, we sacramentally internalize the new covenant and are incorporated into his body.

Christians understand the new covenant as uniting believers as a particular people bound together by the Spirit of Christ. This covenant is the basis of Christian service: "Since God loved us so much, we also ought to love one another" (1 Jn 4:11). The new covenant generates hospitality not only to friends but also to strangers. The love of strangers *(philoxenia)* is an application of Jesus's willingness to offer hospitality to powerless outcasts, the disabled and diseased, and other marginalized people.

This is why Dorothy Day and Peter Maurin took hospitality to the "least" as a central feature of the Christian life. True Christian hospitality is paradigmatically expressed in face-to-face personal care. It provides not only food and drink to visitors but also friendship. "It is so much easier to throw people the clothes, the food or what not that they need, and so hard to sit down with them and listen patiently."[4] A Christian theology of covenant thus places a special emphasis on extending kindness to people on the margins. Day said that we are to serve everyone, "to wash the feet of all men, recognizing our common humanity—we are one flesh, as is said of husbands and wives."[5]

We can offer hospitality in our homes, our neighborhoods, our places of work, and our worship communities. We can only do so appropriately, though, if we are aware of who might feel like an outsider in our midst. We come to acknowledge outsiders not only by noticing them visually, but,

---

[4] Quoted in Jim Forest, *All Is Grace: A Biography of Dorothy Day* (Maryknoll, NY: Orbis Books, 2011), 131–32.

[5] Day, *The Duty of Delight*, 165.

more personally, by going out of our way to listen to their stories and to share our stories with them. Covenant hospitality naturally leads to mutual giving and receiving.

Because we have been formed by an individualistic culture, we are prone to think of hospitality only as something that an individual provides to other individuals. Covenantal theology, though, highlights ways in which communities and institutions can also offer hospitality. What might start as the inspiration of a few individuals or a small community can develop into permanent, organized ways of providing hospitality in the future. We saw this in Mother Teresa's homes for the dying, Day and Maurin's Houses of Hospitality, and Stang's centers for women and children.

The theology of the covenant also grounds a vision of the church as open and welcoming to all people. As Pope John Paul II noted it in his "World Migration Day Message 1999," "The parish, which etymologically means a house where the guest feels at ease, welcomes all and discriminates against none, for no one there is an outsider" (no. 6). Unfortunately, this ideal is not always realized. Some Christian communities, for example, are not very welcoming when it comes to people with disabilities, to Christians of other traditions, or to gays and lesbians. For example, Bishop Robert C. Morlino of the Diocese of Madison questions whether the song "All Are Welcome" is appropriate for Catholic worship services because it suggests that the choice to follow Jesus makes no difference. That isn't the case, the bishop points out.[6]

A more inclusive example of hospitality is found in a story told by Greg Boyle, SJ, from a time when he was the pastor of the Dolores Mission Parish in East Los Angeles. In 1987, his parish declared itself a sanctuary for undocumented migrants. Men, women, and children who had nowhere else to go were invited to sleep in the parish church or convent. One night an angry person spray-painted "Wetback Church" on a wall of a parish building. When Boyle asked his parish leaders if they could get someone to remove the graffiti, one of them, Petra Saldana, objected: "You will not clean this up. If there are people in our community who are disparaged and hated and left out because they are *mojados* (wetbacks), then we shall be proud to call ourselves a wetback church."[7]

Covenant theology suggests that particular congregations must be both inward-facing and outward facing; they have to build up their own internal bonds while also making sure that outsiders feel welcome. We must thus

---

[6] See Bishop's Column, "The Beauty of Our Worship in the Liturgy," *Catholic Herald*, October 20, 2011.

[7] Gregory Boyle, *Tattoos on the Heart: The Power of Boundless Compassion* (New York: Free Press, 2010), 71–72.

avoid two extremes: being warm and supportive toward one another but reserved toward outsiders, or focusing so much on the surrounding community that we ignore our own members.

All of us need to think about whether our acts, attitudes, and use of language communicate, at least in subtle and unintended ways, unwelcoming messages. It is easy for the lay Christians to point fingers at clergy and to ignore our own personal responsibility to show hospitality to guests. The church is the entire community, and not just its formal institutional authorities. We can ask whether estranged people feel welcome in our communities the same way that the "outcasts" felt accepted by Jesus.

The Virtue of Generosity

Hospitality is rooted in the virtue of generosity, a broad willingness to give to others without seeking to receive something in return. A company that pays a huge salary to its CEO is just reflecting market conditions, not being generous. Generosity is not so much marked by the size or costliness of what is given as by the quality of the giver's motivation. The poor widow who gives only a few pennies is more generous than the rich man who gives out of his abundance (Mk 12:38–44).

This understanding of generosity is illustrated in Dorothy Day's description of her friend Marge Hughes:

> When there is nothing in the house but rice and a few vegetables, she can produce a delicious meal consisting mainly of fried rice and onions. Hers is a joyous and uncomplaining spirit, never perturbed, always welcoming. . . . She does not hesitate to use "the last of her meal and oil" for the needy and hungry guest, and somehow there is "always enough for one more."[8]

Christian faith holds that we can only give what we first receive. Christian generosity flows from gratitude for what God has done for us in Christ. The culmination of divine generosity is the incarnation. The Word became flesh so that we could come fully to God. Christ's Spirit is offered freely to each of us. There is nothing we can do to earn this gift. Whereas reciprocity says, "I'll be good to you so that you will help me in the future," Christian gratitude says, "I'll be good to you because I want my life to reflect and pass on the goodness God has shown to me."

Christian faith sees all the particular goods in our lives—from the air we breathe and water we drink to the music that moves us and the friends we

---

[8] Dorothy Day, *Loaves and Fishes* (Maryknoll, NY: Orbis Books, 1997), 143.

love—as gifts given to us by God. Day went so far as to say that gratitude "makes you love people."[9] This suggests that Christian morality is based on a gift mentality rather than on an exchange mentality—the attitude of the extravagant father rather than the prodigal son or his resentful older brother. A gift mentality proposes that we give to others because of what we have been given by God; an exchange mentality reflects a "tit-for-tat" policy that advises us to treat others the same way that they treat us.

Appropriate hospitality gives in a way that fits the needs and respects the limits of both giver and recipient. It is obviously better, for example, to give food rather than cash to an active addict. We have to discern how best to take care of those to whom we are closely bound in life while also remaining attentive to the most needy in our world. In the end we have to exercise good judgment based on our sense of what is fitting in a given situation.

Love leads to concrete actions when we have the resources to undertake them. We might bring a lonely friend home for dinner, spend an hour listening to a colleague's painful story, or go out of our way to give directions to a lost stranger. Since we do not have infinite time, energy, and money, however, we have to decide how best to use our resources. We are not in a position to do the good we wish we could do for every person we encounter—far from it. Yet we can still will the good to them, and at the very least, refuse to treat them unjustly.

Generosity is thus not simply a matter of giving as much of our resources as possible to others. We would not expect the father of the prodigal son to be just as generous with a complete stranger as he is to his own flesh and blood. Wise generosity gives to the right people in the right way; it must always be tailored to particular circumstances.

We must also give with the right attitude. Day captures this point when she writes: "You must know when to open the door to the other, and you must know how to open the door. There's no point in opening the door with bitterness and resentment in your heart." One day she realized that "the best, the very best, I could do for everyone in the community, including our guests, was to stay away, to not fight staying away, which I might have done successfully. There are times when one's generosity is a mask for one's pride: what will 'they' do without me?"[10]

The ability to be exercise appropriate generosity depends on a certain kind of interior detachment. *Detachment* here does not mean indifference, apathy, or aloofness. A balanced love of neighbor seeks to engage rather than withdraw from the world. It is detached in the sense that it is marked

---

[9] Day, *The Duty of Delight*, 51.

[10] Cited in Robert Coles, *Dorothy Day: A Radical Devotion* (San Francisco: Harper and Row, 1989), 130–31.

by a freedom from thoughts, emotions, or attitudes that get in the way of our thinking, speaking, and acting with appropriate generosity. "Appropriate" means neither stinginess, giving too little, nor extravagance, giving more than is needed or than one can afford to give.

We can note two domains where detachment supports hospitality. First, Christian hospitality depends on a certain interior detachment from possessions. Jesus denounced greed, stinginess, and cold-heartedness (Lk 12:15; Mt 6:19). He was especially critical of the disordered love of money that leads people to have a false sense of self-sufficiency and puts them out of touch with those who struggle financially.

Second, authentic hospitality also depends on a kind of freedom from what others think of us. Conformity can be the enemy of Christian hospitality. Caring too much, or in the wrong way, about how others view us can make some people afraid to be seen with the "wrong" people. Or it can make us go along with people who are acting in destructive ways. Looking back over his youth, Augustine lamented his willingness to go along with his friends when they stripped a farmer's pear tree just for the fun of doing what they shouldn't have done.[11] While teenagers are usually seen as especially susceptible to social pressure, adults often crave approval from their peers as well. In principle, there is nothing wrong with wanting to be accepted by our peers. Our desire to belong can draw us into friendships and communities that enable us to develop in good ways. But we can also be drawn into those that require us to sacrifice our integrity as a condition of belonging.

Growing in Hospitality

The two major obstacles to Christian hospitality are egocentrism and fear of the other. We already noted how hospitality can be a form of egoism that gives only to get something back. Hospitality that is generous, on the other hand, comes out of caring for others for their own sake. Jesus asked: "If you love those who love you, what credit is that to you? For even sinners love those who love them" (Lk 6:32). Christian hospitality to the stranger goes beyond the reciprocity of egoism. It includes caring for those who, for one reason or another, will never be able to reciprocate.

This does not mean, of course, that hospitality ought to be withheld from friends. When second Isaiah asks, "What is righteousness?" the answer embraces both stranger and family member:

---

[11] See St. Augustine, *Confessions*, trans. Henry Chadwick (New York: Oxford, 1991), 26.

> Is it not to share your bread with the hungry,
>> and bring the homeless poor into your house;
> when you see the naked, to cover them,
>> and not to hide yourself from your own kin?
>>> (Is 58:7)

Jesus warned his disciples not to love only those who love them, but this does not mean we should neglect our families, friends, neighbors, colleagues, or members of the various communities to which we belong. The New Testament, in fact, accents fellowship within the church. In St. Paul's terms, we are many members of "one body" (1 Cor 12:12). The Gospel of John presents a Jesus who is deeply committed to the unity of his followers: "By this everyone will know that you are my disciples, if you have love for one another" (Jn 13:35).

The second obstacle to hospitality is fear of the other. People throughout the world distinguish "us" from "them." We set up boundaries to feel safe. We are told to be good to our friends and to keep our distance from others. This pattern probably has roots in our remote evolutionary past, when our hunter-gatherer ancestors trusted group members and were suspicious of outsiders, who might harm them.

We hear about "stranger danger." We teach children never to talk to strangers (sometimes with unconscious racial and class overtones), and not to make eye contact with other riders on buses or subways. Mass media gets our attention by scaring us. The more violent television shows we watch, the more we will assume that we are likely to become a victim of violent crime.[12] In this context the Good Samaritan seems like a naive "do gooder."

Perhaps this fear of the other led Fort Lauderdale recently to pass an ordinance banning private groups (like churches) from publicly feeding homeless people. Two ministers and a ninety-year-old homeless advocate were arrested and face sixty days in jail or a $500 fine for doing so.[13] More than thirty other cities have passed or are now considering such legislation.

What begins with innuendo and subtle prejudice can slide into defending the "grain of truth" in ethnic stereotypes. Unchallenged bigotry makes it more acceptable to look down on people who are different, make derogatory comments about them, scapegoat them when something goes wrong, and even overtly persecute them. Demagogues find it easy to get political support by whipping up suspicion of people that are "other."

---

[12] Kathleen Kusters and Jan Van den Bulck, "Mediators of the Association between Television Viewing and Crime: Perceived Personal Risk and Perceived Ability to Cope," *Poetics* 39 (2011):107–24.

[13] Associated Press, "Three Arrested for Feeding the Homeless," *Boston Globe*, November 6, 2014.

Christianity tells us to love wisely rather than recklessly. We have to protect ourselves and our loved ones from con artists, scams, and others seeking to take advantage of us. King didn't welcome members of the Klan into his living room, and Christian hospitality doesn't require us to let anyone who comes to the door into our homes.

At the same time, we have to be careful not to let being "realistic" slide into self-centeredness or indifference to strangers. The gospel calls us to be responsible for both distant and near neighbors—precisely because everyone is our neighbor.[14] Christian hospitality thus does best when it avoids two extremes: both a "drop everything" radicalism that is so unrealistic that it runs out of gas in a few days and an equally extreme "look out for your own" mentality that has nothing to do with Christianity. If we want to be both realistic and generous, we need to cultivate two virtues: the social courage that gives us freedom from being controlled by our wariness of strangers and the practical wisdom to know when and how to extend hospitality in different circumstances.

Hospitality runs a spectrum from weak to strong, depending on both the capacities of the host and the needs of the guest. A homeowner who gives a cup of water to a painter working on his house shows weak hospitality, and one who takes in refugees for a month displays strong hospitality. The former is short term and inexpensive; the latter is longer term and costly.

We can extend our capacity for hospitality in many ways. First, we expand the range of our life experience. People from more individualistic cultures have a lot to learn about hospitality from people who live in more communitarian cultures. Sometimes communities with quite modest material resources display striking generosity.

Americans are often surprised by the hospitality they receive when are invited to stay in the homes of families in places like El Salvador or Guatemala. We are usually moved by the hospitality of hosts who open their homes, prepare beautiful meals, and spend lots of time with their guests. They often provide visitors the best food they can cook, the most comfortable beds in their homes, and heartfelt attention. They extend this hospitality not just as one individual to another, but as families and communities.

Experiences like these challenge us to extend hospitality more generously to strangers who visit our own communities. They help us see that other cultures have strengths that ours does not and that greater economic resources do not always translate into greater hospitality. They can help us to see that sometimes the wealthiest communities can be the least welcoming to outsiders. They protect themselves from outsiders by building gated

---

[14] See Karl Barth, *Church Dogmatics*, vol. 3.4, ed. G. W. Bromiley and T. F. Torrance, trans. A. T. MacKay et al. (Edinburgh: T&T Clark, 1961), 285ff.

communities, wiring their houses with alarm systems, and hiring private security agents. To give a rather extreme example, a 2013 candidate for city council of the affluent Detroit suburb of Hamtramck, Michigan, proposed that his town build a twelve-foot wall to "protect the city" and grant entry only to people who show state-issued IDs.[15]

We can grow in hospitality by cultivating an attitude of openness to the other. Our capacity for hospitality is blocked if we are suspicious of people who are different from us. Hospitality challenges us to make the boundaries of our communities more porous and to allow ourselves to feel awkward, to go out on a limb, and even to be taken advantage of from time to time.

We can also become more hospitable by structuring our communities to be more welcoming. A small-scale example of Christian hospitality is seen in Our Lady of Lourdes Catholic Church in Daytona Beach, Florida. The parish's mission statement is "Loving the God we cannot see by loving the neighbor we can." It begins with a strong affirmation of hospitality: "We strive to provide a welcoming place of worship for everyone: members and visitors alike." Almost all parishes make these kinds of official statements—but most only offer a few vague platitudes and leave it at that.

Our Lady of Lourdes, however, spells out in significant detail the image of hospitality it intends to implement. Instead of the usual generic invitation, the parish bulletin goes out of its way to communicate its commitment to inclusivity:

> We extend a special welcome to those who are single, married, divorced, gay, filthy rich, dirt poor, y no habla Ingles. We extend a special welcome to those who are crying newborns, skinny as a rail, or could afford to lose a few pounds. We welcome you if you can sing like Andrea Bocelli, or like our pastor who can't carry a note in a bucket. You're welcome here if you're "just browsing," just woke up, or just got out of jail. We don't care if you're overdressed, underdressed, cross-dressed, more Catholic than the Pope, or haven't been in church since little Joey's Baptism. We extend a special welcome to those who are over 60 but not grown up yet, and to teenagers who are growing up too fast. We welcome soccer moms, NASCAR dads, starving artists, tree-huggers, latte-sippers, vegetarians, junk-food eaters. We welcome those who are in recovery or are still addicted. We welcome you if you're having problems, or you're down in the dumps, or you don't like "organized religion" (we've been there, too). If you blew all your offering money at the dog track, you're welcome

---

[15] Hunter Schwarz, BuzzFeed, "City Council Candidate in Detroit Suburb Wants to Build a Wall to Keep Detroit Out," July 21, 2013.

here. We offer a special welcome to those who think the earth is flat, work too hard, don't work, can't spell, or came because grandma is in town and wanted to go to church. We welcome those who are inked, pierced, or both. We offer a special welcome to those who could use a prayer right now, had religion shoved down your throat as a kid, or got lost in traffic and wound up here by mistake. We welcome the flexible, inflexible, tolerant, intolerant, those who laughed, and those who gasped at this welcome. We welcome tourists, seekers, doubters, bleeding hearts . . . and you![16]

A more sharply countercultural example of communal hospitality can be seen in the New Sanctuary Movement of the 1980s and 1990s in the United States. The movement began by recruiting parishes and congregations to provide sanctuary to refugees who fled war and violent repression in Central America. Communities found they were changed by the practice of extending hospitality to Guatemalans and Salvadorans. Personal contacts helped them understand how the world looks from the point of view of the marginalized and to see the connection between Christian convictions and collective public action to change oppressive laws and policies.

This kind of religiously based hospitality challenges our wider American society to live up to our national ideals of hospitality. In 1903, words from American poet Emma Lazarus's sonnet "The New Colossus" were mounted on the pedestal of the Statue of Liberty to professes our country's commitment to hospitality:

> Give me your tired, your poor,
> Your huddled masses yearning to breathe free,
> The wretched refuse of your teeming shore.
> Send these, the homeless, tempest-tost to me.
> I lift my lamp beside the golden door.

Working from Catholic social teachings, theologian Kristin Heyer examines immigration patterns and their socioeconomic context. She argues that Christian ethics requires us to offer hospitality to immigrants based on four considerations: (1) the intrinsic dignity of every person requires us to fight the exploitation of immigrants as nothing more than cheap labor; (2) the pervasiveness of social sin alerts us to the ideological justification of

---

[16] See "All Are Welcome," ourladyoflourdesdaytona.com website. The statement is credited to Rev. John Petty of All Saints Lutheran Church, Aurora, Colorado.

structural injustices that harm immigrants; (3) the importance of the family underscores the harm done to women and children by unjust immigration policies; and (4) the Christian ethic of global solidarity (the fifth model of service in this book) calls into question any cultural division of the world into "us" (whom we protect) and "them" (whom we keep out). To be faithful to the gospel, Heyer argues, we need to begin imagining immigrants as extended kin rather than as strangers in our midst.[17]

Christian hospitality is diametrically opposed to popular prejudice against immigrants. Many media figures refer to undocumented immigrants as "illegals" who want to be "parasites" on American wealth and as "undesirables" who refuse to work, pay no taxes, take advantage of free social services, form gangs, and commit crimes to support their drug habits. In the United Kingdom some public figures denounce immigrants as the "reckless and feckless" who want to take advantage of British welfare provisions. These generalizations recall what nineteenth-century Yankees said about Irish and Italian immigrants who were coming into Boston and New York. We often unwittingly absorb these kinds of discriminatory attitudes, and so a commitment to hospitality challenges us to think about the ways in which each of us at least tacitly perpetuates stereotypes, harbors irrational suspicions, and treats strangers in inhospitable ways.

Official church teachings, Christian NGOs, and theologians like Heyer speak out in defense of more inclusive hospitality, but many rank-and-file churchgoers continue to harbor prejudiced attitudes toward immigrants.[18] Modern charity contributes to this gap when it leads us to view immigrants not as agents in their own right but rather as "beneficiaries of forbearance, philanthropy, or pity."[19] Every historic wave of immigrants to our country, and many others, has had to deal with resistance, suspicion, and even xenophobia.

The government has a duty to protect American citizens, but it also has a moral obligation to treat immigrants with respect and fairness. The post-9/11 security apparatus now faced by those entering the country is less than hospitable, particularly for visitors who have dark skin or come from predominantly Muslim countries. Extending good will to the people of every nation and country would enhance rather than compromise our long-term national security.

---

[17] Kristin E. Heyer, *Kinship across Borders: A Christian Ethic of Immigration* (Washington, DC: Georgetown University Press, 2012).

[18] See USCCB, "Welcoming the Stranger among Us: Unity in Diversity," November 15, 2000; and idem, "Strangers No Longer Together on the Journey of Hope," January 22, 2003.

[19] Ibid., 115.

Temptations of Hospitality

The central temptation for people who exercise hospitality is to use it as a way of competing with one's guests or gaining power over them. This happens in a small-scale way when people extend hospitality in ways that put others in their debt. The host can imply, "I've done this for you, now I'd like you to do this for me." In a wider cultural context, hospitality is often assumed to require assimilation, and so implicitly suggests that visitors give up their own cultural identity in order to be accepted by the dominant culture.

Rabbi Jonathan Sacks provides helpful discussion of the social meaning of hospitality.[20] He wrote *The Home We Build Together* after the London bombings of July 7, 2005. Sacks struggled to grasp how people raised in the United Kingdom could be so profoundly estranged from their own country that they would be willing to kill fifty-two and injure seven hundred of their fellow citizens. He offers three models of British society to build a case for an integrated diversity that goes beyond both the conformity of cultural paternalism and the social fracturing of contemporary multiculturalism.

The first model envisions society as a country house. The old Victorian approach to national hospitality welcomed foreigners as long as they recognize that they will only feel at home to the extent that they adopt British culture as their own. This model failed because it routinely undermined the ethnic identity and self-respect of immigrants.

The second model is the multicultural society. It seeks to protect the particular cultural identities of immigrants. This "hotel" model of society allows for every group to have its own space, accents the differences among particular groups within a pluralistic society, and emphasizes noninterference with others and their ways of life.

While the second model is an improvement over the cultural domination of the country-house model, its central value of toleration also has its shortcomings. Toleration is an attitude of merely putting up with a state of affairs that is unpleasant or undesirable. We tolerate a crying baby on a seat behind us on an airplane, but do we also want to say that we merely tolerate Mexican or Iranian immigrants in our society? Such an attitude feeds prejudice and stereotypes and promotes cultural isolation and resentment in the marginalized. It also tends to reduce politics to special-interest activism.

Sacks's third model of hospitality seeks to go beyond both the homogeneity of the first model and the mere coexistence of the second. He argues that conceiving of pluralistic society as "the home we build together" is

---

[20] Sacks, *The Home We Build Together* (New York: Continuum, 2007).

preferable to both the country-house model, in which guests must assimilate to the way of life of the dominant culture, and the hotel model that respects everyone's right to be left alone. Sacks's third model suggests that people with diverse ethnic and racial identities can build common ties in a shared acceptance of the common good rooted in citizenship, community activism, and participatory democracy. We can be bound together by shared projects like raising money to support a local school, cleaning up a neglected city block, or creating a green space downtown. Working together helps to forge a common identity in a way that allows people to retain their cultural and religious identities.

This model also allows us to grow in cross-cultural understanding. It enables us to better identify the strengths and weaknesses of our own society and to begin to correct ways in which we have unconsciously accepted prevailing concepts of cultural superiority or inferiority and imposed them on others. Hospitality that promotes intercultural understanding can help all people lead more examined, socially engaged lives.

Conclusion

Christian hospitality is nurtured in Christian communities that welcome friends and strangers. It embraces people who are like us and those who are different, particularly those who have no home in the world—immigrants, asylum seekers, street children, the severely mentally ill, and others. To show hospitality we must have generosity of heart and a willingness to care for those who may not be able to reciprocate our kindness.

In its fullest sense Christian hospitality helps strangers become friends and coworkers. It seeks friendship on the basis of equality rather than dependency or patronage. It challenges us to develop an inclusive companionship with those whom Christ befriended.

9

Compassion

"Be merciful, just as your Father is merciful" (Lk 6:36). The heart of service lies in compassion. Every act of compassion has three basic features: an agent who *sees* that someone is suffering, *cares* about his or her suffering, and then *does something* about it. Compassion combines empathy, the ability to feel what another person is going through, with good will (or benevolence), wanting what is good for that person.

This chapter discusses (1) compassion in the Bible, (2) theological reflection on Jesus Christ, (3) the virtue of mercy, (4) growing in compassion, and (5) temptations of compassion.

Compassion in the Bible

Jesus of Nazareth is the primary exemplar of compassion for Christians. We can only understand his compassion if we have a sense of Jesus's identity as an ancient Jew from the small town of Nazareth living among a people dominated by Roman rule. According to Rabbi Abraham Joshua Heschel, the Hebrew Bible is marked by a strong sense of the "divine pathos," that is, the "suffering of God" that comes from God's love for us.[1] In steadfast love for Israel, God responds to injustice in different ways at different times. This involves various combinations of righteous indignation, anger, distress, sorrow, a desire to punish, and especially compassion. Divine compassion seeks to protect, forgive, heal, and redeem. Biblical compassion is not meant to replace righteousness, but is rather its highest expression. It demands justice for the exploited and dispossessed.

---

[1] See Rabbi Abraham Joshua Heschel, *The Prophets* (San Francisco: Harper, 1962).

Taking seriously Jesus's Jewishness requires us to grasp three religious convictions central to the Judaism that shaped his identity.[2] First, Judaism is strongly monotheistic; it insists that Jews worship only the one true God. Second, Judaism interprets history in light of divine election, the belief that God chose the Jews to be a special people, and the covenant—the agreement that bound Israel to God and vice versa. Third, Judaism affirms that failure to live up to the covenant leads to punishment, and ought to be met with acknowledgment of guilt. Israelites who violated the covenant were required to repair whatever damage they had done to their victims, repent of their sins, and offer a sacrifice to God. The roots of Christian forgiveness lie in the Hebrew experience of a God who is willing to forgive the sinful people.

These three religious convictions were complemented by five distinctive practices in the Judaism of Jesus's day: first, Jews were to serve God and not other gods (Ex 20:3–4; Dt 5:7–8) at the Temple in Jerusalem; second, their infant sons had to be circumcised to bear the sign of the covenant (based on Gen 17); third, they were obligated to refrain from work on the Sabbath (Ex 20:8–11); fourth, they were bound to abstain from eating certain "unclean" foods like pork and shellfish (Lev 11; Dt 14); and finally, before entering the Temple, Jews had to purify or cleanse themselves of any bodily fluids associated with life or death.[3] These particular customs regulating food, worship, holidays, and the like were ways in which Jews at the time of Jesus protected and affirmed their absolute loyalty to God and their distinctive identity as a people. Jewish law (then and now) runs contrary to the modern assumption that we ought to compartmentalize our faith and piety in a private domain called "religion." It seeks to bring every part of life—one's home, one's workplace, and the public square—"under the authority of God."[4]

This integrative character of Judaism carries major implications for how we think about service. First, God cares as much about compassion and justice as prayer and worship, religious rituals and traditions. Many religious people (not only Christians) tend to assume that God cares primarily about the proper observance of religious rituals and that, if we displease God, we can compensate for our transgression by correctly performing those rituals. Yet the Bible tends to be sharply critical of believers who are religiously observant but hardhearted. The prophets denounced those

---

[2] See E. P. Sanders, *The Historical Figure of Jesus* (New York: Penguin, 1993), 13–14. The Judaism discussed here is that which formed Jesus and his communities. It is important to note that Judaism has continued to develop and grow as a vital and creative religious tradition from this time period up to the present day.

[3] Ibid., 36.

[4] Ibid., 37.

who exploited their weaker neighbors and assumed they could please God by offering sacrifices in the Temple. They saw this kind of manipulative worship as an insult to God.

Second, our responsibility to act compassionately ultimately comes from a God who is moved by compassion and steadfast love, who is "near to the brokenhearted, and saves the crushed in spirit" (Ps 34:18–19). God, moreover, not only *has* compassion, but later theologians have come to hold that since whatever attributes God has, God has completely, absolutely, without compromise, then we can say that God *is* compassion.

The paradigmatic biblical manifestation of divine compassion is God's act of rescuing Israel from slavery in Egypt: "You have seen for yourselves how I treated the Egyptians and how I bore you up on eagle wings and brought you to myself" (Ex 19:4). God's compassion for people trapped in slavery led him to liberate them from Egyptian slavery and to give them the blessings that come with covenantal righteousness. We thus need to avoid the popular dualistic assumption according to which the Old Testament's God of justice, judgment, and punishment is opposed to the New Testament's God of love, compassion, and forgiveness.

The Old Testament is saturated with images of divine compassion. God loves with the tenderness of a father (Hos 11:1–4) or a mother (Is 49:15; Is 66:13). God heals the brokenhearted and binds up their wounds (Ps 147:3) and has a special concern for the poor, orphans, widows, and resident aliens. Nor are divine love and compassion confined to Israel: "The Lord is good to all, and his mercy is over all that he had made" (Ps 145:9).

Third, compassion is not just the responsibility of individuals. In biblical perspective compassion ought to characterize a community overall, including its social, legal, and economic practices. In the ancient world (as today) to be poor was often to be a victim of oppression and violence at the hands of powerful people, and so the prophets insisted that compassion holds everyone accountable to the standards of justice (see Amos 5:10–15). Compassion is not just a matter of feeling for someone who is hurting and then helping him or her; it also demands the institution of just practices and laws. At harvest time, for example, farmers were required to leave the edges of their fields and vineyards unharvested so that those with no land could gather what remained (see Dt 24:19–22).

New Testament compassion emerged within this tradition. Jesus shows compassion to the helpless and confused multitudes, the blind, the hungry, the sick, widows and orphans, and the grieving. When he encounters a man afflicted by leprosy, he is "filled with compassion." He stretches out his hand, touches the leper, and heals him (Mk 1:41). The authors of the Gospels show Jesus to be a man of compassion who realizes the hope of the prophets who came before him. The Gospel of Matthew, for example, connects Jesus's healing of Peter's mother-in-law with the prophecy "he took our infirmities and bore our diseases'" (Mt 8:17; see Is 53:4).

Jesus tells his followers to *do* the compassionate will of God, not just talk about it. Their teacher's compassion does not come from a bland, inoffensive niceness that never renders judgment on anyone's behavior or attitudes. Jesus gets irritated and angry when he sees marginalized people being ignored or mistreated. He acts rudely (at least according to the standards of his culture) at a banquet in defense of a man suffering from dropsy (Lk 14:1–6). He does not hesitate to shame members of a synagogue when they refuse to see that a woman with scoliosis is just as much a daughter of Abraham as they are (Lk 13:10–17).

At the same time the tone of Jesus's ministry is compassionate rather than stern, harsh, and judgmental. He forgives people who slip up, shows patience to the weak, and offers rest for the weary (Mt 11:28–30). Jesus taught compassion through his parables as well as his concrete actions. The Good Samaritan is the iconic Christian depiction of what it means to love our neighbor (Lk 10:25–37). In this story a lawyer asks, "Teacher, what must I do to inherit eternal life?" Jesus responds with a question of his own, "What is written in the law?" The lawyer answers by citing two texts from the Torah: the first command, to love God (Dt 6:5), and then the second, to love one's neighbor as oneself (Lev 19:18). Jesus concurs: "You have answered correctly. Do this, and you will live." Yet the lawyer was not satisfied and "seeking to justify himself," asks Jesus, "And who is my neighbor?'"

Instead of answering this question in a direct way, Jesus tells a story and then poses a question to the lawyer. A man was traveling down from Jerusalem to Jericho when robbers stripped him, beat him, and "left him for dead." Later, two religious figures, a priest and a Levite, come across the victim but choose to pass to the other side of the road and keep moving. Travelers in their situation might well worry about being ambushed by the same robbers who had attacked the victim, or they might have pressing obligations elsewhere. Some readers in the past wondered if the priest and Levite are prevented from helping because a religious law declares that anyone who touches a dead body becomes ritually unclean. If they had become ritually unclean, the argument runs, they would have been prevented from touching the tithe (the religious tax), which would have interfered with their ability to support their families and help the community carry out its obligations. This regulation, however, applied to priests but not to Levites. Moreover, as A. J. Levine points out, ritual purity would not have been relevant here because in going from Jerusalem to Jericho the priest and the Levite were moving away from rather than toward the Temple. But even if they had been going in the other direction, Levine tells us, "in Jewish law saving a life trumps all other laws." The earliest rabbinic law says that even a high priest must care for a neglected corpse.[5]

Whatever their possible thoughts or motives, these figures function as foils for Jesus's story. They show us what it means not to love the neighbor, and stand in contrast to a "certain Samaritan" who comes along the same road. When he sees the victim "he is moved with pity. He goes to him and bandages his wounds, and pours oil and wine on them" (Lk 10:33–34). The Samaritan then puts the victim on his own animal, takes him to an inn, and stays the night to make sure that he begins to recover. Before he leaves the next day, the Samaritan pays the guest's charges and promises the innkeeper that he will make good on any charges incurred during the man's recovery.

Jesus's audience would probably have expected the third figure to be a good Jew or perhaps even one of his own disciples. Instead, he offers a Samaritan, a bitter enemy of the Jews, who considered Samaritans to be "half-breeds and heretics."[6] Jesus's audience would have expected a good Samaritan as much as Americans would expect hearing of a good Taliban fighter who showed compassion to an American. By praising the Samaritan as the positive model, Jesus challenges his listeners' preconceptions about the presumed goodness of their own group members and the presumed wickedness of others.

If we genuinely love God, this story suggests, we will be compassionate to the neighbor in need. Conversely, if we are compassionate to our neighbor, we will please God. The Samaritan is not described as a man of faith, piety, or religious observance, only as a traveler who helps another human being who is in need. The identifiably religious figures in the story fail to love God because they do not love their neighbor. We can see parallels to their attitude in our own society when people think they please God by going to church but have no qualms about ignoring the poor or otherwise oppressed.

After telling this story Jesus turns to the lawyer and asks, "Which of these three, do you think, was a neighbor to the man who fell into the hands of the robbers?" The lawyer answers: "The one who showed him mercy" (Lk 10:36–37). The lawyer's initial question can be interpreted as, What do *I* have to do so that *I* can gain eternal life? His question reveals an egocentric focus that Jesus challenges by shifting his attention to his duty to act as a neighbor to everyone and not just to members of his own group.

---

[5] Amy-Jill Levine, "The Many Faces of the Good Samaritan—Mostly Wrong," *The Journal of Christian Ethics* 85 (Winter 2012): 20.

[6] Ibid., 194.

Luke tells this story in a way that accents Jesus's deliberate shifting of focus from the recipient of love (Whom ought I to love?) to the subject of love (How ought I to love?). It is first told in response to the question "Who is my neighbor?" but in telling the story Jesus shifts the question to: What does it mean to act as neighbor? Jesus's answer is as profound as it is simple: we are to love everyone with humble, generous, and active compassion. Jesus tells the lawyer that to love our neighbor means to act compassionately to anyone in need. The story culminates with an imperative: "Go and do likewise" (Lk 10:37).

Compassion should not be confused with simple kindheartedness or a cheap sentimentality that says, "I feel your pain," but doesn't do anything. Dorothy Day recounted in a letter to a friend in January 1948 the humiliation of being arrested and thrown in jail:

> To perform the works of mercy becomes a dangerous practice. Our Baltimore House was closed as a public nuisance because we took in blacks as well as whites. The [staff] were arrested and thrown in jail overnight and accused of running a disorderly house [a brothel]. . . . It is a good thing to live from day to day and from hour to hour.[7]

This is one of many episodes that taught her that compassion requires courage, patience, and resilience.

Day stressed the radically inclusive nature of Jesus's compassion. When the lawyer asks, "Who is my neighbor?" he is actually asking, in a subtle way: Who is *not* my neighbor? Whom am I *not* obligated to care for? Perhaps this lawyer assumed that the proper response would be that he must love his fellow Jew but could ignore a Samaritan or any other outcast or sinner. This presupposition makes sense because the tradition had earlier understood the *neighbor* to be the "near one," that is, as the people in one's family or community. The Book of Leviticus, for example, commands: "You shall not hate in your heart *anyone of your kin*; you shall reprove your neighbor, or you will incur guilt yourself. You shall not take vengeance or bear a grudge *against any of your people*, but you shall love your neighbor as yourself: I am the Lord" (Lev 19:18, emphasis added). Though it was also extended to resident aliens, the neighbor in Jesus's day usually meant fellow Jews. He stretched his tradition to a universal compassion in which everyone matters. The neighbor is anyone in need with whom one comes into contact and "to whom one can show pity and kindness, even beyond the bounds of one's own ethnic or religious group."[8]

---

[7] Dorothy Day, *All the Way to Heaven*, January, 1948.

[8] Joseph Fitzmyer, *The Gospel according to Luke X–XXIV,* Anchor Bible series, vol. 28A (New York: Doubleday, 1985), 884.

Jesus was merciful not only to the socially acceptable, but also to criminals, prostitutes, beggars, Gentiles, itinerants, and other "undesirables." He extends compassion to people who are unattractive, unable to reciprocate, difficult, and strange. As Martin Luther put it, God "loves sinners, evil persons, fools, and weaklings."[9] We are called to do the same.

We should also note that the Gospels do not depict Jesus simply as a sage who teaches an ethic of compassion. He is a messianic figure whose words and deeds announce the in-breaking of the reign of God. The parable of the Good Samaritan thus offers a "vision of a counter-order" that went well beyond the bounds of conventional thinking about our responsibilities for one another.[10] It suggests that the church ought to be a community whose way of life and mission reflect the radical compassion of God.

Theological Reflection on Jesus Christ

It is easy to see how theological reflection takes its bearings from our understanding of Jesus Christ. We focus now on three important themes: Jesus as the revelation of the Father's compassion, the cross as the culmination of Jesus's loving obedience, and the resurrection and ascension of Jesus as the revelation of the triumphant power of divine love.

First, the Christian interpretation of compassion is fundamentally rooted in the love of God that is revealed throughout salvation history and that reaches its climax in the person and work of Jesus Christ. Jesus's deep communion with his heavenly Father—whom he called Abba, an Aramaic term for Daddy (Mk 14:36)—led him to see that we are all God's children (e.g., Mt 5:44–45). Jesus's intense awareness of the universality of the Father's love inspired his inclusive compassion—healing the wounded, forgiving the transgressor, searching for the lost, and welcoming the outcast. He is the image of what divine compassion looks like when expressed in human form.

St. Paul describes God as the "Father of mercies and the God of all consolation, who consoles us in all our affliction, so that we may be able to console those who are in any affliction with the consolation with which we ourselves are consoled by God" (2 Cor 1:4). Paul proposes an ethic of imitation; that is, just as God has consoled us in our suffering, so we ought to console one another. Compassion makes us want to console one another when we are troubled, especially when our trouble comes from discipleship.

---

[9] Martin Luther, "Heidelberg Disputation," in *Martin Luther's Basic Theological Writings*, ed. Timothy F. Lull (Minneapolis, MN: Fortress Press, 1989), 48.

[10] Ben Witherington, *Jesus the Sage: The Pilgrimage of Wisdom* (Minneapolis, MN: Fortress Press, 2000), 193.

> For just as the sufferings of Christ are abundant for us, so also our consolation is abundant through Christ. If we are being afflicted, it is for your consolation and salvation; if we are being consoled, it is for your consolation, which you experience when you patiently endure the same sufferings that we are also suffering. (2 Cor 1:3–6)

Christians speak of the "paschal mystery" as the way in which Jesus accomplished the salvation of the world. The core of this process is his passion, death, resurrection, and ascension into heaven. Christians believe that the infinite compassion of God is definitively revealed in Jesus's willingness to undergo public shaming, torture, and execution on the cross. The cross represents the bloody destruction of an innocent man who is first broken, humiliated, and abandoned. His death on the cross was the culmination of an entire public ministry in which he had to confront wave after wave of opposition—the scribes and Pharisees, the chief priests, Pilate and Herod, the regional political rulers, the crowd in Jerusalem calling for his crucifixion, and of course, his betrayer, Judas.

Yet Jesus remained obedient and faithful to the Father. The powers arrayed against him destroyed his body but failed to crush his obedient trust in his heavenly Father. He refused to resort to violence to defend himself, and he refused to "curse God and die." By staying faithful to the Father, Jesus was able to do what God alone can do—save people from enslavement to the power of domination, the assumption that we have to control and possess people and things in order to make ourselves safe.

Early Christians understood Jesus's suffering as redemptive, as bringing healing to broken human beings and forgiveness to sinners. They saw Jesus as the Lamb of God, the Passover lamb, whose blood was shed to protect and rescue the people (1 Cor 5:7; Jn 1:29). They also identified him with the Suffering Servant who, rather than obliterating his enemies, took suffering onto himself out of redemptive love. The Suffering Servant passages (see Is 42–53) announce the coming of an innocent and righteous figure, probably representing all of Israel, whose persecution and death would constitute an atoning sacrifice that would restore Israel's relationship with God. Early Christians saw Jesus as this figure.

In Jesus, God took on human vulnerability. Jesus's wounds on the cross are also *God's* wounds. These wounds symbolize two sides of vulnerability: they are the effects of violent assault, the severe damage done to Jesus's body; and they are also breaches that opened his body to the world.[11] The

---

[11] See Vincent Leclerq, *Blessed Are the Vulnerable: Reaching Out to Those with AIDS* (Ellicott City, MD: Twenty-Third Publications, 2010).

depth of Jesus's compassion is seen in what he was willing to suffer out of obedience to his Father and love for humanity. His wounds signified both the damage that was done to him (evidence of his assault) and his willingness to endure that suffering for the sake of love (testifying to his openness and vulnerability).

The challenge of compassion, at least in Christian terms, lies in its willingness to suffer on behalf of and in communion with those who suffer. Unfortunately, the Gospel stories of the passion and death of Jesus have become routine to many churchgoers. Stylized artistic depictions of crucifixes in churches and museums often smooth over the shocking and violent character of the crucifixion.

Vulnerability is difficult in every culture, perhaps especially in those that place a high value on individual strength, power, and independence. Men are still expected to be strong, able to handle anything, always in control. If a man gets hurt, he is supposed to endure it stoically and not feel sorry for himself. The competitive strain of our society says he should never let down his guard in public. Women are also taught these lessons. Feminism is right to insist that we recognize the full equality of men and women. But when equality gets interpreted as a self-sufficient autonomy rather than mutuality, women can be just as discouraged from acknowledging their vulnerability as men. Competition in the workplace leads women as well as men to feel pressured not to admit when they feel stressed, overworked, or uncertain that they can get the job done. They probably have it worse, because men are at least given cultural permission to complain, get angry, and vent their frustrations. But if neither men nor women admit when they are flawed, weak, or wounded, how are we supposed to be compassionate to—rather than just feel pity for—people who are?

To external observers the crucifixion of the "King of the Jews" seemed to prove that Jesus was an imposter and his followers deluded. Christians, though, do not reduce the entirety of Jesus's significance to his passion and death. We view Good Friday within a paschal mystery that culminates in Christ's resurrection and ascension into heaven. In faith, Christians profess that the Father raised Jesus from the dead and that the risen Christ then appeared to the disciples.

What the Father did in raising Jesus cannot be captured in terms available either to common sense or to the sciences. St. Paul describes Jesus as having a radically transformed body (1 Cor 15:45). In continuing to bear the wounds of his passion and death, the risen Christ shows his solidarity with all victims of domination, hatred, and violence. If the cross testifies to the love of a God who is willing to embrace human pain and suffering without reservation, the resurrection reveals God's final victory over them.

Christians believe that what happened to the risen Jesus is God's will for all of us. The love of God overcomes the power of domination and replaces it with love. We have received a "first installment" on an "inheritance" guaranteed to be ours in the future (see Eph 1:14). The Spirit of Christ is given to guide and strengthen us so that we can become "new creatures" who can participate in God's redemption of the world.

Finally, the ascension of the risen Christ signals his exaltation over the powers of evil and foreshadows the destiny of humanity in the eternal love of God. In the Letter to the Philippians, St. Paul speaks beautifully of the exaltation that follows Jesus's humiliation. The Son of God, he writes, "though . . . in the form of God, did not regard equality with God as something to be exploited, but emptied himself, taking the form of a slave, being born in human likeness" (2:6). The cross reveals the full meaning of the incarnation and the radical nature of Jesus's self-transcending love: "Being found in human form, he humbled himself, and became obedient to the point of death—even death on a cross" (2:8). In serving the Father in "self-emptying" humility, Jesus incarnates what it means to give oneself without reservation to God. This self-emptying was accomplished completely on the cross.

Jesus's humility leads to the exaltation of the risen Christ. Because of his radical obedience the Father "highly exalted him and gave him the name that is above every name, so that at the name of Jesus every knee should bend, in heaven and on earth and under the earth, and every tongue should confess that Jesus Christ is Lord, to the glory of God the Father" (Phil 2:11).

In giving himself completely to God, Jesus shows us what it means to be truly human as well as what it means to be truly divine. The heart of both is a radical giving of self. This giving is not partial. Jesus gives everything to the Father, and so his life culminates in his willingness to be killed rather than betray the Father. This suggests that we too are invited to give everything that is ours to God and to our neighbor. Or perhaps, even better, we are invited to acknowledge that everything that exists is already a manifestation of divine love and to live in accord with its true significance. The process of dying to self is fulfilled in a rising to companionship in God that defeats all the powers of selfishness and domination—both internal and external, in the self and in the world.

St. Paul describes the risen Christ as disarming the "powers and principalities" of the world (Col 2:15). Human powers of domination remain in place, but their hold over those who live in the Spirit has been broken (Col 2:15; Eph 1:20–23).[12] Faith in the risen Christ gave figures like Dorothy

---

[12] See Walter Wink, *Naming the Powers: The Language of Power in the New Testament* (Philadelphia: Fortress Press, 1984).

Stang and Oscar Romero the freedom and courage to remain steadfast in the face of persecution, even "unto death."

Christians believe Jesus Christ began a process of redeeming the world that will be fully accomplished in the future. We live now in a time of struggle between Jesus's inauguration of the reign of God and its complete achievement in the transformation of creation. In the reign of God the exploiting powers of this world will have been completely transformed into servants of humanity. Salvation is thus envisioned not as a mass exodus from the world but the transformation of it. As biblical scholar Gerhard Lohfink puts it: "For Jesus, the reign of God first of all means this life, this history within which the rule of God is to expand."[13]

The suffering-dying and rising-exaltation of Christ form the overall pattern for Christian life. This pattern is present in all forms of service as Christians conceive it, especially in compassion. In baptism we enter into Jesus's death and burial so that we can be raised from the dead and live a new life with him (see Rom 6:3–4). Just as we were buried with Christ in baptism, so we are raised with him in baptism (Col 2:8–12). St. Paul thus did not say we are buried *now* and will rise *later*, but rather that we live *now* a new kind of existence with Christ. Christians ought to be hopeful and confident because, "in Christ they have already come to the fullness of life."[14]

Christian discipleship is cruciform, patterned on a cross that takes its meaning from the whole paschal mystery. Because every human being is a brother or sister "for whom Christ died" (1 Cor 8:11), we are to show compassion to everyone without exception. We are to enact the pattern of Jesus's cross in our everyday lives. "Be imitators of me, as I am of Christ," Paul advised the Corinthians (1 Cor 11:1). Just as compassion was central to Jesus's life, so we ought to make it central to ours. Just as the risen Christ radiated joy, so we ought to live joyfully.

Compassion is deeply connected to the Eucharist, the church's liturgical performance of the paschal mystery. *Eucharist* comes from the Greek word for "thanksgiving," and it constitutes a celebration of what Christ has done for us. Eucharistic worship is meant to renew our membership in the church and to reaffirm our participation in Christ's mission to the world. In helping us become more and more as part of the body of Christ in the world, Eucharist draws us more deeply into the compassion of Christ.

Liturgy is meant to focus our attention on what is most important in our lives and to challenge us to embrace its meaning more deeply. Unfortunately,

---

[13] Gerhard Lohfink, *Jesus of Nazareth: What He Wanted, Who He Was*, trans. Linda M. Maloney (Collegeville, MN: Michael Glazier, 2012), 354.

[14] Colin G. Kruse, *Paul's Letter to the Romans* (Grand Rapids, MI: Eerdmans, 2012), 272.

Christians often just show up at church as if they were attending a performance. The Eucharist, however, is not meant to be a spectator sport; it is a communal spiritual practice in which every member of the congregation plays an active role. We act in and through the actions of the celebrant, but we are also invited to engage in the prayer of the worshiping community. When we say "Amen," we are actively and personally committing ourselves to the truth of what has been said and to acting on the basis of that truth in our daily lives.

Finally, the paschal mystery also calls the church, both as a whole body and in all its parts, to imitate the compassion of Christ. We are to be present to people caught in all forms of suffering. As we will see in the chapter on witnessing, the church itself is called to be a sacrament in the broad sense—a symbol that makes present what it symbolizes. It can only do so it if embodies the compassion of Jesus. Just as he came to serve and not to be served (Mt 20:28), so the church exists to serve rather than to be served. Unfortunately, as Pope Francis has repeatedly pointed out, the official leaders of the church sometimes act more like masters than servants. But just as Christ came to serve not only his own disciples but the whole world, so the church must be a servant of humanity and not only of its own members. As servant the church must be open, outward facing, and responsive to the deep human needs of the world, particularly those of the outcast and oppressed.

Christian compassion includes care for our fellow believers and the church itself. We were all baptized into this "one body," St. Paul wrote, and "whether Jews or Greeks, slaves or free persons" we are all given to "drink of one Spirit" (1 Cor 12:13). Each part of the body is needed by the whole and by all the other parts. When one part suffers, "all the parts suffer with it; if one part is honored, all the parts share its joy" (1 Cor 12:26). There should thus be no division in the body and all the parts should have the same concern for one another. In the church, as elsewhere, compassion seeks to forgive and repair damaged relationships.

The Virtue of Mercy

Speaking of love of neighbor, fourth-century theologian Gregory of Nazianzus wrote: "I must conclude that love of the poor, and compassion and sympathy for our own flesh and blood, is its most excellent form. For God is not so served by any of the virtues as he is by mercy, since nothing else is more proper than this to God."[15] It is important to note that God's mercy

---

[15] "Oration 14: On the Love of the Poor," in *Gregory of Nazianzen*, ed. and trans. Brian Daley, SJ (New York: Routledge, 2006), 78.

is not focused on those who are marginalized because God does not care about those who are prosperous and powerful. As economist-theologian Daniel Finn points out, the Christian tradition insists on giving "a special focus on the poor and marginalized, not because God loves them more than others but because God's attention has been most focused on those whose human flourishing is most threatened."[16]

Anyone can act compassionately on a given occasion, but not everyone has the virtue of mercy. Even a cruel person can act compassionately once in a while, and even selfish people want to relieve the suffering of their loved ones. Mercy is the virtue of people who are truly and habitually compassionate.

The traditional Christian works of mercy illustrate the range and focus of this virtue. As we saw in Dorothy Day, corporal works of mercy address basic human bodily needs for food and drink, clothing and shelter, physical health and safety, and companionship. Spiritual works of mercy are directed to people needing an education, encouragement, forbearance, guidance, forgiveness, consolation, or prayer. This list of works of mercy is illustrative, not comprehensive. These works are relevant to the general needs of people in every society. But how we act on them in concrete ways can vary from culture to culture. Day, for example, insisted in her time that the spiritual works of mercy include "picket lines and the distribution of [Catholic Worker] literature."[17]

The virtue of mercy is not just a willingness to help others. It is based on a love that appreciates the goodness in every person we encounter or, as Day liked to say, that sees Christ in the other. Doing so requires attentive empathy. Day wrote:

> Love means answering the mail that comes in—and there is a fearful amount of it. That person in the hospital, that person suffering a breakdown of nerves, the person lonely; far-off, watching for the mailman each day. It means loving attention to those around us, the youngest and the oldest (the drunk and the sober).[18]

The late United Nations Secretary-General Dag Hammarskjöld was asked by a journalist about what traits enable a person to serve others. He responded that such a person must "push his awareness to the utmost limit without losing his inmost quiet, he must be able to see with the

---

[16] Daniel Finn, *Christian Economic Ethics: History and Implications* (Minneapolis, MN: Fortress Press, 2013), 337.

[17] Dorothy Day, *The Long Loneliness* (New York: Image, 1959), 214.

[18] Dorothy Day, *The Duty of Delight: The Diaries of Dorothy Day*, ed. Robert Ellsberg (Milwaukee: Marquette University Press, 2008), 395.

eyes of others from within their personality without losing his own."[19] He believed that spiritual development occurs when our interiority opens us to the beauty and goodness of the neighbor. The problem is that we don't always see it.

A recent example of the inclusive character of Christian mercy comes from Father Frans van der Lugt, a Dutch Jesuit who lived for decades in Homs, Syria. Like the other Jesuits working in Syria, his inclusive humanitarian commitment gave him widespread credibility. He voluntarily choose to share the plight of ordinary Syrian people. After learning Arabic in Lebanon, he moved to Syria to minister to Christians and to be present to anyone who needed help. He founded the Al Ard Center near the city of Homs to provide care for disabled people and to foster interreligious understanding.

As violence in the region escalated, many people fled. Father Frans was urged to leave, but he stayed behind to help people who could not or would not leave. When government forces laid siege to the insurgent-held Old City, he stayed to provide refuge and aid to anyone who needed it, whether they supported the rebels or the regime. As the only priest left in the Old City to help the people there with their suffering, he said, "How can I leave? This is impossible." Despite the threats Father Frans said that when someone knocked on his door, "I don't see Muslims or Christians, I see, above all, human beings" who "hunger to lead a normal life."[20] Some of the rebels tried to protect Father Frans, but on April 7, 2014, at the age of seventy-five, he was assassinated by masked gunmen.

Father Frans showed that the virtue of mercy is not only a matter of providing people with the material supplies they need, but also a giving of oneself in a way that helps others appreciate their own dignity. Australian Bill Yeomans learned this crucial point by serving for many years in the Asia Pacific region of the Jesuit Refugee Service:

> Working with refugees, I realize more and more that unless I give my-self, it would be better that I gave nothing. People who are starving, homeless, friendless, so easily lose the sense of their human dignity. It is not enough to give them what they need. I must give in such a way that my giving restores their self-worth, their human dignity, in such a way that their hope and trust in mankind are rekindled.[21]

---

[19] Cited in Roger Lipsey, *Dag Hammarskjöld: A Life* (Ann Arbor: University of Michigan Press, 2013), 607.

[20] See Anne Barnard, "A Long Survivor in Syria, A Lone Dutch Priest Is Slain," *New York Times*, April 6, 2014.

[21] Danielle Vella, "Two Fathers General in the Service of Refugees," in *In the Footsteps of Pedro Arrupe: Ignatian Spirituality Lived in the Service of Refugees,* ed. Danielle Vella (Rome: JRS, 2007), 14.

People like Father Frans and Bill Yeomans, or Dorothy Day and Dorothy Stang, show us the power of mercy. But their lives also suggest that the virtue of mercy does not stand alone. We must also have the virtues of patience, courage, and equanimity to provide that stability of character that enables us to resist getting overwhelmed by the stress of dealing with another's suffering.

We also need to be able to exercise the virtue of practical wisdom, the ability to make good choices in difficult circumstances. People with compassionate intentions sometimes act in ways that worsen a situation they mean to improve. Strong feelings are no substitute for good judgment. We can only effectively address the suffering of other people if we have a fairly accurate grasp of what they are going through and if we can identify concrete actions that would improve their situation.

The importance of good judgment cannot be underestimated. Consider the case of a student under pressure from his parents to get good grades. He cheats on his chemistry final, gets caught, and flunks the course. Now he has to face his parents. A well-intended roommate wanting to comfort his friend might blame the entire event on the chemistry professor for being too demanding, or on his friend's parents for putting too much pressure on their son, or on the university for requiring him to take so many courses in a semester.

The roommate means well but is actually making matters worse for his friend. He does not help him think about the difference between honest and dishonest ways of dealing with the pressures in his life. The roommate naively assumes that compassion for his friend means defending and rationalizing his behavior. This "support" only confirms the very attitudes that led to the cheating in the first place. Friends function like enemies when they act against our true good. In this case appropriate compassion would empathize with the friend but see his cheating for what it is: dishonest, unjust, and self-destructive. The wisely compassionate roommate would try to find a way to help his friend think about how he wants to lead his life and how much he wants his life to be controlled by expectations dictated by authority figures and peers.

Practical wisdom helps us identify when, where, and how to act mercifully. James F. Keenan, SJ, describes mercy as the "willingness to enter into the chaos of another."[22] Chaos signals some kind of personal or social disorder. We can see this in people who suffer from compulsions, addiction, or severe mental illness, or those who live in seriously dysfunctional

---

[22] Daniel J. Harrington, SJ, and James F. Keenan, SJ, *Jesus and Virtue Ethics: Building Bridges between New Testament Studies and Moral Theology* (Lanham, MD: Rowman and Littlefield, 2002), 126.

families or neighborhoods that put them in constant fear of violent crime. But chaos also occurs in a broader way when the order and peace of our lives gets seriously compromised.

Entering into the chaos of another is riskier and more demanding than to feel pity as a detached observer. It suggests a form of attention that avoids the condescension and judgmentalism associated with "charity" in its modern sense. Pope Francis sees mercy as the heart of pastoral commitment: "The ministers of the Gospel must be people who can warm the hearts of the people, who walk through the dark night with them, who know how to dialogue and to descend themselves into their people's night, into the darkness, but without getting lost."[23] The key qualification here is "without getting lost." It is not enough to enter someone else's chaos. We also need to bring with us an emotional stability and inner peace that can calm the one in chaos rather than just make a chaotic situation worse.

An example of what I mean might help here. I know a student, I'll call her Jane, who had a very difficult upbringing mainly due to her father's absence and her mother's internal turmoil and alcoholism. Her mother lived in a constant state of anger, resentment, and bitterness. She was angry at her ex-husband, manipulated her colleagues at work, and acted insultingly to everyone. She also constantly criticized Jane. When she was drunk, she would tell Jane that she was ugly and fat, that no boy would ever like her, and that she would never amount to anything. Jane tried countless times to talk to her mother when she was sober, suggested that she get help, and even tried a few interventions with members of their extended family, but nothing helped. Jane couldn't invite friends to her house, didn't take care of her body, and felt anxious and depressed all the time. She slowly discovered that she had come to hate not only her home but also herself.

After a long struggle Jane finally decided that, for her own sanity, she had to move out of the house and get away from her mother. The last year of high school she moved in with relatives, and after that she went away to college. After a few months at college she made some good friends and began to get more sleep, concentrate better, and take better care of herself. Her inner anxiety and self-loathing began to subside. For the first time since she was a child, she began to feel good about herself and her life.

Jane decided to spend her Christmas break at a friend's house rather than return home. Her mother was still belligerent and drinking heavily and said she didn't care whether Jane came home or not. Jane knew that home was too chaotic for her to handle without sliding back into the old negativity. She knew her limits. She decided she couldn't live at home as long as her

---

[23] "A Big Heart Open to God," interview with Pope Francis by Antonio Spadaro, SJ, September 30, 2013.

mother was out of control. Jane acted mercifully by staying in touch with her mother through phone calls, texts, and emails. Her mother never did find a better way to live. In Jane's case, returning to the chaos at home, even for three weeks, would not have been an act of mercy. It would have been an act of self-destruction.

Growing in Compassion

There are many ways we can become more merciful people, such as developing better judgment by learning from experience, cultivating greater attentiveness to others, increasing our powers of empathy, and generally leading more informed, reflective lives. Here we examine three more ways.

First, we can become more merciful by expanding our range of life experience so that we can come to a better understanding of the struggles of other people. This is especially important for those who socialize, live, and work in segregated "bubbles" populated mostly by people like us. As Pierre Claverie learned, we can challenge ourselves by getting out of our comfort zones.

There are different ways to expand our range of experiences. An immersion or service trip to the developing world can help, especially if it is done thoughtfully and with plenty of time for reflection and conversation. Yet traveling somewhere exotic can be problematic, especially if it involves "poverty tourism." Dr. Paul Farmer, the cofounder of Partners In Health, worries about what he calls "medical voluntourism," in which "untrained individuals travel to the developing world to provide health-related aid for short-term stints." It is easy for such a venture to amount to nothing more than a sentimental gesture. Yet Farmer recognizes how an intense experience can be a catalyst for a new kind of social consciousness and commitment. Sometimes, he says, "young people who are not trained—if they do no harm—do become engaged in a lifelong and much more serious manner because of these initial, very ill-conceived efforts." This is what happened to Farmer himself as a result of his first trip to Haiti.[24]

We do not have to travel far from home to expose ourselves to challenging situations. We can cultivate relationships with people on the margins of our own towns and neighborhoods. We can decide to make a point of visiting a shut-in in our neighborhood or to pay attention to someone in our apartment building who is socially isolated.

Reaching out to other people doesn't have to be restricted to an exercise of a "have" helping a "have-not." Consider the case of a college senior I

---

[24] Jennifer Yang, "Paul Farmer, the 'Good Doctor' of Haiti, Talks Global Health in Toronto," *The Star*, June 11, 2014.

will call Phil. Phil volunteered in a service program that set him up as a tutor for a twelve-year-old named Maurice. Phil tutored Maurice twice a week and took him to dinner about every other week. Phil got used to dwelling in two separate worlds: one on campus with his friends and the other in his inner city placement. He enjoyed both roles and was comfortable in both settings. In a moment of spontaneous generosity Phil invited Maurice to visit him on campus.

Yet almost as soon as he invited him, Phil started to feel uneasy; when he actually showed up, Phil began to feel downright uncomfortable. On the one hand, walking around campus with Maurice was different from hanging out with him in the city. Feeling self-conscious at the affluence of his campus, he worried that Maurice would see him as just another rich kid who, out of curiosity, was "slumming" a few hours a week to see how people live on the "other side of the tracks." Phil also found himself worrying that Maurice would say or do something around Phil's friends that would make them think less of him.

After thinking through it, Phil recognized that his misgivings were misplaced. He realized that welcoming Maurice to campus was one of the best things he could have done for their friendship. The experience, though minor, helped Phil both to see how compartmentalized his life had become and to acknowledge that he cared a lot more about his image and popularity than he had ever realized. Phil grew by disrupting the well-defined boundaries that protected his comfort zone—this time not by going out, but by bringing in an "outsider."

We feel most comfortable when we control our environment. But recall the connection between compassion and vulnerability, and particularly the compassion revealed in the wounds of Christ. Since those who are supremely strong do not have first-hand knowledge of what it is like to be weak, to be deeply confused, or to fail, it is hard to see how they can be compassionate. They can be generous, considerate, and kind, but not compassionate. Since to be compassionate is to "suffer with" another person, we can only do so if we have had experiences of our own weakness, neediness, and failure. This suggests that expanding the range of our experiences will not help us to become more compassionate unless we enter into them with an openness to what they have to teach us about our common human dependency, vulnerability, and fallibility.

Second, we can grow in compassion by getting some distance from our culture's obsession with winning. From the time we are young children, we are constantly compared to other people and told that we need to distinguish ourselves from them. Our culture places great emphasis on personal autonomy, financial success, prestige, and power. Many people feel constant pressure to become more physically fit, more popular, and more wealthy. It is easy to push others out of the way to get where we want to go.

We can cultivate supportive and cooperative rather than competitive relationships with our peers. Competitive drive is often fueled by insecurity and fear. There is nothing wrong with challenging ourselves and making the most of our abilities, but many of us don't know the difference between excelling in competition and winning at all costs. Even service can be an occasion for gaining a competitive edge. Indeed, some volunteers find service to homeless people or inmates a way of showing their superiority to others. If we can't learn to set aside our self-involved ambition, our attempt to serve will be a charade. Thus, often the first step to becoming more merciful is recognizing that there is more to life than competition, to see what we have in common with one another, and to cultivate cooperative relationships.

The Christian affirmation of our intrinsic worth is especially valuable here. Because we are loved by God, and created in God's image, we don't have to earn our dignity. If we accept that we are saved by faith, then we do not have to spend our time trying to defeat others to show that we are worth something. This leaves us free to love ourselves and one another without ulterior motives.

A third way we can become more merciful people is by participating in organizations dedicated to serving marginalized people—soup kitchens, shelters, civil rights organizations, and so on. Institutions like these not only provide valuable services to underserved people, but can help us translate our social concern into specific actions.

Organizations are one thing; communities are another. Organizations without community become mere bureaucracies. At their best communities support compassion, build morale, and help us maintain a healthy set of priorities. All of the exemplars discussed in Part I of this book either founded or worked with organizations, but they were also supported by particular communities. Recall King and the African American churches, Dorothy Stang and the Sisters of Notre Dame de Namur, and Day and the Catholic Worker communities. Communities reflect our nature as intensely social beings. The people with whom we spend our time inevitably shape us. And we have a role in gradually forming ourselves primarily by our choices about what communities we join and what friendships we cultivate. As a friend of mine likes to say, "The company you keep is the air you breathe." So if we want to be people of mercy, we ought to build friendships with merciful people.

We have to be deliberate about the kinds of friendships we build. Fellowship is an especially strong part of the Christian life. Churches and congregations are meant to be communities of compassion, but unfortunately they often function as the equivalent to spiritual gas stations that we visit one hour a week. Jesus never told anyone to go to church for an hour. He gathered disciples, formed them into a community, and taught them to take care of one another. He sent them out in twos rather than alone (see Mk 6:7). In the Gospel of John, Jesus describes discipleship as friendship: "Love one another as I have loved you" (Jn 15:13). Though the disciples abandoned him when he was arrested, the resurrected Lord brought them back and formed them into community of compassion whose members were empowered by the Spirit to perform "signs and wonders" (Acts 5:12). The same Spirit was alive in Dorothy Day, Oscar Romero, and our other exemplars.

Temptations of Compassion

Compassionate people can be tempted in a variety of ways. Here we focus on reducing morality to compassion, nepotism, depoliticizing compassion, and burnout.

First, even in our highly individualistic culture, compassion is a widely respected value. It is compassion that led Wesley Autry, the Subway Samaritan, to risk his own life to save a complete stranger who had fallen onto a subway track in Manhattan. Compassion is so obviously good that we can be tempted to think it constitutes the whole of morality. Yet compassion can get us only so far. It rests on our capacity for empathy, and even in the best people empathy has its limits. Research in social psychology suggests that our capacity for empathy is very context sensitive. We are more likely to feel empathy for someone we encounter when we are rested or in a good mood than when we are tired or in a bad mood. We are more prone to empathize with individuals who are connected to us, or whom we perceive as similar to us, or to whom we feel some kind of a personal connection.[25]

Some people can be generous and caring to a person they meet face to face but do not seem to care about similarly situated people whom they never personally encounter. While interpersonal compassion is necessary, it is not sufficient for addressing either the scale of human suffering or its systemic, institutional causes. We can give water to a thirsty child, but we can't personally give water to all the children in a village whose water supply has been polluted by a copper mine. Yet if we truly care about people

---

[25] See, for example, Jennifer Gutsell and Michael Inzlicht, "Empathy Constrained: Prejudice Predicts Reduced Mental Simulation During Observation of Outgroups," *Journal of Experimental Social Psychology* 46 (2010): 841–45.

who suffer, we will support policies that promote their well-being, for example, by working to pass laws holding corporations accountable for toxic dumping. "True compassion," according to Martin Luther King, Jr., "is more than flinging a coin to a beggar. It comes to see that an edifice which produces beggars needs restructuring."[26] This "edifice" must include the law and the socioeconomic order, culture and morality, and religion and politics.

As Dorothy Day insisted, if you care about slavery you will seek, "not just to minister to the slaves but to do away with slavery."[27] The moral concern that begins with particular acts of compassion must be translated into socioeconomic, political, and legal justice. The larger the scale, the more we need to translate compassion into just institutions.

Compassionate institutions give caregivers avenues for acting compassionately. Paul Farmer says,

If there is one thing that I think is true after 30 years of doing this work, it's that there are probably also structural ways to help people be compassionate. . . . I believe anybody can be pushed, structurally, into thinking compassionately. And setting up systems so that people have a chance to be merciful, just, kind, compassionate, loving—all that is possible.

And what does that mean?

Well, if you set up a system where you have 100 people standing in line in the hot sun, and one doctor and one nurse . . . that is set up to just exclude any kind of compassion. . . . That's the way to structurally determine that people be hardened. So you actually need *time* to be compassionate.[28]

Institutions can thus either encourage or discourage compassion.

The second temptation that attracts compassionate people is nepotism—confining their quite intense and generous empathic concern to friends, family, and their own groups. All communities involve networks of reciprocity. We all tend to follow an implicit policy of reciprocity that directs us to be good to people when they are good to us and not to get entangled with others. In Plato's *Republic* the character Polemarchus captures the

---

[26] King, "Beyond Vietnam: A Time to Break Silence," address delivered to Clergy and Laymen Concerned about Vietnam, Riverside Church, New York City, April 4, 1967.

[27] Day, *The Long Loneliness*, 43.

[28] Yang, "Paul Farmer, the 'Good Doctor' of Haiti, Talks Global Health in Toronto."

ethic of reciprocity when he defines justice as benefiting one's friends and harming one's enemies.

Christian ethics, on the other hand, insists that we show compassion to people whether or not they are members of our group. In fact, some texts in the Gospels stress our responsibilities to outsiders precisely because most people are not drawn to go out of their way to help them. Jesus routinely challenges exclusions and pays attention to outsiders. "If you love those who love you, what credit is that to you? For even sinners love those who love them" (Lk 6:32). His actions showed what it means to have faith in a God who loves absolutely everyone without exception.

We can work against nepotism by training ourselves to be ready to consider things from the point of view of others. Powerfully displayed in the life of Oscar Romero, the preferential option for the poor challenges us to view both church and society from the perspective of people in marginalized communities. As we will see in the chapter on solidarity, this change of vision only happens when we stand with the poor as their companions rather than from a social distance.

A third temptation, especially in our own society, is to depoliticize compassion. Compassion seems pure, noble, and cooperative, but politics seems dirty, competitive, and divisive. Many student activists throw themselves into service but keep all political questions at arm's length.

Exemplars like King and Romero, on the other hand, understood compassion as leading to a commitment to justice that had serious implications for how we structure our communities and society at large. Both biblical prophecy and Christian compassion judge any society in terms of how well it treats its least well-off members. But even more broadly, most citizens recognize that a decent society is one in which everyone has enough to eat, decent shelter, and access to medical care. Whatever views they have about religion, most people do not want to live in a society that tolerates people starving to death on the street or forces children to drink polluted water.

The attempt to depoliticize compassion tries to maintain that if needs like these cannot be met through the working of the market, they are the responsibility of individual charity. King, Romero, and Stang, on the other hand, represent central strands of Christian social ethics when they maintain that government plays a key role in establishing equity when other sources fail. Compassion and justice constitute the moral criteria of our political life. The prophets condemned not only the injustice and heartlessness of individuals, but also the failure of political rulers who turned their back on the poor. The Good Samaritan, in short, is necessary but not sufficient for addressing the needs of people that come with large-scale societies. As King said: "We are called to play the good Samaritan on life's roadside, but that will be only an initial act. One day we must come to see that the whole Jericho Road must be transformed so that men and women will not be constantly beaten and robbed as they make their journey on life's highway."[29] This transformation can only take place if both government and civil society are committed to compassion and justice.

At times large-scale structural problems can only be addressed adequately through laws and public policies administered by the government. The government is better positioned than either nonprofit organizations or individuals to address large-scale human needs and the essential elements of the common good of society as a whole. When all other forces fail, the government bears responsibility to promote the essential features of the common good—the conditions that give people access to a decent level of human flourishing and an opportunity to participate in the public life of their communities.

The ethic of compassion can be misleading, then, if cut off from concern for justice in the political and legal as well as social and economic orders. Government, civil society, and individual citizens must work together for the common good. This is not to give a blanket endorsement to help the poor by just "throwing money" at social problems; no one thinks this is a good idea. Identifying how best to structure and run particular programs is a matter of prudent judgment. Christian ethics insists that such programs must meet the standards of justice. Instead of dismissing all government programs, the politics of compassion seeks to modify or eliminate inefficient programs while supporting programs that can meet the demands of justice with greater efficiency.

Finally, the temptation that most afflicts compassionate people is burnout, a state of physical, mental, and emotional exhaustion. Referring to burnout as a "temptation" is meant to signal the fact that we can act in ways that we think are good but actually turn out to be self-destructive (and harmful to other people as well). Serving others in very demanding ways for long periods of time without sufficient support can lead to a state of personal debilitation that undermines our ability to be compassionate. It affects nurses, first responders, therapists, pastors, and teachers, and many other people as well. Burnout interferes with sleep, disrupts concentration, saps energy, and compromises mental health—all of which can make us feel disillusioned, mistrustful, discouraged, and cynical. So striving to be compassionate in the wrong way can undermine one's long-term ability to be compassionate.

Burnout is often occasioned by mismanaged and impersonal bureaucracies. Its long-term, systemic solution requires reform of dysfunctional institutions. Yet people threatened by burnout can't just wait for the enact-

---

[29] King, "Beyond Vietnam."

ment of necessary organizational reforms. They need to make choices that will advance their own physical, mental, and spiritual well-being: proper nutrition, exercise, sleep, spending time with supportive friends, and participating in the activities of healthy communities.

Christianity provides both spiritual and social resources for helping us prevent or recover from burnout. First of all, Christian faith resists unfair expectations some people put on themselves to do all the good they can possibly do every day of the week. The gospel reminds us that there is only one Savior. As Boyle puts it, "none of us can save anybody."[30]

Second, active participation in a vital worship community helps us to celebrate the goodness of life and to cultivate an attitude of gratitude for our blessings and gifts. Social psychologists have discovered that people who are more thankful tend to have better mental and physical health, stronger relationships, and greater self-esteem than people who are less grateful. They also tend to be more sociable, less materialistic, more resilient, and more altruistic.[31] Active participation in a religious community also connects us to a social network that can provide support, guidance, and encouragement.

Third, the Christian ethic of love includes not only God and our neighbor, but also ourselves. Indeed we have a duty to take care of ourselves. The command "Love your neighbor as yourself" (Lk 10:27) presupposes healthy and virtuous self-love. We ought to love our neighbor as we love ourselves, but only if we love ourselves the right way. Some Christians brand all forms of self-love as sinful. They are right that selfishness in all its forms—arrogant pride, self-aggrandizement, and willfulness, for example—is harmful to oneself as well as to others. But proper self-love is good for both us and our neighbor. The more we love ourselves in response to God's love for us, the more it will be right. The more healthy and rightly formed our love for God and our love for ourselves, the more healthy and rightly formed will be our love of our neighbor. Whereas selfish love makes true friendship impossible because it uses the neighbor as nothing but an instrument for the self, proper self-love reaches out to the neighbor in true good will and mutuality.

One of the worst kinds of harm is done to people when they are treated in ways that make them feel degraded, shameful, and humiliated. As Boyle points out, "The principal suffering of the poor is not that they can't pay their rent on time," but rather a "toxic sense of shame—a global sense of

---

[30] Gregory Boyle, *Tattoos on the Heart: The Power of Boundless Compassion* (New York: Free Press, 2010), 127.

[31] See Robert A. Emmons and Michael E. McCullough, eds., *The Psychology of Gratitude* (New York: Oxford, 2004).

failure of the whole self."[32] Distorted versions of Christian piety have made people feel they have acted in ways that put them permanently and irreversibly outside of God's love. Advocates of this kind of distorted theology do not see that Christianity lacking forgiveness is not authentic Christianity.

We encourage burnout when we view the gospel as demanding unending generosity with no acknowledgment of our finitude. The virtue of practical wisdom knows where to draw the line between healthy generosity and neurotic, compulsive altruism. Ultimately, we have to trust in divine providence rather than get trapped into assuming that everything is up to us.

Pope Saint John XXIII displayed the serenity that comes with deep faith. At the end of the day he was able to pray: "I've done the best I could in your service this day, O Lord. I'm going to bed. It's your church. Take care of it!"[33]

Conclusion

This chapter indicated some of the richness of the third model of service, compassion. Scripture points to compassion as an essential dimension of the nature of God. Jesus built on the tradition of the prophets in teaching the compassion of the Good Samaritan, and on the cross he embodied the radical compassion of God. The divine compassion of the Spirit of Christ reaches out to all human beings everywhere today. This compassion is described as the fundamental expression of the virtue of mercy. We grow in mercy by learning to pay attention to others, engaging in the give and take of honest dialogue, participating in communities of mercy, building friendships with compassionate people, and constructing merciful institutions. We do so with "open eyes" about the dangers of reducing morality to compassion, nepotism, depoliticizing compassion, and burnout.

---

[32] Boyle, *Tattoos on the Heart*, 52.
[33] Cited in Diana Jean Lopez, "Divine Prioritization," *Patheos* (November 13, 2014).

10

Advocacy

The prophet Isaiah explained what God wants from us:

> Wash yourselves, make yourselves clean.
> Remove the evil of your doings
> > from before my eyes;
> cease to do evil,
> > learn to do good;
> seek justice,
> > rescue the oppressed,
> defend the orphan,
> > plead for the widow (Is 1:16–17)

In a commencement speech in Oxford, Mississippi, William Faulkner told high school graduates: "Never be afraid to raise your voice for honesty and truth and compassion against injustice and lying and greed. If people all over the world . . . would do this, it would change the earth."[1] Faulkner's advice captures the essence of advocacy: to speak up for what is right, especially in the face of injustice. This chapter examines five dimensions of advocacy as a model of service: (1) advocacy in the Bible, (2) theological reflection on the Holy Spirit, (3) the virtue of courage, (4) growing in advocacy, and (5) temptations of advocacy.

Advocacy in the Bible

Biblical advocacy begins with God, who hears the cry of the poor and comes to their aid. The prophets remind the people of what God desires:

---

[1] William Faulkner, commencement address, University High School, Oxford, Mississippi, May 28, 1951, in William Faulkner, *Essays, Speeches and Public Letters,* ed. James B. Meriwether (New York: Modern Library Classics, 2004), 123.

> Is not this the fast that I choose:
>> to loose the bonds of injustice,
>> to undo the thongs of the yoke,
> to let the oppressed go free,
>> and to break every yoke? . . .
>
> If you offer your food to the hungry
>> and satisfy the needs of the afflicted,
> then your light shall rise in the darkness
>> and your gloom be like the noonday. (Is 58:6, 10)

Israelites were to defend those without the power to protect themselves: "Speak out for those who cannot speak, for the rights of all the destitute. Defend the rights of the poor and needy" (Prov 31:8–9). Their rulers had a special duty to "defend the cause of the poor of the people, give deliverance to the needy, and crush the oppressor" (Ps 72: 4).

The prophet Nathan exemplifies biblical advocacy (2 Sam 11-12). As a court prophet he had access to King David. But because he could not be so bold as to confront the king directly, he tells him a fictional story about a rich man who has many flocks and herds and a poor man who has only enough money to buy one lamb, whom he loved tenderly. Visited by a guest, the rich man takes the poor man's lamb, has it killed, and then has it cooked to feed his guest. When David hears this story, he is outraged and declares that such a man ought not only to give a fourfold repayment to the poor man but also, because he had shown no pity, be put to death.

The prophet then turns to David and tells him: "You are the man!" Now the king cannot avoid acknowledging his own guilt. The prophet is then free to remind him of all the blessings he has received: "Thus says the Lord, the God of Israel, 'I anointed you king over Israel, and I delivered you out of the hand of Saul; and I gave you your master's house, and your master's wives into your bosom, and gave you the house of Israel and of Judah; and if that had been too little, I would have added as much more'" (2 Sam 12:8). Nathan then asks, speaking in the Lord's name, "Why have you despised the word of the Lord, to do what is evil in his sight?" He lists David's offenses: "You have struck down Uriah the Hittite with the sword, and have taken his wife to be your wife, and have killed him with the sword of the Ammonites" (2 Sam 12:9). Once David sees his own lack of compassion, Nathan can speak as advocate for Bathsheba and her husband, Uriah. At the end of this story, after their baby dies, David goes to Bathsheba, now his wife, and comforts her (2 Sam 12:24).

Jesus also engaged this kind of prophetic advocacy, but he did so as an expression of his mission to inaugurate the in-breaking of the reign of God.

At the beginning of his public ministry he proclaims: "The Spirit of the Lord is upon me, because he has anointed me to bring good news to the poor. He has sent me to proclaim release to the captives and recovery of sight to the blind, to let the oppressed go free, to proclaim the year of the Lord's favor" (Lk 4:18–19; also Is 61:1–2).

Many Christians have tried to read this message as purely spiritual and other-worldly. They have assumed that what Jesus teaches is good news to the poor because he tells them that they too can be saved and go to heaven. Seeking heaven in their view has nothing to do with changing this world. Christians who follow this line of thinking often invoke the famous passage in which Jesus says, "you always have the poor with you" (Mk 14:7; Mt 26:11). Yet to understand this passage, we need to see it in context. Jesus speaks these words a few days prior to Passover and his arrest. Both Mark and Matthew place him at a dinner party in Bethany at the house of Simon the Leper, someone he had cured. When a woman puts costly perfume on his head, some people who were there complained that the ointment was expensive. It could have been sold to get funds to help the poor. Yet Jesus defends her action: "she has anointed my body beforehand for its burial" (Mk 14:8). This woman treats Jesus with great honor, and she alone seems aware of the ordeal he is about to endure.

To the complaint that the money could have been used for the poor, Jesus says: "For you always have the poor with you, and you can show kindness to them whenever you wish; but you will not always have me" (Mk 14:7). Jesus here cites the Book of Deuteronomy, which says that because we will always have poor people, we ought to be "openhanded" with them (Dt 15:11). Rather than indifference to the suffering of the poor, Jesus reminds the woman's critics that they "have the power to do good for them."[2] Dorothy Day interpreted this message to mean: "'The poor you will always have with you,' *but* you must not be content that there should be so many of them. The class structure is *our* making, not God's, and we must do what we can to change it."[3]

In one of his most important acts before he was arrested, Jesus acts as an advocate for the poor at the Jerusalem Temple. Around the time of Passover pilgrims from all over Palestine traveled to Jerusalem to offer sacrifice in the Temple. Merchants exchanged Greek and Roman coins for local currency that could be used to pay Temple taxes and fees and to buy materials to be sacrificed. When Jesus goes to the Temple, he is outraged at what he sees, accuses the merchants of turning a "house of prayer" into

---

[2] John R. Donahue, SJ, and Daniel J. Harrington, SJ, *The Gospel of Mark* (Collegeville, MN: Liturgical Press, 2002), 387.

[3] Jim Forest, *Love Is the Measure: A Biography of Dorothy Day,* rev. ed. (Maryknoll, NY: Orbis Books, 1998), 67.

a "den of robbers" (Mk 11:17, citing Jer 7:11), overturns their tables, and drives them out of the Temple.

This act seems to be more about the purity of religious worship than advocacy for the poor, but these two concerns are related. Jesus denounces the merchants as "robbers," which suggests not only religious commercialism but also dishonest dealing. Perhaps they were overcharging or defrauding their customers, or convincing people that their ability to please God was proportionate to the cost of the materials they were willing to sacrifice. Perhaps the expense of paying for sacrificial animals was especially hard on poor pilgrims. In any case, Jesus's insistence on a purified and renewed Temple worship went hand in hand with his insistence on justice. This incident increased his enemies' desire to get rid of him.

In the Gospel of John, Jesus promises his disciples that the "Father will send you another Paraclete, to be with you forever" (Jn 14:16). The Paraclete would inspire, guide, and strengthen the disciples after he is no longer physically present to them. The Paraclete can be an advocate, a mediator, or an intercessor. The word *paraclete* is usually translated "advocate," an image taken from a judicial context in which a lawyer pleads a client's case to get a favorable verdict.

The New Testament envisions the Holy Spirit as an advocate sent by the Father to teach and to dwell in the followers of Jesus. The Christian term *Spirit* is based on the Hebrew word *ruah*, which can refer to "wind," "spirit," or "breath." It carries connotations of the powerful wind that parted the waters for the Hebrews as they fled Egypt but also, more generally, the quiet and steady breath that sustains our bodily life. As "spirit," it refers to the personal core of a human being. In this sense, the Gospel of John describes Jesus as "deeply moved in spirit" when he saw Mary weeping over the death of her brother, Lazarus (11:33). St. Paul used the image of spirit as a way of talking about discipleship when he explained that we fulfill the law when we walk "according to the Spirit" (Rom 8:4).

Many texts indicate the importance of the Holy Spirit in the life of the Christian community (Acts 4:28–31; 1 Thess 1:4–7; Gal 4:4–7). The Holy Spirit is a comforter, counselor, and advocate who gives Christians strength to deal with adversity. The Spirit today continues the work started by Jesus: to announce the reign of God, to build a community that manifests that reign in its worship and service, and to preach the gospel throughout the world.

Theological Reflection on the Holy Spirit

The Holy Spirit is the eternal love of the Father for the Son and the Son for the Father. The Spirit is the power of divine love in the world. God as Trinity, Michael Himes writes, is an "eternal explosion of love."[4] The Spirit of Christ heals and builds up the spiritual health of the Christian community. It also empowers Christians to participate in God's transformation of the world.

The Spirit, then, strengthens Christians to be advocates for justice in both the church and the world. "The church is also in the world for the benefit of humankind,"[5] insisted Romero. We see a church envisioned as engaged in the world in King's "beloved community" and in Pope Francis's image of the church as a "field hospital" after a battle. This dual empowerment is expressed in the traditional prayer known as *Veni Sancte Spiritus:* "Come, Holy Spirit, fill the hearts of your faithful and kindle in them the fire of your love. Send forth your Spirit and they shall be created. And you shall renew the face of the earth."

Truthful and appropriate advocacy is often no easy thing. To the extent that we are not properly and fully formed human beings, our advocacy will be compromised. Most of us display a complex blend of selfishness and loving generosity, insecurity and healthy confidence, immaturity and emotional development. The Holy Spirit tries gently to pull us from the former to the latter, but this movement happens only to the extent that we willingly cooperate with grace. The Holy Spirit is the source of the grace that heals, renews, and transforms the heart of each Christian. We can think of the Spirit as the "oxygen" of our spiritual "breathing." Just as we die physically if we stop breathing, so we die spiritually if we stop responding to the Holy Spirit.

The Spirit binds the members of the faith community to one another as "one body" (1 Cor 12:27; Eph 4:4). The church is called to facilitate our response to the presence of the Spirit in our lives. Religious practices like sacraments, prayer, and retreats are intended to form us into believers who can hear what God is trying to say to us in our everyday lives. Spiritual discernment is a crucial basis for advocacy because it attunes us to what reflects divine love and justice.

Friendship and community are essential for discernment. Given our capacity for self-deception, it is easy for us to talk ourselves into thinking that the Spirit wants us to do what *we* want to do. This is why we need the Bible, teachers, clergy, tradition, and friends to figure out what it means to be faithful to the Spirit in our circumstances. All of our exemplars engaged in processes of spiritual discernment. King was convinced that the Spirit was present in the civil rights movement, Romero believed that the

---

[4] Michael J. Himes, *Doing the Truth in Love* (Mahwah, NJ: Paulist Press, 1995), 103.

[5] Romero, *Voice of the Voiceless* (Maryknoll, NY: Orbis Books, 1985), 66.

Spirit was calling him to speak prophetically in El Salvador, and Mother Teresa trusted that the Spirit led her to dedicate herself to the poorest of the poor.

The Virtue of Courage

In the Acts of the Apostles the Spirit comes to the disciples at Pentecost, and they are filled with courage. They are able to speak in public without fear and persevere in the face of obstacles, misunderstanding, and trials. They show that advocacy depends upon courage, the virtue that helps us remain steadfast in the face of what threatens us and those we love. Courage is not oblivious to danger, but neither is it controlled by it.

In a speech have gave in Selma on March 8, 1965, King drew the following contrast between courage and cowardice:

> Courage is an inner resolution to go forward despite obstacles; cowardice is submissive surrender to circumstances. Courage breeds creativity; cowardice represses fear and is mastered by it. Cowardice asks the question, is it safe? Expediency asks the question, is it politic? Vanity asks the question, is it popular? But conscience asks the question, is it right? And there comes a time when we must take a position that is neither safe, nor politic, nor popular, but one must take it because it is right.[6]

King had the courage to raise questions about the justice and decency of popular opinion, local customs, and civil authorities. He did not just resign himself to injustice. He could easily have said, "The system of racial oppression is much bigger than I am, and it's been going on for decades, and there's nothing one person can do about it." Instead, he accepted the risks of working to mobilize people to change what he saw as intolerably evil.

King's courage enabled him to fight injustice at great personal cost to himself and his family. He went willingly to jail and risked his life many times for the sake of the movement. On January 30, 1955, his house in Montgomery was bombed. On September 28, 1962, he was assaulted as he was delivering a speech at a church in Birmingham; the same person attacked him four months later in Chicago. King said that he was able to be strong in these and other occasions because of the power of God.

---

[6] Martin Luther King, Jr., *A Testament of Hope: The Essential Writings and Speeches of Martin Luther King, Jr.*, ed. James M. Washington (San Francisco: Harper, 2003), 512–13.

Courage generates two virtues that are particularly relevant to advocacy: patience and magnanimity. The passion for justice can lead advocates to refuse to suffer in silence in the face of intolerable injustice. In his "Letter from a Birmingham Jail," for example, King defended the "legitimate and unavoidable impatience" of civil rights activists. In *Why We Can't Wait* he criticized the inappropriate patience of both liberals and moderates who said they valued equality while advising civil rights workers to slow down and not be so disruptive.

At the same time, advocacy also requires a patient willingness to put up with discomfort to achieve one's goals. We exercise the virtue of patience when we absorb suffering without allow it to distort our priorities or change our course of action. It enabled our exemplars to deal with shortsighted allies as well as formidable opponents. Again, Christian advocates often describe themselves as able to bear suffering patiently because of the power of the Holy Spirit.

Courage also generates an appropriate kind of proper moral ambition, or what Thomas Aquinas called the virtue of magnanimity, the "stretching forth of the mind to great things."[7] A magnanimous person appreciates his or her gifts and seeks to use them for the sake of a noble cause.

In the Christian tradition, magnanimity has to be complemented by humility. The magnanimous person needs to be wary of what the Christian tradition calls vainglory, a love of praise from other people, and from acts motivated by a desire to gain fame, power, or status. Magnanimity can become corrupted into ambition, as when advocates who work for a good cause begin using it for their own gratification.

Growing in Advocacy

There are many ways to increase our capacity for advocacy, but here we will focus on three: transforming anger into commitment, exercising the "see-judge-act" method of social engagement, and exercising power responsibly.

Transforming Anger into Commitment

Christians are sometimes suspicious of anger because it seems at odds with Jesus's meekness and gentleness. Yet like the prophets Amos and Jeremiah, Jesus did get angry. We see this in the story of his "cleansing" of the Temple (Mk 11:15), but also in his response to Pharisees (Mk 3:5), in his rebuke of Peter (Mk 8:33), and elsewhere.

---

[7] *Summa Theologiae* II-II, 129, 1.

Anger is a natural response to seeing someone we care about treated unjustly. King recalled the pain of having to tell his young daughter, Yolanda, that she could not go to the Funtown amusement park because of racial prejudice.[8] He rightly resented not only white supremacists, but also white liberals who professed sympathy for the victims of racial injustice but refused to do anything about it.

King's anger motivated him to work against injustice. Anger can provide an antidote to deep sadness, fatalist resignation, fear, and personal animosity. Journalist Jonathan Kozol praises the "focused indignation" that leads activists to become involved in "organized political activity that makes it possible to galvanize a neighborhood to fight for its collective good." Indignation can lead to social commitments that provide a constructive alternative to the "self-laceration" and despair that often leads poor people, as Kozol puts it, to "collude in their own ruin."[9]

Anger is only constructive when expressed in the right way. Kozol writes about "Kim," who is outraged at injustice but chooses not to demonize individuals like her landlord: "She voices anger at injustice, not contempt for individuals."[10] There is a big difference between King's prophetic anger toward injustice and the Klan's racist-fueled anger at civil rights advocates. If our love is virtuous, then our anger will be appropriate; if our love is disordered, then our anger will be inappropriate. This anger can fuel social action when it is transformed into a compassion for those hurt by unjust institutions.

Political activist Mary Beth Rogers notes that the working poor most often get angry when they feel "ignored, invisible, left out, overlooked, dismissed, and burdened by the small frustrations and daily humiliations of a constant struggle to get by." Social activism becomes most effective when "new political participants take the hot impulse of their anger and cool it down so that it can become a useful tool to improve individual lives and the quality of the common community."[11]

Christian ethics suggests two caveats when it comes to anger. First, we shouldn't confuse anger with hatred. Anger is simply emotional energy that responds to a perceived unjust harm. Hatred is a settled attitude of antipathy that wishes to damage or destroy its target. Some Christian writers also use the word *hatred* to express their adamant rejection of some evil.

---

[8] Washington, *A Testament of Hope*, 342.

[9] Jonathan Kozol, *Rachel and Her Children: Homeless Families in America* (New York: Crown Publishers, 1988), 99.

[10] Ibid., 100.

[11] Mary Beth Rogers, *Cold Anger: A Story of Faith and Power Politics* (Denton: University of North Texas Press, 1990), 9, 10.

St. Paul encouraged Roman Christians to hate sin (Rom 12:9). Dorothy Day hated what she called the "filthy rotten system" that causes so much human misery.[12] While she tried hard not to hate powerful people who did not lift a finger to help the masses trapped in destitution, Day confessed: "as I thought of our breakfast line, our crowded house with people sleeping on the floor, when I thought of cold tenement apartments around us . . . it was impossible not to hate, with a hearty and with a strong anger, the injustices of this world."[13]

Anger is appropriately directed at structural sin operative in unjust institutional patterns and the ideologies that legitimate them. Dorothy Stang saw the personal injustice of Brazilian landowners who stole land from settlers and murdered community leaders. But she also saw evil in the way local economies are structured to disenfranchise small farmers and recklessly exploit the natural resources of the Amazon. Structural sin is both a condition and an effect of the sins of individuals.

Illegal narcotics are a good example of structural evil. People who use cocaine don't think about the fact that the drug they are using was smuggled across the US-Mexico border after it was produced in Colombia, or that the path it took to get to them is literally a trail of death for thousands of people in places like Guatemala, El Salvador, and Honduras. They don't consider the horrible crimes committed—bribery, extortion, political corruption, kidnapping, rape, and murder—to get them the product they want to use. Recreational drug users have no intention of causing such mayhem; they just want to have a good time. But their use of the drug is what sustains the system by making it profitable. This example underscores the *social* in social sin; the whole is much worse than its individual parts.

Christian ethics calls this destructive behavior sin, not just evil, because it harms our relationship with God as well as with our neighbors and ourselves. All sins, personal as well as social, involve some degree of destructiveness. This leads to the larger question of complicity. We are all beneficiaries of some kind of institutional and structural injustices inflicted on others. Even very poor people in this country benefit from the low wages paid to migrant laborers who harvest the food they eat and from the sweatshop laborers who make the inexpensive clothes they are wearing. Men have historically benefited because equally talented women were not considered for the jobs that they held. Whites who graduate from elite universities do so in part because many other talented people do not have

---

[12] Day, "C.W. States Stand on Strikes," *Catholic Worker*, July 1936.

[13] *Dorothy Day: Selected Writings*, ed. Robert Ellsberg (Maryknoll, NY: Orbis Books, 1992), 82.

the opportunity to go to such schools. Beneficiaries of white privilege not only receive the benefits of unjust systems, but they also perpetuate them by their participation in them.

Complicity is daunting because we are so enmeshed in many unjust social systems. The more aware we are, the more likely we are to feel overwhelmed and to slide into social apathy. Yet if we care about the people whose suffering somehow benefits us, we need to do what we can to change those systems or at least to reduce our participation in them.

The key issue for readers of this book is not whether we are privileged, but whether we want to use our privilege to become socially engaged for the benefit of those who have been left out. The choice is either comfortable entitlement or pro-active social responsibility. The latter sees privilege as an opportunity for advocacy. The alternative to fatalism and indifference is to live more conscientiously. Even if we as individuals can't solve global problems, we can try to live as justly as possible and act as advocates for just social change wherever we live and work.

Exercising the See-Judge-Act Method

A second way we can become more effective advocates is by becoming more skilled at the see-judge-act method of social action. As noted in an earlier chapter, this approach was initially crafted by a Belgian priest, Joseph Cardijn, who began to provide pastoral care for industrial laborers around the turn of the twentieth century. His leadership was critical for the formation of the social action organizations in the 1920s like the Young Christian Workers (YCW) and the Young Christian Students (YCS) in Belgium and France. At the end of World War II these movements inspired the formation of the International Young Catholic Students (YCS) to coordinate eighty-five national movements devoted to social action, global solidarity, and the deepening of Christian faith. These movements draw their inspiration for Cardijn's see-judge-act methodology. Put in the simplest terms, this method begins by objecting to a particular problematic situation (see), trying to understand it in greater depth (judge), and then deciding what to do about it (act).

The first stage, *see,* begins when a group identifies a concrete form of injustice that comes out of their experience. It gets their attention enough to make them object to it and want to change it. This seeing involves not only an intellectual grasp of a negative situation, but also an affective reaction to it. It might be triggered by hearing about the troubles of a homeless teenager encountered in an urban plunge or the story of a family one meets in a soup kitchen.

The second stage, *judge,* is complex and multifaceted. It begins when we start thinking about the wider conditions that shaped the unjust situation that bothers us. We ask: What happened? Why is this teenager living in a shelter? Why is this family eating all its meals at the soup kitchen? These questions can be approached in two ways: one concerns the specific people, and the other considers the broad patterns found in similar cases. Most of us tend to be drawn to personal stories. We learn that the people we meet are usually not struggling because they are lazy or lack talent or have bad character. Even when they act in self-destructive ways, we begin to understand that we might have acted in the same way or worse if we were in their shoes. We begin to think about how their behavior reflects the wider social and economic circumstances within which they live.

Judging thus involves social analysis, that is, an examination of the patterns that characterize the functioning of groups, organizations, and societies. These patterns shape the attitudes and acts of individuals and groups. Unjust situations, of course, sometimes result from bad choices. But many unjust situations involve more than the poor choices of particular individuals. They reflect a broader problem in social institutions: neighborhoods, family structure, schools, the job market, and the like.

For example, consider the case of an undocumented farm laborer who is poisoned from working with pesticides and is taken to an emergency room and given medical treatment. One can blame the worker for mishandling the chemicals or the boss for unsafe conditions, but doing so misses the larger set of issues that affect countless other farmworkers who work in dangerous conditions: the failure of lawmakers or law enforcement agencies to ensure that farmworkers are protected by proper occupational health and safety measures. In other words, the problem is systemic.

Social institutions are structured by the distribution of power. If we want to understand power, we need to understand who makes decisions in a particular situation, how they make them, and why. We also need to understand who is affected by their decisions. Social analysis is thus focused on how power is exercised within various institutions. To understand how power gets distributed, we also have to know something about a given situation's historical, economic, social, political, legal, and culture context.

In the case of the farmworker, we need to know where he works, what he does, and what kind of machinery and chemicals are used there. We also need to understand the farm owner's point of view. This includes an awareness of the economic pressures on his or her business, whether it is a corporate or family owned farm, the farm's day-to-day management practices, how supervisors are trained and monitored, and a host of other factors. An adequate social analysis needs to consider the laws that pertain to the handling of pesticides, the marginal status of migrant farmworkers, methods for monitoring chronic pesticide exposure, the political debate over immigration and undocumented workers, and the economic pressures facing that particular farm from its competitors and the wider market. We also have to consider possible reasons that poisoning incidents may be underreported, including, among others, the language barrier, the risk of job loss, fear of deportation, lack of health insurance, exclusion from workers' compensation benefits, and other factors.[14] Finally, farmworker advocates argue that violations of current Environmental Protection Agency regulations are usually met only with warnings or insufficiently punitive monetary fines. This case merely illustrates the wide-ranging set of issues that might be considered in social analysis.

Social analysis is the domain of social scientists, policymakers, politicians, and community activists. But the see-judge-act method came out of the church, and when Christians employ it they naturally raise spiritual and religious as well as political, legal, social, and economic questions. Social analysis can be developed from many different normative perspectives. Christian social analysis draws its central norms of compassion and justice from the Bible, the Christian tradition, and the ongoing life of the Christian community. The prophetic strain of the Christian tradition calls us to resist the tendency to assume that injustice is just the way of the world and can never change. The priestly strain of the Christian tradition calls us to celebrate the presence of goodness, courage, and self-sacrifice in people who dedicate themselves to justice and peace.

How we analyze social structures depends a great deal on where we stand. The church is always called to stand with the marginalized and underserved. Romero's social analysis of El Salvador, for example, was motivated by his option for the poor and his strong belief in the dignity of every person. The social analysis seen in Day's columns in the *Catholic Worker* reflected her identification with the working class and her commitment to the works of mercy. Claverie began his social analysis only after he decided to extract himself from the culture of his youth and to see the world from the point of view of Arab and Muslim Algerians. This shift to the perspective of the marginalized is essential for Christian social analysis. It also has to be committed to justice for everyone and to take into account the rightful claims of all parties. Christian social analysis is not a form of class-based ideology.

Social analysis is not sufficient for social action. Once we come to a deeper grasp of the problematic features of social institutions, we need

---

[14] See the Farmworker Justice website, at http://www.farmworkerjustice.org/content/pesticide-safety.

to figure out how to produce constructive change. Social analysis helps by shedding light on the assets available for addressing the problematic situation.[15] This includes determining how to influence decision makers through either positive or negative incentives. Social action can create conditions for change when it mobilizes people in a specific direction and then constructively leverages their collective power.

Consider again the civil rights movement. King and other leaders were motivated by their experiences of racial oppression. They saw that racial injustice was not caused simply by individual racists or white supremacist organizations, but was rooted in complex historical factors that had come to dominate socioeconomic structures, political and legal arrangements, religion, and every other aspect of the wider culture. They mobilized people to march, boycott, publicize their grievances, and put economic and political pressure on decision makers to change their policies. These changes were the beginning of a long process of social transformation that continues, albeit haltingly and imperfectly, today.

The final stage, *act*, depends on a concrete and practical plan for addressing the challenge at hand. We have to decide whom to influence, how to do so, and with what goal in mind. This stages asks: Of the options available to us, what should we do? What actions should we take to attain justice here? What can we do, concretely and practically, to improve this situation? What do we need to do to ensure long-term success?

Acting flows from decisions about the specific action that needs to be undertaken, including the appropriate tactics, stages, components, and goals. It includes a number of sub-stages: formulating a specific plan of action, preparing the participants through awareness raising and practical training, and mobilizing them to fulfill the plan. It also includes efforts to influence key decision makers to promote the goals of the campaign.

Though often easier said than done, advocacy at its best offers constructive solutions that accommodate the legitimate concerns of all relevant parties. Successful advocates know that significant social change requires more than changing particular laws. It also involves transforming attitudes, moral sensibilities, and cultural assumptions. These kinds of changes are best accomplished by patient, respectful dialogue that slowly builds shared understanding. King repeatedly tried to persuade the public, his allies as well as his opponents, that justice is good for all Americans, not just for African Americans. His Christian-based advocacy aimed ultimately not at defeating its opponents but enlightening and enlisting them in a collaborative enterprise.

---

[15] See John L. McKnight and John P. Kretzman, *Building Communities from the Inside Out: A Path toward Finding and Mobilizing a Community's Assets* (Evanston, IL: Northwestern University, Institute for Policy Research, 1993).

In complex circumstances, social change results from pragmatic, interactive processes, improvisational decision making, flexibility, and bargaining. It usually depends on competitors' willingness to make tradeoffs to attain their most important goals. All sides have to be willing to compromise for the sake of making a deal that everyone can live with. King and other civil rights activists did not want to compromise in the face of manifest injustices like workplace discrimination or unequal schooling. They had certain fundamental norms of love, justice, and self-respect, but they also realized that, under some circumstances, it was necessary to delay the achievement of some goals for the sake of attaining others.

Exercise Power Responsibly

Third, we can grow as advocates by learning how to gather and utilize various forms of power. Each phase of the see-judge-act process takes power into account. Christians can be squeamish about *power*. The word can sound harsh and domineering, as indeed it is when people unjustly use their power to harm others. But this does not mean all forms of power are bad.

We can distinguish two forms of power: power *over* and power *with*. Power over forces people to do what they don't want to do. We see this in the power of some officials and leaders, but also in impersonal forces like the market or even the weather. Power of this sort is a fact of life, and we are surrounded by it all the time. It can either enhance our lives or diminish them; it can be exercised transparently or in secrecy; it can be put to just or unjust ends.

The SCLC mobilized people to seek goals that sometimes could only be attained by exercising power over uncooperative people who were not interested in changing racially segregated legal, social, and economic institutions. It made beneficiaries of the old system do what they did not otherwise want to do: make good jobs accessible to everyone, allow open seating in restaurants and buses, and admit black as well as white students to universities.

Coercive power can thus be used for good as well as bad ends. Sometimes it takes the threat of coercion to bring competing parties to the negotiating table. All institutions wield some kind of coercive power; for example, the church has the power to grant contracts to some businesses rather than to others and to allow some but not other people to exercise official ministries. At their best, leaders of institutions exercise power as a form of service pursued in justice. King exercised power from within the SCLC, Romero as an archbishop, and Mother Teresa as head of the Missionaries of Charity.

The businesses in Birmingham did not just change their policies because they "saw the light." As King pointed out,

History is the long and tragic story of the fact that privileged groups seldom give up their privileges voluntarily. Individuals may see the moral light and voluntarily give up their unjust posture . . . but groups tend to be more immoral, and more intransigent, than individuals. We know through painful experience that freedom is never voluntarily given by the oppressor; it must be demanded by the oppressed.[16]

If the financial leaders of Birmingham had not been put under enormous pressure by the marches, they would never have agreed to desegregate their businesses. As a general rule leaders of powerful institutions do not usually reverse profitable but unjust policies out of the goodness of their hearts. Power over others is morally tricky because, among other things, it has a coercive side. It is especially dangerous when its users are not accountable to others.

Most politicians seem to do the right thing only when doing so will not harm their chances of reelection. Community organizer Ernesto Cortes says some politicians he has had to confront "refuse to give you respect. They don't recognize your dignity. So we have to act in ways to get their attention." Getting their attention doesn't mean laying out a good moral argument or utopian social vision. Sometimes, Cortes explains, "what we have going for us is the amount of fear we can generate. We got where we are because people fear and loathe us. They fear us not because we turn out votes for them, but for what we can do to them."[17] Strong advocates need to know who to use power over. Social advocates must be persistent in their demands, vigilant in holding elected officials accountable, and willing publicly to reveal the incompetence or dishonesty of public office-holders. They also have to be willing to confront not only opponents but also allies who are confused or wavering.

Comfortable majorities who benefit from an unjust status quo tend to resist those who demand change. From the 1950s until now, Americans have slowly been brought into greater awareness of the evil of racism. Such progress only comes about when we are willing to put aside our psychological denial and moral defensiveness. Most whites in the 1960s did not see the pervasive and pernicious character of racism until the media exposed its violent and dehumanizing nature in graphic and undeniable ways.

In addition to "power over," we can also talk about "power with," the power of effective agency, the ability to get something done. Effective agency can be either individual or collective. People acting together as effective

---

[16] King, in Washington, *A Testament of Hope*, 292, 374. King here draws from Reinhold Niebuhr, *Moral Man and Immoral Society.*

[17] In Rogers, *Cold Anger*, 27.

agents can do more than they can as individuals working in parallel. Mother Teresa was highly effective as an individual agent of compassion, and her religious communities have been highly effective as collective agents of compassion. "Power with" involves equality and mutuality.

Effective advocates understand the importance of bringing people together to engage their collective agency for the sake of justice. As one community organizer puts it, "What you go through when you're a nobody and don't have any status or money made me realize that you need to be together with other people to have some kind of power."[18]

We can also distinguish the informal "people power" of ordinary citizens taking action for the good of their own communities from the formal institutional power wielded by major corporations or governments. Cortes distinguishes the relational power of a community that acts effectively and responsibly from the brute power of bullying, aggression, and violence.[19] The ethically sound exercise of citizen power employs coercive power only within a framework of justice.

Popular movements exert lasting influence when they are institutionalized. Citizen power is made possible by voluntary associations or mediating institutions that lie between the individual and the state. The SCLC emerged in the early civil rights movement, Pax Christi grew out of a movement to bring reconciliation to post-World War II Europe, and the Community of Sant'Egidio was organized by lay Christians to implement the ideals of the gospel in light of the Second Vatican Council.

Social advocates have to counter two powerful threats to citizen empowerment: bureaucratization and individualism. First, modern society has led to the construction of bureaucracies run by elites. The heightened status we give to so-called experts can discourage ordinary people from getting involved in political decisions, even when they concern the well-being of their own communities.

Second, the mentality of contemporary individualism presents a major obstacle to grassroots political mobilization. It encourages us to see people as "I" and "you" rather than as "us." It reduces politics to elections and tends to unite people according to special interests. These and related forces tend to undermine our sense of the common good.

Advocates are most likely to achieve success when they have gained sufficient power to influence decisions and to mobilize people to achieve goals. The locus of such power varies. Some of the most successful advocates have institutional power that they can use to achieve their goals. A chief executive has the power to raise the wages of employees, a military

---

[18] Ibid., 39.
[19] Ibid., 49.

officer can assign armed protection to a vulnerable community trapped in a war zone, and a judge has the power to give a juvenile offender a sentence that might give him a chance for a better life in the future.

It is a mistake, however, to say that one has to have significant institutional power before engaging in advocacy. In fact, institutionally powerful people are usually defenders of their own institutions, not advocates for outsiders. Outsiders can also act as successful advocates. King, while powerful within the civil rights movement, was regarded very suspiciously by much of the country's white power structure. He sought to "speak truth to power" as an outsider. He had enough credibility to get the attention of ordinary citizens, yet enough independence to be free to issue strong challenges to those in positions of institutional power.

Temptations of Advocacy

Advocates face certain characteristic temptations: paternalism, fanaticism, and self-righteousness.

First, social advocates can be tempted to think they know more about what is good for others than the people themselves do. "Do gooders" who see themselves as helping the poor, meeting their needs, and solving their problems might be well intentioned, but their actions can reinforce passivity and dependency in the very people whom they want to help. In this vein Dorothy Day once told an interviewer that "it's a grave temptation—to want to help people." She did not think it wrong to serve people out of love, of course, but she was suspicious of people who think they are "God's gift to humanity."[20]

Just because we take the side of marginalized people doesn't mean that we know what is best for them. Even well-intentioned paternalism ignores their capacity for agency, their intelligence and judgment, and their leadership potential.

Many people assume that those who have more money are somehow superior to, or more intelligent than, those who are less well off. In an international context this assumption is at play when Americans assume they know best what people of other countries ought to do to remedy the ills of their society.

Advocates who seek to avoid paternalism do well to adhere to Saul Alinsky's "Iron Rule" of community organizing: we ought never do for others what they can do for themselves.[21] Advocacy at its best is not smart,

---

[20] Robert Coles, *Dorothy Day: A Radical Devotion* (San Francisco: Harper and Row, 1989), 115–16.

[21] In Rogers, *Cold Anger*, 15.

organized people trying to "organize the disorganized"; rather, it comes from the marginalized themselves. This point is sometimes expressed in terms of empowering the poor, but even the word *empowerment* is paternalistic in that it suggests that those who have power are giving some to people who don't. Everyone has some degree of agency, and only children should be treated as children. The challenge of advocacy is to see how people can use their collective power to make positive changes in their communities. Advocacy enables people to develop and exercise their own agency through building trustful, cooperative relationships among people who see and want to work for their own good.

King once proposed that, "Life's most persistent and urgent question is: 'What are you doing for others?'"[22] Yet an even better question is: How are you supporting others in doing *for themselves?* The kind of advocacy envisioned here is best conducted by people who take matters into their own hands to get rid of the structures that harm them and replace them with structures that can benefit them.

A second temptation of advocacy is fanaticism. Love can give rise to healthy zeal and passionate devotion, but it needs to be formed properly and expressed appropriately. One can be so convinced of the rightness of her cause that she becomes blind to the truth seen by others. Fanatics are be reluctant to deal with complicated questions; they tend to see careful and critical reflection as a threat to their agenda. Some are even willing to lie, cheat, and otherwise manipulate others to accomplish their goals. People who are excessively devoted to a cause are often driven by their own ego needs. Fanatics have a hard time seeing their adversaries as anything but "the enemy."

We can avoid becoming fanatical by developing mental habits that allow us to see things from perspectives different from our own and give us the freedom to acknowledge the complexities and ambiguities of real life. King wrote: "Never must the church tire of reminding men [and women] that they have a moral responsibility to be intelligent."[23] We can widen our perspectives by developing friendships with people who think differently than we do and taking their points of view seriously.

Finally, advocates can be prone to self-righteousness. Someone who has just had a powerful social conversion can look down on family members and friends who seem to be (and perhaps are) complacent about social injustice. Once we have met a person who works long hours to support a family at

---

[22] Cited in *The Domestication of Martin Luther King, Jr.,* ed. Lewis V. Baldwin and Rufus Burrow, Jr. (Eugene, OR: Wipf and Stock Publishers, 2013), 253.

[23] Martin Luther King, Jr., *Strength to Love* (Cleveland: William Collins and World Publishing., 1963), 44.

the most basic level, it can be hard to spend $200 for drinks, dinner, and a cab on Saturday night—or even to be comfortable with anyone else doing so. Once our eyes are opened to ecological problems, it can be hard to deal with overconsumption in your family members or friends.

Passionate advocates are often seen as preachy. A person who feels an urgent desire to live more simply, if not in poverty, can come across as "holier than thou" to friends. Judgmental attitudes generate alienation, imperil friendships, and create isolation. Turning to likeminded friends can also come across as rejecting others. We can become more persuasive advocates for social justice if we stay connected to our friends and family members rather than isolating ourselves or withdrawing into a clique of those who think as we do.

We often tend to grade ourselves leniently while holding others to stricter standards. It is easy for a new social convert to exaggerate his connection to the poor. It is one thing to have strong opinions about an important cause for a few weeks, and another to sustain a serious, disciplined commitment to addressing that cause over the long haul.

Honest self-examination can counter the temptation to self-righteousness. So does deliberately paying more attention to the goodness of our friends and family members than to their weaknesses and shortcomings. As Jesus puts it, "Why do you see the speck in your neighbor's eye, but do not notice the log in your own eye?" (Mt 7:3).

Habits do not change overnight. Even St. Paul had to lament, "What I do, I do not understand. For I do not what I want, but I do what I hate" (Rom 7:15). Significant personal change is hard, and cultivating an awareness of its difficulty can make us less judgmental.

The virtue of humility helps us resist all three of these temptations—paternalism, zealotry, and self-righteousness. Day pointed out that "we would not see our brother's faults so clearly if they were not a reflection of our own."[24] A similar insight came to Dag Hammarskjöld, the Swedish diplomat who was the secretary-general of the United Nations from 1953 to 1961. His journal revealed a man whose deep spiritual life made it possible for him to deal wisely with big egos, constant pressure, and occasional international crises. "To have humility," he once said, "is to experience reality, not in relation to ourselves, but in its sacred independence. It is to see, judge, and act from the point of view of rest in ourselves. Then, how much disappears, and all that remains falls in place."[25] Hammarskjöld understood that humility flows from a contemplative attitude of openness to

---

[24] In Ellsberg, *Dorothy Day*, 182.

[25] Cited in Roger Lipsey, *Dag Hammarskjöld: A Life* (Ann Arbor: University of Michigan Press, 2013), 610.

the world and ourselves. Humility is not self-disparagement, but an attitude that frees us to be honest about our own limits, shortcomings, weaknesses, and need for help.

Christian humility is grounded in faith in a God of love who reaches out to "the least." Martin Luther put it dramatically when he wrote that we believe in "the God of the humble, the miserable, the afflicted, the oppressed, the desperate, and of those who have been brought down to nothing at all." This God is infinitely giving and wants "to exalt the humble, to feed the hungry, to enlighten the blind, to comfort the miserable and afflicted, to justify sinners, to give life to the dead, and to save those who are desperate and damned."[26]

Good people are not tempted as much by stealing, adultery, or murder as by the "deadly sin" of arrogant pride. Self-righteousness is a religious as well as moral temptation. Jesus was critical of the Pharisee who paraded his piety in public saying, "O God, I thank you that I am not like the rest of humanity—greedy, dishonest, adulterous—or even like this tax collector. I fast twice a week, and I pay tithes of my whole income" (Lk 18:11). An idealistic social activist might think along similar lines, praying: "O God, I thank you that I am not like other people—selfish, shallow, and materialistic. I tutor a child in the projects every Friday, and I just spent my spring vacation building a house for a family in Tijuana." In his story Jesus contrasts the Pharisee with a repentant tax collector who "stood off at a distance and would not even raise his eyes to heaven but beat his breast and prayed, 'O God, be merciful to me a sinner'" (Lk 18:13). This prayer is especially applicable to those who would be advocates.

In the story of the self-righteous Pharisee, it is the repentant tax collector who is accepted, "for everyone who exalts himself will be humbled, and the one who humbles himself will be exalted" (Lk 18:14). Jesus did not praise the tax collector because he was a sinner, but rather because he recognized his own need for forgiveness and mercy. We all make bad decisions from time to time and wrongly harm people. We all harbor unjust attitudes and stubbornly disordered affections that lead us to act in ways we wish we had not. Yet *guilty* is not the final word for Christians. Forgiveness brings not only humility but also a hope that empowers advocacy.

Conclusion

Advocacy means speaking up for victims of injustice or on behalf of the common good. The Bible suggests that properly developed love of God

---

[26] Luther, *Lectures on Galatians*, in *Luther's Works*, vol. 26, trans. Jaroslav Pelikan (Saint Louis, MO: Concordia Publishing House, 1963), 314.

and love of neighbor generates advocacy for the marginalized. Christian advocates like King and Romero relied on the Holy Spirit to empower their work. We can grow in advocacy by transforming anger into constructive commitments, becoming more skillful in exercising the see-judge-act method of social action, and learning to utilize power responsibly. Those who seek to do so face three abiding temptations: paternalism, fanaticism, and self-righteousness. To avoid these faults, we must deliberately cultivate the virtue of humility.

This book has tried to show that service can take place on many levels. We can engage in immediate, short-term service, for example, by volunteering to help at a food pantry that distributes food to impoverished families. Or we can engage in long-term service, for example, by teaching in a school in a poor area. These commitments help people in important ways, but they do not change the structures that put people in a position to need help in the first place. We can also act for others by engaging in a campaign to change a particular unjust institution, for example, by working for an organization that lobbies state legislators to enact policies that significantly improve schools that serve students in poverty-ridden areas. People engaged in this kind of advocacy promote systemic change, but they can be tempted to stop there; even in this sense advocacy is still a form of "doing for" the poor. The next level of service moves beyond paternalism to respect the rights of people to speak for themselves and to act as the agents of their own lives. This kind of advocacy comes from a strong commitment to solidarity, the topic of the next chapter.

11

Solidarity

*For just as the body is one and has many members, and all
the members of the body, though many, are one body, so it is
with Christ. For in the one Spirit we were all baptized into one
body—Jews or Greeks, slaves or free—and we were all made to
drink of one Spirit. . . . If one member suffers, all suffer together
with it; if one member is honored, all rejoice together with it.*

—1 COR 12:12–13, 26

The word *solidarity* refers to loyalty to a cause or a community. Because
we are social beings, solidarity comes naturally to us. We see it among coal
miners, fire fighters, and bricklayers, recovering alcoholics and cancer sur-
vivors, veterans and Peace Corps volunteers. Solidarity is found wherever
people are connected to one another in some way or other. Connections run
a spectrum from weak to strong. We see relatively strong forms of solidarity that come with bonds of membership and community. These bonds are
sustained by certain kinds of virtues and protected by particular obligations.
The key question of this chapter is not *Are* we in solidarity? but rather *With
whom* are we in solidarity? Considering this question in a Christian context
leads to us to ask, With whom *ought* we to be in solidarity? and What kind
of solidarity *ought* to mark the Christian life?

In the last few decades the church has spoken quite often about solidarity with the poor. It is possible to be in solidarity with the poor, of course,
without being Christian. Since many Christians seem to be entirely separated from the lives of poor people, it is also possible to be a Christian and
at least in a sociological sense not be in solidarity with the poor.

This chapter hopes to show that Christian conviction assigns an important
place to solidarity in two senses: solidarity with fellow Christians (ecclesial
solidarity) and solidarity with the marginalized. It discusses (1) solidarity in

the Bible, (2) the church as the basis of Christian solidarity, (3) the virtue of justice, (4) growth in solidarity, and (5) the characteristic temptations of solidarity.

Solidarity in the Bible

Scripture does not use the term *solidarity,* but it does offer images, stories, and standards that encourage loyalty to particular people and communities. The biblical archetype of solidarity is the covenant, the bond of loyalty between God and Israel. Biblical prophets insisted that the standard used to judge communities is how well the marginalized, especially the poor, widows, orphans, and resident aliens, are treated.

The Book of Deuteronomy, for example, says that because the land is so plentiful, there should be no poor in Israel (Dt 15:4). It required Israelites to lend to needy neighbors (Dt 5:7–11), to cancel debts every seven years (Dt 15:1–2), and not to charge interest on loans to fellow Israelites (Dt 23:19–20). Farmers were not to harvest to the edges of their fields so that something would be left for the poor (Lev 19:9–10). For the same reason, they were to leave their fields unplowed and unharvested once every seven years (Ex 23:11; Lev 23:22).

The prophets denounced the behavior of the rich "who oppress the poor [and] crush the needy" (Amos 4:1). They told the powerful to stop exploiting their fellow Israelites and urged kings and other rulers to enact social legislation to cancel debts, free slaves, and restore land taken from its true owners. As we saw in the chapter on hospitality, Israelites were commanded to extend this concern to resident aliens because they, too, count in the eyes of God.

Christians are in the unfortunate habit of drawing a sharp contrast between the Old Testament's inwardly focused tribal focus and the New Testament's concern for strangers and love of enemies. God liberated the Hebrews from oppression in Egypt but then commanded them to take over the land of Canaan regardless of the wishes of its prior occupants. Strong religiously authorized solidarity is accompanied by exploitation of others. Jesus, the same line argues, changed the equation by teaching the disciples to care for those who suffer regardless of their group affiliation.

If we look more closely at particular biblical texts, however, we see the options are more varied than is depicted in the simple dichotomy of Jewish partiality versus Christian universalism. The Pentateuch traces the movement of the chosen people from Mount Sinai to a land that was already occupied by others. Subsequent narratives describe God wielding power to help a fairly small band of Israelites subjugate much stronger occupants of the land (Jdg 1:28; 1 Kgs 9:20–21). Some biblical texts speak of God demanding very harsh treatment of non-Israelites, even to the point of exterminating entire groups of men, women and children (see 1 Sam 15:2-3; Dt 2:34). Historians tell us that the occupation of this land actually took place over a few hundred years and was more complicated than simple conquest. It probably involved migration, gradual infiltration, and uprisings of dissatisfied peasants. However the Israelites came to possess the land, they were often tempted to drift into Canaanite ways and to forget their pledge to remain faithful to the covenant. Many biblical passages underscore Israel's need not to be compromised by assimilation to the surrounding pagan cultures and their religions (see Jdg 13:1; Joshua 24:14-15; 1 Kgs 18:21).

Common sense suggests that the more secure, comfortable, and confident a people, the less they have to deliberately reinforce its boundaries with outsiders. Conversely, the more threatened a people feels, the more they will want to close ranks and the harder it will be for them to empathize with strangers. The challenges faced by a small nomadic tribe trying to survive, as in the stories about Abraham and his family, are quite different from the challenges that confronted the Twelve Tribes of Israel as they were struggling to establish themselves in the region. These challenges were, in turn, radically different from those facing the sixth century BCE inhabitants of Jerusalem who were taken captive and transported to Babylon.

Covenantal solidarity occupies many points along a spectrum from strong to weak. While Israelite law prohibited the oppression of resident aliens, it also differentiated them from Israelites. The Book of Deuteronomy prohibits Moabites and Ammonites from entering the Temple because of the way they had treated Israelites (Dt 23:3–8) and it allows Israelites to charge interest on loans to resident aliens (Dt 23:21). Texts written in one context allow for the assimilation of resident aliens into a future idealized Israelite society (Ezek 47:21–23), but texts from another time demanded the expulsion of the "peoples of the lands" (Ezr 10:2–3). A similar context-sensitivity is seen in other matters as well.

The tendency to draw sharp boundaries, though, has to be seen alongside the development during the Second Temple period (530 BCE–70 CE) of an awareness of the Jews as a blessing to the whole world (see Is 42:3). The later emergence of post-biblical Jewish ethics of responsibility to outsiders is captured in the Hebrew expression *tikkun olam*, meaning the duty to "heal," "repair," or "perfect" the world.

This expression carries two connotations. One is that the world will be healed one day when all its people acknowledge and live according to God's law. A second is the suggestion that all people must work together to transform the world and especially to help those who are most in need. Jews are supposed to live in a way that makes them constant and visible witnesses to God. Rabbi Jonathan Sacks points out that by "transforming ourselves into a people we transform the world."[1] He draws from the Book of Isaiah:

> You are my witnesses, says the Lord,
>   and my servant whom I have chosen,
> so that you may know and believe me,
>   and understand that I am he. (Is 43:10)

The roots of this concept originate in God's command that Israel become a "holy nation" (Ex 19:6) and a "light to the nations" (Is 42:6). The Roman defeat of a Jewish insurrection in 70 CE culminated in the destruction of most of Jerusalem, including the Temple. The brutal Roman repression of a second Jewish revolt in 135 CE led to the dispersion of the Jewish people throughout the ancient world. Jews had to learn how to survive as an exiled and often persecuted minority. *Tikkun olam* calls Jews to be obedient to God, whose providence works not only for the sake of Jews but for all human beings. Jews must use their energy and resources to assist one another but also to care for the wider world.

The modern interpretation of *tikkun olam* includes everything from small acts of personal caregiving to philanthropic gifts and promoting just social policies. Sacks stresses the practical and worldly locus of this command: "Many people worry about their own stomachs and the state of other people's souls. The real task is to do the opposite: to worry about other people's stomachs and the state of your own soul."[2]

The meaning of solidarity for Christians and Jews includes but goes beyond what is found in their scriptures. Subsequent Christian theology shows a range of views about solidarity. The earliest Christians did not think of themselves as starting a separate religion but as a sub-community within Judaism centered on following Christ as the one who has fulfilled Israel's messianic hopes. Jesus himself went to the synagogue and Temple, and Paul continued to do so after his conversion. Jesus, though, radically recast solidarity by centering it on fellowship in the reign of God. As we have seen, he displayed the radically inclusive nature of the reign of God by his special concern for the sick, the poor, the outcast, and other marginalized people. His message was first addressed to fellow Jews, but then extended to Gentiles.

---

[1] Jonathan Sacks, "Tikkun Olam: Orthodoxy's Responsibility to Perfect G-d's World," address delivered at the Orthodox Union West Coast Convention, December 1997.

[2] Sacks, "Why Fighting Poverty and Hunger Is a Religious Duty," *Huffington Post*, January 26, 2013.

Specific challenges faced by particular Christian communities shaped the ways in which they practiced solidarity and care for the poor. St. Paul underscored the importance of building the internal bonds within particular Christian communities. He advised the Galatians: "Whenever we have an opportunity, let us work for the good of all, *and especially for those of the family of faith*" (Gal 6:10). This is the *church-based* or *ecclesial* side of Christian solidarity that is often forgotten by Christian social activists. We should be concerned about all human suffering ("let us work for the good of all"), but we have a special responsibility to those who suffer within our own particular religious communities (the "family of faith").

Paul demonstrated ecclesial solidarity when he writes to Christians in the Greek city of Corinth that it is "by one Spirit are we all baptized into one body, whether we be Jews or Gentiles, whether we be bond or free; and have been all made to drink into one Spirit. For the body is not one member, but many" (1 Cor 12:13–14). Christians are united not by membership in one ethnic group, observance of the law, or circumcision, but because they all belong to one Spirit. As members of one body, we must care for one another, especially for weaker members. Paul was critical of Christian communities where the Lord's Supper was followed by a banquet at which the wealthy dined but the poor were left out (1 Cor 11:17–34). If they want to have parties with their friends, he tells them, they should do it in their own places and not in a way that is associated with the worshiping community: "Do you not have homes to eat and drink in? Or do you show contempt for the church of God and humiliate those who have nothing?" (11:22).

Healthy group solidarity generates compassion for fellow members. St. Paul spent nearly ten years raising money from Gentile Christian communities to send to the poor of Jerusalem (Rom 15:26), some of it desperately needed because of famine in Palestine. This charity reflected both his Jewish identity and his faith in Christ.

The Synoptic Gospels show a similar concern to build up solidarity within Christian communities. They depict Jesus inviting followers to a renewed covenantal community formed in expectation of the reign of God. Disciples learn from him to travel together, share meals, and take care of one another. Their primary form of solidarity is no longer familial or tribal but religious. Jesus praises those who leave their homes and families to follow him (Mk 10:28; Mt 19:29). The Gospel of Luke, for example, tells of a time when Jesus's mother and his brothers were trying to talk with him but were prevented from doing so because of the crowds. When informed that they wanted to see him, Jesus responds, "My mother and my brothers are those who hear the word of God and do it" (Lk 8:21). Thus the Christian disciple, as Lisa Cahill writes, is "not one who was born in the family of faith, but one who heard the word of Jesus and was transformed by the new kingdom life."[3]

Jesus saw his mission as directed first to his people, the Jews, who were like "sheep without a shepherd" (Mk 6:34; 8:2). But he also taught and healed Gentiles. He did not reject ties of kinship, but, like the prophets, he insisted that loyalty to God takes precedence over them: "Whoever loves father or mother more than me is not worthy of me; and whoever loves son or daughter more than me is not worthy of me" (Mt 10:37). All other forms of solidarity are subordinated to the highest priority, the reign of God.

As we saw in the chapter on compassion, Jesus extended concern to the poor, lepers, prostitutes, tax collectors, and various other outcasts. To follow Jesus means to forgive those who do us harm, to extend hospitality to strangers, not to return evil for evil, and to love our enemies. He showed his disciples what it means to see people as God seems them rather than as they are defined by group membership and social hierarchies (including religiously based hierarchies). He reserved his sharpest criticism for those who marginalize and exploit outcasts and who care more about ritual purity than mercy. Following Jesus, Christians are to be concerned about social outcasts whether or not they believe in Jesus.

We also see a special concern for fellowship within the community of Jesus's followers most sharply in the Gospel of John. The first followers of Jesus constituted a movement with Judaism and they attended synagogues. At some point in the late first century, however, Jewish leaders of a particular synagogue in Asia Minor expelled members who were part of the Jesus movement (see Jn 9:22), most likely because they included Gentile and Samaritan Christians who did not fulfill the requirements of the Jewish law.

The Gospel of John was probably written by one of these expelled Christians, which might explain why it speaks so harshly about "the Jews" Jn 5—12) and "the world" (Jn 13—17) while also holding many elements of the Jewish tradition in high esteem. Written in the face of a bitter divide, this Gospel tried to strengthen its members' group solidarity. In this Gospel, Jesus gives his disciples a new commandment: "Just as I have loved you, you also should *love one another*" (13:34, emphasis added). His farewell address describes his disciples as "friends" (15:15). And shortly before he is arrested, Jesus prayerfully asks the Father to protect his disciples "*so that they may be one*, as we are one" (17:11, emphasis added).

The Hebrew and Christian scriptures thus display a variety of views about solidarity. This diversity suggests that particular communities must weigh the demands of solidarity in light of their own particular

---

[3] Lisa Sowle Cahill, *Women and Sexuality* (Mahwah, NJ: Paulist Press, 1992), 31.

circumstances. As one biblical scholar puts it, the "primary mandate" for Christians was to "manifest love and service within the community," but they could not follow Christ and be "indifferent to those outside the community of faith."[4]

Christians in the first centuries were known for their care for the needy, whether Christian or not. The last non-Christian Roman emperor, Julian the Apostate (360–63), worried about the number of former pagans who had converted to Christianity. In a letter to the pagan high priest of Galatia, the emperor complained that even in hard times "no Jew ever has to beg, and the impious Galileans [Christians] support not only their own poor but ours as well."[5] In attempting to bolster public relations, the emperor ordered Roman priests to start imitating Christian charity for the poor. It was far too little, and far too late.

Church as the Basis for Christian Solidarity

How we understand Christian solidarity is closely related to our conception of the church, and how we think of the church is closely related to what we make of Jesus Christ. Christian traditions that emphasize the incarnation tend to see the church as called to be highly engaged in the world. In the second half of the twentieth century Christian activists drew a strong connection between the incarnation and the church's involvement, as Oscar Romero put it, in the "world of the poor." Since the deepest meaning of the incarnation is revealed in the cross and resurrection, these were interpreted in light of the experience of the poor. The cross came to be seen as revealing Christ's solidarity with the excluded, the victims of domination, and the vanquished. The resurrection, accordingly, came to be seen as God's redemptive overcoming of the suffering and death of the victims of the world.

Pedro Arrupe described the incarnation as revealing the "most profound meaning of the poverty of the poor Christ, whom we want to imitate and follow."[6] He regarded Christian "insertion" into marginalized communities as a kind of incarnation. "To know reality, to change our attitudes, and achieve a true discernment," he said, "we must first be inserted into reality in an effective way." Personal contact allows us to be in "solidarity with those who suffer, even to be identified with their lives." This identification

---

[4] Richard B. Hayes, *The Moral Vision of the New Testament* (New York: Harper, 1996), 145.

[5] Julian the Apostate, "Letter to Arsacius, High-Priest of Galatia."

[6] Kevin Burke, ed., *Pedro Arrupe: Essential Writings* (Maryknoll, NY: Orbis Books, 2004), 87.

means that solidarity is first and foremost a matter of *being with* rather than *doing for* the poor.

So far we have seen two senses of Christian solidarity: solidarity among Christians (*koinonia*, community) and solidarity with the poor. Christian solidarity with the poor has at least two meanings. First, it can refer to ecclesial solidarity with poor Christians. This was St. Paul's concern when he solicited donations for the poor of Jerusalem (1 Cor 16:1-4). We see it today when small groups of parishioners gather to care for a sick or dying member.

Second, Christian solidarity with the poor more commonly refers to a social commitment regardless of religious identity. In the United States, Catholic social ministries began by helping poor Catholic immigrants from Italy, Ireland, and Eastern Europe, but over time they were expanded to offer care to anyone who needs it. The Paulist Center in Boston, for example, has a weekly Supper Club not just for parishioners but for anyone who wants to join them for a meal and company.

Christian solidarity is not just a matter of helping the poor, but also a deliberate choice to adopt their cause as our own. Even more deeply, it is an identification with the poor. When Martin Luther King, Jr., visited Chicago, he saw intense racial hatred. The ferocity of white supremacists in the so-called liberal North, and the ensconced power of city hall, led him to reflect on his own solidarity with the poor:

> I choose to identify with the underprivileged. I choose to identify with the poor. I choose to give my life for the hungry. I choose to give my life for those who have been left out of the sunlight of opportunity. I choose to live for those who find themselves seeing life as a long and desolate corridor with no exit sign. This is the way I'm going. If it means suffering a little bit, I'm going that way. If it means sacrificing, I'm going that way. If it means dying for them, I'm going that way, because I heard a voice saying, "Do something for others."[7]

King's comments echo what Albert Nolan says about Jesus:

> The remarkable thing about Jesus was that, although he came from the middle class and had no appreciable disadvantages himself, he mixed socially with the lowest of the low and identified himself with them. He became an outcast by choice.[8]

---

[7] Martin Luther King, Jr., August 28, 1966, cited in David J. Garrow, *Bearing the Cross: Martin Luther King, Jr., and the Southern Christian Leadership Conference* (New York: William Morrow, 1986), 524.

[8] Albert Nolan, *Jesus Before Christianity* (Maryknoll, NY: Orbis Books, 1967), 34.

Solidarity with the poor is rooted in particular bonds of friendship with marginalized people. The decision to identify with the poor led Stang, Day, and Mother Teresa to live in the midst of seriously impoverished people. "We can't talk about the poor," Stang wrote in a letter. "We must be poor with the poor and then there is no doubt how to act."[9] She referred to the Amazonian settlers as "my people." "She identified with them, body and soul," wrote a friend. She did not do this only out of sense of duty, but out of desire to be with people who had become her friends: "I have to be with these people," she wrote. "If it means my life, I want to give my life."[10]

The solidarity exercised by our exemplars supports a vision of the church as a radically inclusive community. Whereas most forms of ordinary human solidarity tend to be exclusive, Christian love demands an ethic of inclusive solidarity. Jesus did not select particularly heroic individuals and teach them a set of spiritual secrets reserved to them alone. He gathered disciples into a circle of friends (Jn 15:13–15), what early Christian writers described as community *(koinonia)* (1 Cor 10:16; Acts 2:42), but their community was meant to have open doors. It was gathered to imitate a founder who sought out the lost, announced good news to the poor, and welcomed the stranger.

As Christian communities attracted new members and spread geographically, they began to take institutional forms—rituals, teachings, leadership structures, and the like. Institutions help to sustain communities. Charismatic leadership is crucial, but it is not sufficient for the long haul. Suspicion of institutions pervades our society. Yet while there is no doubt that institutions can become corrupt, so can anything human. Families, hospitals, and universities can be dysfunctional, but that doesn't mean we ought to abandon them. There is no real and lasting community without some set of norms, patterns of organization, and common practices. This is as true of Christian communities as it is of a neighborhood bowling league, a Boy Scout troop, or Little League baseball.

The key question is not *whether* we ought to have institutions but *how* they ought to be organized. The key criterion, Timothy Radcliffe says, is whether our religious institutions *empower* people or *weaken* them.[11] He deliberately uses the plural; the church is not a single massive institution, but a community served by a multitude of institutions that range from parishes and retreat houses to colleges and diocesan social services. The

---

[9] Cited in Roseanne Murphy, *Martyr of the Amazon: The Life of Sister Dorothy Stang* (Maryknoll, NY: Orbis Books, 2007), 63.

[10] Cited in Binka Le Breton, *The Greatest Gift: The Courageous Life and Martyrdom of Sister Dorothy Stang* (New York: Doubleday, 2007), 111, 185.

[11] Timothy Radcliffe, *Why Go to Church? The Drama of the Eucharist* (New York: Bloomsbury Academic, 2009).

healthier the life of the community, the more it produces institutions that serve people's needs and enhance their agency.

There are specifically theological reasons for wanting to create good institutions. The incarnation provides a strong Christian basis for affirming the value of institutions, the communities they serve, and the church itself. The incarnation of God's love for us in the particular person of Jesus of Nazareth implies that the love of Christ must be embodied in tangible, visible ways in our own communities. This is the rationale for the continued existence of the Christian community and why Christians ought to have a strong commitment to it.

Because institutions are necessary for the health of a community, we ought to work, whenever possible, to *reform* church institutions rather than just abandon them. The reform can take place at a high level, as seen in Pope Francis's efforts to reform the Roman Curia, but also on a smaller scale at a local level. Each Christian can make a difference by getting involved in parishes or congregations and helping them function better as participatory communities. To give up on institutions altogether is not only to mistrust human beings but also to lack faith in what the Holy Spirit can do in and through us. Christian churches at their best engage in a "creative fidelity" that is rooted in the past while also willing to assimilate contemporary insights and face contemporary challenges.

The Church as Servant to Christians—Ecclesial Solidarity

All this is to say the church is to follow the example of Jesus, the one who "came not to be served but to serve" (Mt 20:27). Acting as servant, the church has two focal points: internally, on building up the body of Christ, and externally, promoting justice and peace in the world.

People often think church refers to a building where people assemble for religious services, but it refers primarily to the community of disciples of Christ. The church follows Christ not just as a prophet, teacher, and exemplar, but also, and most decisively, as Savior of the world. It thus exists in order to help us see and respond to the presence of the Spirit of Christ in our lives, our communities, and the wider world.

Some forms of service are specially directed to building up the Christian community and deepening the spiritual and moral lives of Christians. All believers have this responsibility, but pastors have it in a special way. Jesus envisioned authority within the community of his disciples as a way of serving others. He instructed the Twelve not to follow the pattern of worldly rulers who use their authority to "lord it over" their subjects but rather to serve them in humble love. Disciples are to serve rather than to be served (Mk 10:42–45; Mt 20:25–28).

Every official position within the church is a specific form of service. In the Catholic church, priests and bishops perform a special service when they preside at the ministry of the word and administer the sacraments. Ministers are called to special service in Protestant preaching and worship as well. The office of deacon calls particular Christians to a special ministry in service of needy members of their communities, but every disciple is expected to serve the community in some way. The Letter to the Ephesians describes Christ as giving leaders to the church to enable them to care for the needs of its members, to enhance the unity of its faith, and to build up the whole body of Christ in love (Eph 4:11–16). Solidarity is based on Christ: "We must grow up in every way into him who is the head, into Christ, from whom the whole body, joined and knit together by every ligament with which it is equipped, as each part is working properly, promotes the body's growth in building itself up in love" (Eph 4:15–16).

At the same time, religious communities should not become comfortable enclaves whose members are indifferent to the outside world. Pope Francis offers a warning that "whenever we Christians are enclosed in our groups, our movements, our parishes, in our little worlds, we remain closed, and the same thing happens to us that happens to anything closed: when a room is closed, it begins to get dank."[12] The mark of authentic Christian solidarity is openness to the other in what we might call "social self-transcendence." As Pope Francis reminds us in his 2013 apostolic exhortation *Evangelii Gaudium (The Joy of the Gospel)*, "To go out of ourselves and to join others is healthy for us" (no. 87).

The Church as Servant to the World—Christian Solidarity with the Poor

The church is thus also called to be servant of the world. The church's service is seen in orphanages, schools, homes for the elderly, hospitals and hospices, shelters and refugee centers. As Stang, Romero, and other exemplars show, the church has a role to play not only in charitable activities but also in promoting justice in political, legal, and socioeconomic institutions.

We can trace three positions Christians take regarding the social responsibility of the church, which we can call the "vertical," the "horizontal," and the "integrated" positions.[13] First, *verticalists* hold that the church ought to evangelize unbelievers so they can be saved and go to heaven. They view

---

[12] Pope Francis, "Address to Participants in the Pilgrimage of Catechesis," September 27, 2013.

[13] Pedro Arrupe speaks about the vertical and horizontal dimensions of Christian love in his talk "The Social Commitment of the Society of Jesus," in Burke, *Pedro Arrupe*, 158–60.

the gospel message as forming personal piety and private salvation—"Jesus and me." The pure verticalist thinks that love of neighbor has nothing to do with altering social structures because salvation is a strictly individual and entirely otherworldly matter. Christ died to save our souls, and if we confess that Jesus is Lord, we will be saved (Rom 10:9; Jn 3:15). They believe we ought to share what we have with the truly needy because it is "more blessed to give that to receive" (Acts 20:25), but they point out that scripture provides no blueprint for a just society or state. During the 1950s and 1960s, for example, verticalist Christians were on both sides of the desegregation debate.

Second, *horizontalist* Christians think the church ought to be concerned primarily with fighting social injustice rather than redemption from personal sin. The reign of God is collective, not solitary, and it is earthly, they hold, not a heavenly "pie in the sky." We do not move to God only as individuals, but also as communities. As St. Paul said, "If one member suffers, all suffer together with it" (1 Cor 12:26). Horizontalists think we ought to be concerned with providing food for the hungry rather than praying that God will feed them. They want us to change the policies that leave families having to choose between buying food and paying their heating bill, rather than hoping that lawmakers will be divinely inspired to change those policies.

Third, an integrationist approach includes both the transcendence of the vertical position and the immanence of the horizontal position. "There is no brotherhood," Dorothy Day wrote, "unless we recognize each other as creatures of body and soul." For this reason she insisted: "You can't preach the Gospel to men with empty stomachs."[14]

The integrationist position holds that God wills both the salvation of individual persons and the transformation of the world. True evangelization, Romero taught, has to be concerned with comprehensive "human advancement."[15] Just as the prophets identified the implications of divine justice in their day, so we must seek justice in ours. The integrationist regards justice as a constitutive aspect of the mission of the church. "Constitutive" means the social mission is not a mere supplemental add-on to its real purpose, but actually essential to it. Pedro Arrupe put it bluntly: any faith that claims to love God but "does not issue in justice for others is a farce."[16] To this end it promotes structural conditions that give everyone

---

[14] Dorothy Day, *The Duty of Delight: The Diaries of Dorothy Day*, ed. Robert Ellsberg (Milwaukee: Marquette University Press, 2008), 88, 12.

[15] Archbishop Oscar Romero, *Voice of the Voiceless* (Maryknoll, NY: Orbis Books, 1985), 60.

[16] *Pedro Arrupe: Selected Writings,* ed. Kevin Burke (Maryknoll, NY: Orbis Books, 2007), 173.

access to the kinds of goods—for example, just wages, healthcare, and decent education—that enable people to lead decent lives.

The solidarity of the integrationist position supports the dignity of the marginalized and protests against their marginalization. As Greg Boyle puts it, we ought to "stand with the demonized so that the demonizing will stop."[17]

Oscar Romero defended popular organizations in El Salvador because he wanted to support "the people themselves who are working to shape their own destiny."[18] Solidarity in this sense approaches God, Christ, and the church not just in light of the poor but *from the perspective of the poor.* Christian solidarity here finds Christ in the poor. It is based on confidence that divine grace is *already present* in the lives of marginalized people and calling them, as individuals and as communities, to a fuller human existence through the exercise of their own agency. It thus does not seek to do *for* others, but rather to work *with* them for the betterment of all. The spirituality that accords with this form of solidarity does not attempt to *bring* God to people as much as to *find* God in them.

We now turn to two images of solidarity that have become especially prominent in recent years: accompaniment and kinship. These images have captured the imagination of Christians engaged in service.

Accompaniment

In the last few decades the ethic of solidarity has been intensified in the ethic and spirituality of accompaniment. *To accompany* means not only to walk with someone but also to encounter that person and become his or her companion.

Accompaniment has deep roots in the Christian tradition. Oscar Romero had faith in the God who now, as in biblical times, "accompanies his people in history."[19] The God of the covenant was present to the prophets and in an unsurpassable way in Jesus of Nazareth. Christian faith is not so much a matter of believing that Jesus is the Savior as it is a willingness to accompany Christ, and to be accompanied by Christ, in daily life. Jesus accompanied the marginalized, and the Spirit of Christ is found among the marginalized today. As Day puts it, "Christ is in our midst—not a tidy, well-scrubbed, church-on-Sunday Christ, but a Christ for weekdays, a Christ in

---

[17] Gregory Boyle, *Tattoos on the Heart: The Power of Boundless Compassion* (New York: Free Press, 2010), 190.

[18] Oscar Romero, *A Shepherd's Diary*, trans. Irene B. Hodgson (Cincinnati, OH: St. Anthony Messenger Press, 1986), 507.

[19] Ibid., 255.

patched clothing, a Christ of slums and flop houses, a Christ homeless and jobless, a Christ of soup lines."[20]

Accompaniment is a particularly intense form of solidarity. The term is used by the Jesuit Refugee Service (JRS) to describe the distinctive style of its service to forced migrants. Pedro Arrupe, then superior-general of the Jesuits, founded JRS in 1980 to address the needs of hundreds of thousands of refugees fleeing southeast Asia in the wake of the Vietnam war. JRS seeks to fulfill a threefold mission: to accompany, to serve, and to advocate for refugees. Its agents seek to serve refugees by helping them get access to emergency assistance, education, healthcare, and legal assistance, and to skills that can help them become economically self-sufficient. JRS now serves half a million refugees and internally displaced people in over fifty countries around the globe.

Many forms of solidarity are exercised from a distance. We see it when someone in the United States buys only Fair Trade coffee as a way of acting in solidarity with Guatemalan coffee farmers. Accompaniment, on the other hand, cannot be at a distance. It only happens when physical, social, and interpersonal presence allows for the creation of companionship. Those who practice accompaniment know the meaning of poverty not just by reading books, listening to lectures, or watching documentaries, but by sharing in the daily lives of particular marginalized people. Thus, for JRS, accompaniment involves "breaking bread" with refugees, knowing their names, hearing their stories, and becoming familiar with their struggles through face-to-face conversations. Those who accompany come to know the joys, hopes, and dreams of refugees as well as their worries and sorrows. Accompaniment builds partnership. Intimate knowledge and lived experience provide the basis for cooperation. As Mark Raper, SJ, international director of JRS for ten years, explains: "You cannot doubt the experience of a person whose wounds you dress. If we wish to serve the poor, we must meet them and know them. If we allow the poor to touch our hearts, there is no end to what we will undertake together with them and for them."[21]

Closer to home, the ethic of accompaniment led in 2009 to the establishment of the Jesuit-run Kino Border Initiative (KBI) in Nogales, Arizona, and Nogales, Sonora, Mexico. Every week the Immigration and Naturalization Service busses hundreds of undocumented migrants to the US Border Patrol Station in Nogales, Arizona, and then escorts them to the border. Deportees simply walk across the border, usually bringing scant resources with them. Few are greeted by family or friends who can help. This makes

---

[20] Cited in Jim Forest, *All Is Grace: A Biography of Dorothy Day* (Maryknoll, NY: Orbis Books, 2011), 127.

[21] Ibid.

them highly vulnerable to exploitation by human traffickers, drug cartels, and other criminals.[22]

The KBI was founded with four goals in mind: (1) to provide immediate humanitarian assistance to migrants and deportees, (2) to offer social and pastoral education about migration on both sides of the border, (3) to support research on topics that affect migrants, including documentation of their experience, and (4) to collaborate with other organizations to advocate for just immigration reform. The KBI runs an outreach center for migrants and a shelter for women and children in Nogales, Sonora, Mexico. In addition to providing deportees with food, clothing, and shelter, it also tries to find ways to help them become self-supporting.

Accompaniment gives the staff of KBI personal knowledge of the emotional, physical, and social damage done to migrant families by the enforcement of current US immigration policy. They have a higher degree of credibility than advocates who work from a distance. This approach to solidarity is relevant not only to refugees and deportees, but to any people who find themselves in a position of marginalization due to poverty, cultural exclusion, bigotry, ecological disasters, or any other causes.

Accompaniment has three additional components worth mentioning. First, it is based on a deep affirmation of the intrinsic dignity of every human being. Accompaniment involves a ministry of presence that tells marginalized people that they are precious in the eyes of God. This is no small matter to people who have been so mistreated that they feel worthless.

Accompaniment is only possible if we are willing to listen and share one another's stories. Stories give us a unique window into what their narrators have been through, what they need, and what they want to do about their situation. Advocacy in the context of accompaniment enables the poor to speak for themselves, often in ways that give rise to unexpected insights and creative solutions to problems.

Second, accompaniment seeks to assist marginalized people to expand their own capacities for agency. These include enabling people to acquire the skills they need to make a living, to construct a new way of life for their families, and to develop their own leadership capacities. Those who accompany can treat asylum seekers as individuals rather than as objects of charity. Deogratias M. Rwezaura, SJ, project director of JRS in the Kibondo region of Tanzania, points out that exiles have "as much to offer as those who serve them have to receive." We should not therefore view them "simply as being at the receiving end of national, non-governmental, and international humanitarian aid agencies." Rwezaura points out that, contrary to popular stereotypes, people who live in highly uncertain circumstances

---

[22] For the Kino Border Initiative, see the kinoborderinitiative.org website.

can often, in fact, be quite "hopeful, happy, talented, and hardworking, especially when they are given support and opportunities."[23]

Finally, accompaniment seeks to inspire hope in people whose way of life has been shattered by violence and geographical displacement. The ministry of personal presence can arouse hope in people who are on the verge of despair. Rwezaura captures some concrete ways in which this was pursued in Tanzania:

> Our goal and vision was to build a community of hope. . . . We did not offer services to the refugees; we responded to their needs together with them. We built a place of worship and classrooms, organised workshops and seminars on leadership and peer education, planned social and pastoral services and evaluated our activities. We worked together and through this experience, we recognised one another's strengths and weaknesses. We created a stimulating atmosphere in which to offer service and advocacy. Refugees identified with JRS and were part of our mission and family.[24]

Kinship

Kinship normally refers to family connections, but Greg Boyle, S.J., uses it to describe our common humanity and how we live up to that humanity in compassion and friendship. Boyle is the director of Homeboy Industries, an organization dedicated to helping former gang members and at-risk youth receive the job training, social services, and skills they need to lead rewarding lives. Boyle started his ministry in the 1980s in an area of Los Angeles heavily populated by gangs. Extensive experience with gangs has proven the truth of the saying, "Nothing stops a bullet like a job." Homeboy Industries includes Homeboy Bakery, Homeboy Silkscreen, Homeboy/Homegirl Merchandise, and Homegirl Café. The aim of Boyle's work is to enable at-risk teens and adults to develop their own agency. Despite the bureaucratic sound of "Industries," Homeboy's heart and soul are friendship and community. Participation in community provides the context and confidence for capacity building.

Boyle's work with former members of rival gangs is based on compassion. This compassion takes its cue from God: "If we love what God loves, then, in compassion, margins get erased."[25] His account of compassion is based in a Christian faith that carries powerful social implications: "'Be

---

[23] Deogratias M. Rwezaura, "I Have Called You by Name," in *In the Footsteps of Pedro Arrupe*, ed. Danielle Vella (Rome: JRS, 2007), 26.

[24] Ibid., 25–26.

[25] Boyle, *Tattoos on the Heart*, 75.

compassionate as God is compassionate,' means the dismantling of barriers that exclude."[26] Compassion thus leads to an inclusive hospitality that
welcomes those who have been "written off" by much of American society.

Homeboy Industries provides structured contexts in which former rivals
can work together and learn mutual respect. Respect opens the door to
cooperation, and cooperation typically leads to friendship. Respect, compassion, and hospitality are ultimately rooted in love: "There is no force
in the world better able to alter anything from its course than love."[27] The
power of love slowly works in this context to turn enemies into friends.
Boyle thus shares King's conviction that love is the only force capable of
transforming an enemy into a friend.[28]

Boyle distinguishes service, solidarity, and kinship in a distinctive way.
He describes service as a relationship in which "haves" help "have-nots."
Solidarity moves beyond this superiority-dependency polarity and into
common cause, but, as noted above, it can take place at a distance. Boyle
invites his readers to go a step further: from solidarity to kinship. People in
solidarity can take the right stand on issues, he says, but those who experience kinship stand in the right place.[29] Compassion at its most powerful is
not merely good will and support from a comfortable and secure distance
but friendship within a community of interdependent equals: "Kinship—not
serving the other, but being one with the other."[30]

Boyle uses the terms *service* and *solidarity* in his own distinctive ways,
but the substance of his position is very similar to what is proposed here.
Solidarity runs a vast continuum from weak to strong. In Boyle's terms,
weak solidarity is when our heart is in the right place and strong solidarity—call it accompaniment or kinship—is when our feet are in the right
place. Strong solidarity challenges weak: "So you say you love the poor:
name them."

Boyle's vision echoes those of King, Stang, and our other exemplars. His
tone resonates with Day's description of how the first House of Hospitality
got up and running. Though she did not use the language, she was living
the substance of kinship:

> We started with a soup kitchen, and in no time we had a community
> of us, living together. . . . It wasn't "us" versus "them," a few with
> "ideas" and "ideals" and the hungry poor "we" worked to feed; it was

---

[26] Ibid.
[27] Ibid., 124.
[28] King, *Strength to Love*, 48.
[29] See Boyle, *Tattoos on the Heart*, 72.
[30] Ibid., 188.

a mix of people—some who had no place to stay, and "us," who were searching, you could say, for *our* place to stay![31]

This vision of strong solidarity is based on a commitment to fundamental human equality, respectful partnership, and active co-responsibility. It moves from "men and women *for* others," Boyle says, to "men and women *with* one another." It sees that "Jesus was not 'a man for others'; he was one with them. There is a world of difference in that."[32]

Boyle uses kinship to point to the fact that we all share a fundamental vision of humanity. His vision resonates with Paul's accent on the fundamental equality of the baptized: "You are all sons of God through faith in Christ Jesus, for all of you who were baptized into Christ have clothed yourselves with Christ. There is neither Jew nor Greek, slave nor free, male nor female, for you are all one in Christ Jesus" (Gal 3:26–28). Boyle would say that there is neither Mexican nor Guatemalan, neither migrant worker nor farm owner, neither straight nor gay, neither Jew nor Muslim, for all are one as human beings whom God loves "without measure and without regret."[33]

Boyle's image of kinship might be challenged by social psychologists who claim that human beings are deeply limited by an innate moral parochialism. We naturally care for close relationships and group members but not much for outsiders. Psychologist Paul Bloom, for example, points out that "it is impossible to empathize with seven billion strangers, or to feel toward someone you've never met the degree of concern you feel for a child, a friend, or a lover." He goes on to argue, "our best hope for the future is not to get people to think of all humanity as family—that's impossible." Instead of trying to expand our empathy for distant suffering strangers as our brothers or sisters, we ought to acknowledge, rationally, that, "their lives have the same value as the lives of those we love."[34] If this is true, then we ought to focus on crafting the policies and laws that will promote the greatest good for the greatest number of people on the planet. Right now we rely much too strongly on individuals acting compassionately. We will do more good overall, Bloom thinks, if we focus more on policy assessments based on the big picture of utilitarian costs and benefits than on the acting as good Samaritans.

---

[31] Day, cited in Robert Coles, *Lives of Moral Leadership: Men and Women Who Have Made a Difference* (New York: Random House, 2000), 135–36.

[32] Boyle, *Tattoos on the Heart,* 72.

[33] Ibid., 22.

[34] Paul Bloom, "The Baby in the Well: The Case against Empathy," *The New Yorker,* May 20, 2013.

Boyle might respond that Bloom's reasoning assumes a false dichotomy between empathy and justice, whereas, in fact, the more compassionately we care about the neighbor we encounter, the more we ought to care about justice for the remote neighbor. Kinship is a metaphorical way of talking about both near and distant neighbors as fellow human beings rather than as "others."

The ethic of accompaniment and anthropology of kinship moves us beyond the ever-present temptation to paternalism (a recurring problem, by the way, for Bloom's utilitarianism). Jim Petkiewicz and his wife, Mags, spent eight years working in Oaxaca, Mexico, as Maryknoll lay missioners. They were so committed that they raised their two children there. Jim and Mags cofounded T & C Imports, a Fair Trade import firm, and Frog Tree Yarns, a wholesaler of yarns. He is also the cofounder of Community Links International, an organization that provides immersion trips to delegations that want to visit some communities in Latin America.

During their years in Oaxaca, Jim and Mags saw many delegations of Americans go down to Mexico with what he calls the "Great White Santa Claus from the North" syndrome. Participants from schools or universities visit and volunteer for a week or so in a community in Mexico and then go back home. The syndrome kicks in when their behavior reinforces power dynamics based on a division of the world into competent "haves" and incompetent "have-nots." "Do gooders" think they are helping when in fact their behavior can implicitly communicate harmful messages. Paternalism distorts the vision of the visitors, and they treat locals as if they can do little or nothing for themselves. This behavior, Jim says, is both pervasive and pernicious. Visitors need instead to be brought into a mutually respectful relationship with communities they visit. Most important, they need to have an opportunity to listen to their hosts' stories and share their own stories with them.

The Virtue of Justice

Every form of service is accountable to standards of justice, fairness, and human decency. The ethical legitimacy of Christian solidarity with the poor is established on the basis of justice, which is defined most basically as a stable commitment to give each person what is his or her due. Justice thus requires that we treat each person with the respect that is due to him or her as a human being, which means, at the very least, that we do no harm. This is no small thing.

Christians understand what is due to another in terms of every person's status as created in the image of God rather than, say, primarily as consumers to whom we want to sell something, or competitors we strive to defeat, or animals we try to train, or cogs in a bureaucratic machine we intend to manipulate.

If we are all created in the image of God, then we must honor that image in one another. This means we treat one another with respect, love, and care. There are some things we should never do to another person, even if doing so might benefit other individuals or larger groups. The fact that we are all equally created in the image of God implies that no person counts more than any other person. This obviously rules out all forms of discrimination based on race, gender, ethnicity, or other factors.

Justice based on a Christian view of human beings emphasizes our duty to respect the dignity of every person. We must honor every person's intrinsic worth, freedom, and capacity for self-responsibility. Communities are thus most aligned with justice when they enable their members to develop their own capacity for agency and decision making. Finally, how people contribute to the well-being of that community and how they participate in its decision-making process have a decisive impact on their experience of solidarity. Justice is essential to what King called the "beloved community" and Romero called "the common good."

Created in the image of a trinitarian God, we are called to right relationship with one another. Justice as right relationship is the basis of all forms of authentic and healthy solidarity, whether remote or proximate, large scale or small. Right relationship includes, but goes beyond, simply obeying the law. It requires us to build up the common good by paying special attention to those who are most marginalized. This is what is usually meant by "social justice.

This is not to deny that we have stronger responsibilities to some people than to others, particularly those to whom we are most closely bound, but we also bear responsibility for family members and friends, neighbors, colleagues, and others with whom we have a relationship. All of these responsibilities have their own particular texture. What we owe our spouse is different from what we owe our child, and both are different from what we owe a colleague at work. We act unjustly when we deliberately fail to meet these responsibilities. Particularly intense types of close interpersonal friendships have been characterized as prone to "parochial altruism." It is true that the natural ordering of our affections leads us to be more generous to some people more than others. Justice, however, challenges any tendency that leads us to ignore our other responsibilities and broader duties.

Justice is not only a matter of willing what is due to other individuals, but also of willing the good of our larger communities. It is precisely for the sake of the common good that the church gives priority to the poor. Rich and poor are not created as two separate categories of people. As Romero explained: "There aren't some people who were born to have everything, leaving the rest with nothing and a majority of people who have nothing and cannot taste the happiness that God has created for all. The Christian society that God wants is one in which we share the goodness that God has given to everyone."[35]

Justice coordinates a commitment to various bonds of solidarity with what Catholic social teaching calls the principle of subsidiarity—what can be done as well by a smaller, lower level organization should not be done by a larger, higher level organization. As Daniel Finn explains, the principle of subsidiarity is based on the insight that "each person is called to flourish and to take responsibility for themselves and their dependents—and that this frequently requires assistance from society or government." Finn rightly points out that the preference for the local provides a "strong endorsement for markets, where cooperation among individuals, and not government central planning, solves many economic problems."[36] Subsidiarity respects the intelligence, freedom, and agency of all participants, and it supports the right of people to make decisions about matters that directly affect their lives. It aims at the full participation of as many people possible in the economy, civic organizations, and political processes.

At the same time, subsidiarity requires higher level, complex organizations to fulfill responsibilities that they alone are equipped to meet.[37] It thus rejects both over-reaching and domineering bureaucracies and any anarchism that wants to dismantle all large-scale institutions.

Subsidiarity and solidarity thus go hand in hand. Solidarity without subsidiarity leads to conformism and smothering "group think," but subsidiarity without solidarity generates social fragmentation. Intermediate associations within civil society provide a context for the development of both individual and communal agency.

Christian solidarity with the poor is a special way of promoting the common good. The moral value of a policy depends on whether it ultimately serves the common good, not just the good of a particular group. A teachers' union, for example, cannot be concerned only with teachers' salaries and

---

[35] Oscar Romero, Homily, December 16. 1979, in *The Violence of Love*, ed. James R. Brockman, SJ (Maryknoll, NY: Orbis Books, 2004), 177.

[36] Daniel K. Finn, *Christian Economic Ethics: History and Implications* (Minneapolis. MN: Fortress Press, 2013), 341. Cf. John Paul II, *Solicitudo rei socialis,* no. 38; *Centesimus Annus,* no. 15; Benedict XVI, *Caritas in veritate,* no. 58

[37] Cf. John Paul II, *Centesimus Annus,* no. 48.

benefits. It also has to take seriously the needs of students and their families, the district's budget, and the good of the school district.

Justice also applies to solidarity within the church. Here, as elsewhere, institutional solidarity is good only as long as it takes place within the bounds of justice. Loyalty to God places the duties of justice, inside as well as outside the church, above duties to any human institutions, including the church. The church, Romero writes, "will raise questions about what is sinful in the world, and it will also allow itself to be questioned by the world as to what is sinful in the church."[38] This is advice that we have not sufficiently taken to heart. Loyalty to the institutional structures of the church is secondary to the loyalty to the whole community, the people of God. Christians, laity as well as clergy, are not only entitled but required to be alert to injustice within the church and to work to overcome it in whatever way we can. Justice is due first of all for the sake of potential or actual victims, but also to keep the church true to its mission.

Healthy self-critical Christian ecclesial solidarity promotes a proper loyalty to the church. Blind loyalty identifies the church with Christ and regards all criticism as wrongheaded. Its exact opposite, a knee-jerk anti-institutional prejudice, is just as extreme and just as unhelpful. It is important to keep in mind that anything good—from sports and education to medicine and law—can be used for destructive purposes. We are able to live well because we are beneficiaries of networks of relationships. As noted above, these relationships are made possible by institutional structures, and so institutional solidarity, rightly understood, is appropriate and good. Instead of throwing out the good with the bad, it is better to work to reform and develop what is good. Doing so is the mark of mature solidarity.

Justice requires the church to build an internal culture that accords with a Christian understanding of the meaning of power. We can distinguish *positional power* attached to offices and roles in institutions from the *relational power* that comes from the exercise of joint agency within networks of reciprocity. Positional power is good when exercised by virtuous people who serve the common good. We cannot have organizations without it, but it must be put at the service of relational power. If positional power tends to be paternalistic, relational power tends to be egalitarian. The Christian ethic of love and the common good have been used to support both kinds of power, but it leans more strongly in the direction of relational power.

These views of power are at play in competing accounts of the Catholic priesthood.[39] The cultic model of the priesthood stresses the priest's sacred

---

[38] Romero, *Voice of the Voiceless*, 65.

[39] Dean Hoge and Jacqueline Wenger, *Evolving Visions of the Priesthood: Changes from Vatican II to the Turn of the New Century* (Collegeville, MN: Liturgical Press,

status and his difference from the laity, and it often sees ordination as warranting ownership of positional power within the church. The servant model, on the other hand, sees ordination to the priesthood as conferring a relational power that enables the priest to provide a special kind of service to the Christian community. The servant model of the priesthood supports the empowerment of the laity, a ministry of listening as well as teaching, and open and accountable standards of church governance. Whereas the cultic model sees priests and bishops as authorized for (ideally) benevolent and well-informed, top-down decision making, the servant model sees them as facilitators of diverse forms of agency and consensus builders who accompany the people. As Pope Francis put it at the Chrism mass at St. Peter's on March 28, 2014, priests must not think of themselves as "middle managers," but as servants of "the poor, prisoners, the sick, for those who are sorrowing and alone." They must be like "shepherds living with the smell of the sheep."

Growth in Solidarity

We can distinguish between building solidarity in communities and building it in ourselves, as individuals. Members of groups build solidarity when they learn to identify their shared concerns and then organize and mobilize themselves to address them. Community organizations try to form a collection of individuals into one social body that can act effectively. They begin with face-to-face meetings, small-group conversations, and community-building exercises. If successful, they lead people to go from thinking in terms of "me" and "mine" to "us" and "ours." As our exemplars have shown, faith-based institutions can produce particularly effective forms of solidarity that lead to social action in the public arena.

People who undertake a commitment to live in greater solidarity with the poor usually do so because of powerful, face-to-face encounters. As Mother Teresa pointed out, "to know the problem of poverty [only] intellectually is not to understand it."[40] We have seen many examples of the transformative impact of ongoing personal contact. Day noted how easy it is to tune out the problems of the poor, especially when we are removed from them: "It is so much harder to see poverty when one is not living with it."[41] Experience is crucial, but so are reflection and conversation. Contact alone is not enough.

2003). See also Richard Gaillardetz, *Theology of the Diaconate* (New York: Paulist Press, 2005), 67–97.

[40] *Mother Teresa: Essential Writings*, ed. Jean Maalouf (Maryknoll, NY: Orbis Books, 2008), 20.

[41] *All the Way to Heaven: The Selected Letters of Dorothy Day*, ed. Robert Ellsberg (Milwaukee: Marquette University Press, 2010), 115.

Concrete commitments, even small ones, make the crucial difference—for example, even those as simple as reading a newspaper every day, refraining from using racial stereotypes, volunteering with a local advocacy group, or living in an intentional community.

Individuals who want to grow in solidarity with the poor must overcome a number of obstacles—moral, social, and psychological. First, affluence tends to dull our social conscience. "To be drugged by the comforts of privilege," Pedro Arrupe writes, "is to become contributors of injustice as silent beneficiaries of the fruits of injustice."[42] This theme is repeatedly developed by our exemplars.

Second, we can be drawn away from solidarity by the intensely competitive nature of our culture. It is difficult to develop strong connections with others if we see them either as threats or as people whose needs give us an opportunity to feel good about ourselves. The faith-based acceptance of our own intrinsic worth discussed in the chapter on stewardship is particularly relevant here.

Third, people from privileged backgrounds often underestimate the difficulty and costliness of strong solidarity with the poor. Those who have received higher education, for example, are unlikely to know what it's like to be poor. It is easy to romanticize poverty from a comfortable distance. As Mother Teresa once observed, "Nowadays people want to be poor and live with the poor, but they want to be free to dispose of things as they wish. To have this freedom is to be rich. They want both and they cannot have both."[43]

Even less demanding forms of solidarity with the poor can be challenging: going to a rally for the human rights of immigrants, working on a telethon to raise money for inner-city schools, and so on. As a general rule, the more conscientiously we engage in actions with companions, the stronger our solidarity with them.

The strongest forms of solidarity involve long-term commitments to marginalized communities and working full time to promote social justice. Most people are not called to the radical solidarity of Stang, Day, or Mother Teresa. But solidarity can come in less demanding but still significant forms. Consider the case of a student, call her "Mary," who travels to rural Mexico on a campus ministry-sponsored delegation. In talking with people in the host community, she finds out that Coca-Cola processing plants are taking the water from rural communities that had been used for irrigation. Mary learns that it takes up to three gallons of water to make one gallon of Coke and that the Coca-Cola corporation takes this water from aquifers and riv-

---

[42] Burke, *Pedro Arrupe*, 179.
[43] Maalouf, *Mother Teresa*, 108.

ers with the full approval of the government of Mexico. She also learns that indigenous organizations have organized a boycott of Coke products and she decides to participate to be in solidarity with the impoverished Mexican farmers. Her commitment is small and by itself will not affect Coca-Cola policy. But she acts out of a commitment to solidarity with the farmers who hosted her delegation. As the movement expands, she hopes collective action will make a difference.

Another form of solidarity is seen in someone who is committed to purchasing coffee from companies that use Fair Trade sources. They sell coffee that comes from small farmers who form cooperatives to process and then export their produce. Buying Fair Trade coffee has limitations, especially when it comes to influencing the policies of large farms. Though no substitute for labor rights, healthcare insurance, or education for agricultural workers, supporting Fair Trade coffee is a modest way of contributing to the well-being of some small-scale coffee farmers. Many people undertaking small commitments can have a positive cumulative effect on some coffee growers.

Parishes and congregations can help their members grow in solidarity with the poor by availing them of specific opportunities for concrete action. Some North American Christian communities have engaged in the practice of twinning or partnering with sister communities in the global South. The Archdiocese of Milwaukee, for example, has over fifty parishes with some kind of partnership with sister parishes in Central America, the Caribbean, or Africa. The goal is to enable members of both communities to develop significant levels of mutual understanding, communication, and sharing.

Parishes in the United States typically raise funds or gather materials (for example, educational or medical) to make targeted contributions to their sister parishes. Some parishes send volunteers on healthcare missions or construction projects, such as digging a well for a village. This approach is different from paternalistic charity because it centers on developing ongoing relationships through personal visits, group exchanges, and networks of communication. Like all true friendships, these relationships help all the participants learn and grow. They still have a tendency, however, toward paternalism and it takes a great deal of effort to prevent them from drifting into the "Great White Santa Claus from the North" syndrome.

The stronger the form of solidarity, the greater its costs and rewards. Strong solidarity requires significant time commitment, self-denial, and self-discipline, but it also brings more profound levels of friendship and joy. Long-term engagement in strong solidarity is sustained by the close interpersonal bonds of companionship that Boyle calls "kinship" and JRS calls "accompaniment."

Temptations of Solidarity

Christian solidarity with the poor faces a number of significant temptations. Here we can briefly examine four: idealizing poor communities, elitism, the "drop in the bucket" syndrome, and communal suffocation.

First, people striving for strong solidarity can be tempted to idealize marginalized communities. It is especially easy for young, short-term visitors to view poor communities as more generous, humble, and humane than others. The South African theologian Albert Nolan notes that among such visitors an initial rush of social enthusiasm often leads to an inflated estimate of the moral virtues and wisdom of poor people.[44] Negative experiences, however, can easily turn naive romantics into disillusioned cynics. Realistic appraisal recognizes that poor people can be as greedy, shortsighted, and corrupt as anyone else. They can be foolish as well as wise, competitive as well as cooperative, self-preoccupied as well as altruistic. Poor communities, similarly, can be as cold and clannish as any other communities.

We can acknowledge the goodness of a community without exaggerating its virtues. It is best to take people (regardless of socioeconomic class) one at a time rather than lumping them all into one "type" of person. At the end of the day, we are all fallible human beings and each of us has our own limitations and struggles.

Second, those who strive to be in solidarity with the poor can become snobby, narrow-minded, and arrogant. A passion for solidarity, especially right after a set of intense experiences, can tempt a person to believe that there is only one correct perspective from which to see the world. One-sided, ideological thinking can lead to a "good guys" *vs.* "bad guys" mentality. This can generate a dualism that implicitly divides the world into the few who have made the preferential option for the poor and the many who have made the preferential option for themselves. Such a perspective fails to see one's own oversights and weaknesses, as well as the insights and strengths of others. This can appear in either the intellectual elitism of the know-it-all or in the moral elitism of those who think their lifestyles transcend consumerism and popular hedonism.

Christian solidarity can also lead to a kind of religious elitism. No one wants to come across as "holier than thou," but social converts can at times believe they have discovered the true altruistic core of Christianity, judging all other Christians as "fakes." Such people typically overestimate their own level of solidarity with the poor and exaggerate their spiritual or moral differences from other privileged people. Consider, for example, the words

---

[44] See "Spiritual Growth and the Option for the Poor," presentation, Catholic Institute for International Relations (1984).

of Dorothy Day. After decades in the Catholic Worker, Day confessed in her diary, "I cannot say . . . that I yet share the poverty and suffering of the poor. No matter how much I may live in a slum, I can never be poor as the mother of three, six, ten children is poor (or rich either)."[45]

Solidarity with the poor distorted by elitism can begin to function like a cult that tempts one to cut ties with family and friends. Perhaps some people are not as curious and thoughtful as others. Others may not be ready or willing to make the significant personal changes needed to meet the demands of a more developed social conscience. The question is, how do we best love them?

Here again, cultivating a sense of our commonality with others can help. In Christian terms the mystery of the incarnation reminds us that God entered into our humanity with all its ambiguity, vulnerability, and imperfection. The Word did not "become flesh" because we are virtuous, but on the contrary, because of our need: "Those who are well have no need of a physician, but those who are sick" (Mt 9:12). All of us, no matter who we are, need this physician.

Some people do not have the freedom or opportunity to take time away from their paid work to volunteer in the inner city a few days a week. They have families to feed, bills to pay, and other commitments. This does not mean that they are bad Christians, let alone corrupt human beings.

The radically inclusive reign of God sets the framework for all forms of genuinely Christian solidarity. It excludes unjust attitudes, conduct, and policies, but it does not exclude people as such. Dorothy Day wrote these instructions to herself: "Just to serve others, because we see Christ in them, with no criticism. . . . To criticize the social order is one thing, people another."[46]

True Christian solidarity does not separate people on the basis of their moral goodness. Shortly before he was assassinated, Romero gave a homily in which he appealed directly to the soldiers who were doing most of the killing in El Salvador. They included members of specially trained units that engaged in massacres of entire villages of innocent men, women, and children. In his homily the archbishop implored the soldiers to remember who they are and where they come from: "Brothers, you came from our own people. You are killing your own brothers."[47] His solidarity was at the same time both prophetic and inclusive.

---

[45] Dorothy Day, *On Pilgrimage* (Catholic Worker Books, 1948), 204.

[46] Day, *The Duty of Delight*, 184.

[47] Homily, March 23, 1980, cited in Marie Dennis, Renny Golden, and Scott Wright, *Oscar Romero: Reflections on His Life and Writings* (Maryknoll, NY: Orbis Books, 2001), 95.

Romero wanted the leaders of El Salvador to understand the truth about their country, acknowledge the suffering they were imposing on the poor, move beyond their own fear, stop the repression, and begin social and economic transformation. He urged the powerful to enter into the world of the poor in a way that would promote their understanding, respect, and solidarity. He thought that this transformation would be best for them as well as for the poor. It would have come at a financial and political cost to the wealthy, but money is not what matters most.

A third temptation for people striving to be in solidarity is to get discouraged and dismiss one's efforts as just a "drop in the bucket." A person who has a powerful experience with the suffering of one poor family in a slum soon realizes that similar deprivation is harming tens of thousands of similar families living in the same slum, and, indeed, in thousands of other slums all over the world. One person can only do a small bit, she might wonder, so what's the point? Even a good-willed person devoted to solidarity with one particular community can't do anything about all the other people in all the other slums. Why bother?

The "drop in the bucket" temptation calls for a realistic appraisal of our finitude. We do not have infinite resources. One person cannot be in strong solidarity with prisoners on death row in Egypt *and* refugees in northern Kenya *and* recovering addicts in Cleveland *and* internally displaced people in Colombia *and* aboriginal people in Australia. Giving one's all to a particular cause leaves all the others untouched. While we want justice for billions of people, conditions of finitude make it impossible for us to be dedicated to the well-being of everyone or even to the majority of people.

We can counter the "drop in the bucket" syndrome by cultivating an awareness of the practical good that we can do in our own circumstances. Gratitude ought not to be just a mood we enter into from time to time. It is an attitude that we can nurture in ourselves by developing disciplined practices like prayer, meditation, worship, and spiritual reflection. We can feel grateful for the small but real good we can do. At the age of sixty-one, Day wrote: "If we start by admitting that what we can do is very small—a drop in the bucket—and try to do that well, it is a beginning and really a great deal."[48]

Disappointment over the good we cannot accomplish should not distract us from the good that we *can* do. Gratitude can help us appreciate the good of caring for particular people. If we really care about Jack and Amy, or Antoine and Lisa, then what we do with them matters. The fact that doctors cannot help everyone in the world afflicted with cancer doesn't stop them

---

[48] Day, *The Duty of Delight*, 248.

from trying to cure their particular patients. Their ability to appreciate the good that they do in their medical practice helps to keep them motivated and focused. "Do what comes to hand,"[49] Day suggested.

Each of us has to figure out what kind of commitment to solidarity with the poor is suitable and sustainable for us, given our particular needs, talents, and circumstances. There is a difference between the solidarity of a nurse working for years in a refugee camp and the lawyer who takes time from private practice in real estate law to be involved in local community organizing. Both cases involve accompanying people with whom they identify, for whom they seriously care, and with whom they share an ongoing commitment to justice.

What works for one person might not work for another. King was deeply committed to the disenfranchised, but he and his wife wanted to provide material comforts to their children. A high school religion teacher who brings students to Peru every summer but lives in a comfortable suburb takes intentional steps to live in solidarity with the poor but doesn't have to worry about finding potable water at home. He does the good he can do. It is useless to try to figure out which is "objectively" better or to seek the most heroically difficult challenge we can find. Each of us has to consent to do what we can in our own lives and not compare ourselves, favorably or unfavorably, to the service performed by people who are not us.

Finally, people engaged in solidarity with the poor can be tempted to spend so much time in community that they drift into communal "suffocation." They can become so busy with meetings, activities, and assignments that they lose touch with themselves. They fall into "solidarity overload."

Technology can make matters worse. Many people today rarely set aside time for genuine solitude. How much we feel a need for time alone varies according to our cultural background and individual personality, yet we all need a healthy balance of solitude and solidarity. Day, King, Mother Teresa, and even Jesus needed time alone. Kinship wants to dismantle unjust barriers between people, but we also need solitude for our mental and spiritual health. An appropriate sense of personal boundaries protects both our own integrity and our relationship with others.

French philosopher Blaise Pascal once said that "all of humanity's problems stem from man's inability to sit quietly in a room alone."[50] He would no doubt be shocked at the hyper-social nature of the world in which we

---

[49] *Dorothy Day: Selected Writings*, ed. Robert Ellsberg (Maryknoll, NY: Orbis Books, 1992), 64.

[50] Blaise Pascal, *Pensées,* trans. A. J. Krailsheimer (New York: Penguin Books, 1966).

now live, especially if we consider our constant attachment to electronic devices and the "virtual" people who constantly inhabit our mental space.

We are in an odd situation in which, as psychologist Shelly Turkle points out, we have become a society in which "we ask less of people and more of technology." Accompaniment and kinship in contrast demand more of people but also promise much more in terms of human connections. Pascal would also be concerned at what students call FOMO—fear of missing out. We are never supposed to be out of touch. Many teenagers say they feel uncomfortable when they don't have their cell phones within reach. "They need to be connected," Turkle says, "in order to feel like themselves." She maintains that constant reliance on technology for social contact makes it easy for us to be "hyper-other-directed," that is, in a state of needing constant validation from other people (even when they are at a great physical and emotional distance).[51]

The corrective to this temptation is not radical autonomy, but a balanced rhythm of well-spent solitude and solidarity. The experience of Christians throughout the ages suggests that spiritual growth depends upon both the solidarity of communal worship and service and the solitude of personal prayer in which we can listen to God with fewer distractions. Day worked long days but set aside time to be close to God whenever she could: sometimes she prayed "on the fly . . . at the kitchen table, on the train, on the ferry, on my way to and from appointments and even while making supper or putting Teresa to bed."[52] Technology and social media can be useful in a support role for friendships and social solidarity, but they do not substitute for face-to-face relationships. Sometimes we just have to turn off our phones.

Conclusion

We can think of the challenge that Christian solidarity presents to us in a number of ways. The beginning of this chapter pointed out that we are all in solidarity with various communities. The key question is not *whether* but *with whom* we are in solidarity. We have a tendency to associate with people who like what we like and who think the way we think. Christianity involves solidarity with fellow Christians within the church, but it also sends us out into the world to make connections with those who are marginalized. Both forms of solidarity are deeply rooted in the gospel. Some Christians care about the life of their religious community, others devote themselves to the marginalized. If we want to live in Christian solidarity,

---

[51] Shelly Turkle, *Alone Together: Why We Expect More from Technology and Less from Each Other* (New York: Basic Books, 2012), 176.

[52] Dorothy Day, *House of Hospitality* (New York: Sheed and Ward, 1939), 3.

we need to embrace both. Ecclesial solidarity runs against the grain of our anti-institutional bias and solidarity with the poor runs against the grain of our tendency to judge people on the basis of their wealth and income. The moral quality of our solidarity depends on its connection to the virtue of justice. We can resist its characteristic temptations by cultivating the virtues of gratitude, humility, and love. The next and final model of service turns to how we can serve by living as witnesses to the one who embodied such humility, gratitude, and love.

12

Witness

The sixth and final model of service is witness. In the Gospel of Matthew, Jesus teaches his disciples: "You are the light of the world. A city built on a hill cannot be hid. No one after lighting a lamp puts it under the bushel basket, but on the lampstand, and it gives light to all in the house. In the same way, let your light shine before others, so that they may see your good works and give glory to your Father in heaven" (Mt 5:14–16).

A witness testifies to something he or she has seen. *Witness* can mean observing an event or it can mean telling other people about what we have seen. This "telling" can be direct, explicit, and verbal or indirect, implicit, and non-verbal.

In the spring of 1964, Martin Luther King, Jr., spoke to an assembly of people who had just been beaten by rampaging white extremists in St. Augustine, Florida. After a mob had attacked nonviolent marchers, he encouraged assembled protesters to continue to demonstrate their commitment to nonviolent social change. King told them: "Let them beat us, let them kick us—we will *continue* to present our bodies in peaceful witness for justice, we ain't gonna let *nobody* turn us around."[1] In Christian terms, the highest form of witnessing is manifested by the martyr. Stang, Romero, King, and Claverie presented the ultimate testimony to the power of their faith—a willingness to die rather than to abandon the truth to which they had devoted their lives.

Five aspects of what it means to serve others as a witness are examined in this chapter: (1) the biblical basis of witnessing, (2) theological reflection on sacraments and sacramentality, (3) the virtue of integrity, (4) growing in the capacity to witness, and (5) the characteristic temptations of witnessing.

The Biblical Basis of Witnessing

We usually think of a witness as one who gives evidence for or against another person who is accused of wrongdoing. But the central role of a

---

[1] Marshall Frady, *Martin Luther King, Jr.: A Life* (New York: Penguin, 2002), 141.

biblical witness is to testify to the goodness of God. Witnesses to the God of Israel reminded people to be faithful to the covenant. This is seen in individuals, like Abraham or Moses, or in a particular tribe, or in the whole people of Israel. In general, the act of witnessing reinforces commitment, bolsters loyalty, and elevates the morale of a group. As we saw in the previous chapter, some biblical texts speak of God as working through Abraham and his tribe for the good of the whole world. God says to Abraham: "In you all the families of the earth shall be blessed" (Gen 12:3). His descendants are called to form a new kind of society that makes visible what God wants for all people: "nonviolence, freedom, peace, salvation."[2] The suffering servant of second Isaiah is thus described as "a witness to the peoples" (Is 55:4; 43:10–12) and a "light to the nations" (Is 49:6).

New Testament accounts of witnessing build on this foundation. Early Christians relied on the testimony of the first witnesses to the risen Christ. "The apostles," one church historian writes, "were and are, first and foremost, witnesses to the mighty works of God."[3] St. Paul writes of receiving the gospel and then handing it on to others (see 1 Cor 15:3). His Epistle to the Corinthians testifies to the truth of what Paul considered the central Christian proclamation: that Christ died for our sins, was buried, and was then raised on the third day. The risen Jesus, Paul explains, appeared to Cephas (Peter), then to the Twelve, and then to over five hundred disciples, including himself. Paul does not offer a detailed account of what occurred in his revelatory experience, but it is clear that he believed that the authenticity of his message rested on his personal encounter with the risen Christ.

The Acts of the Apostles also appeals to the testimony of eyewitnesses to the risen Christ. Peter's willingness to speak to Gentiles gathered at the house of the "God-fearing" Roman centurion Cornelius signals an expansion of his sense of mission to include Gentiles as well as Jews. In his speech, Peter explains that he and the other disciples were witnesses to what Jesus did in his public life: "doing good and healing all who were oppressed" (Acts 10:38). Jesus was executed, but "God raised him on the third day and allowed him to appear, not to all the people but to us who were chosen by God as witnesses, and who ate and drank with him after he rose from the dead" (Acts 10:40–41). The risen Lord instructed his disciples to "preach to the people and to testify that he is the one ordained by God to judge the living and the dead" and that "everyone who believes in him receives forgiveness of sins through his name" (10:42). After Peter's

---

[2] Gerhard Lohfink, *Jesus of Nazareth: What He Wanted, Who He Was*, trans. Linda M. Maloney (Collegeville, MN: Michael Glazier, 2012), 46.

[3] Eamon Duffy, *Faith of Our Fathers* (New York: Continuum, 2004), 61.

speech, Acts reports, the Holy Spirit was "poured out even on the Gentiles." Peter and the other Jewish Christians were "astonished" (10:45).

These texts from Paul and Acts suggest that the first Christians were witnesses in two senses: they had some kind of indescribable firsthand experience of the risen Christ and they shared this knowledge with others. The same pattern also appears in the Synoptic Gospels. Jesus taught his disciples primarily by allowing them to share in his daily life and work. When a few disciples of John the Baptist try to find out who Jesus is and what he is doing, Jesus tells them to go back and tell John what they have seen with their own eyes: the blind see, the lame walk, the deaf hear, lepers are cured, and the dead are raised to life (Mt 11:2–5). The Gospel of Luke describes witnessing these works of compassion in joyful terms: "Blessed are the eyes that see what you see! For I tell you that many prophets and kings desired to see what you see, but did not see it, and to hear what you hear, but did not hear it" (Lk 10:23–24).

Finally, John's Gospel gives the same pattern. Early in that Gospel two of John the Baptist's disciples see Jesus and recognize him as the "Lamb of God" for whom they had been waiting. When they begin to follow him, Jesus sees them, turns, and asks: "What are you looking for?" (1:38). They respond with a question of their own: "Rabbi . . . where are you staying?" He replies: "Come and see" (1:39). Jesus says, in effect: "Come, and witness." Only after they see for themselves can they testify about Jesus and what he had done for people.

In John's story of Jesus's healing of the blind beggar (9:1–12), the man runs to tell his neighbors what this stranger had done for him. One can imagine the neighbors responding with some combination of amazement, disbelief, shock, and apprehension. They bring the healed man to their religious leaders, who in utter disbelief promptly throw him out. When word of what happened gets back to Jesus, he finds the beggar and asks him, "Do you believe in the Son of Man?" (9:35). The beggar asks, "And who is he, sir, that I may believe in him?" Jesus replies: "You have seen him, and it is he who speaks to you." The healed beggar immediately proclaims: "'Lord, I believe.' And he worshiped him" (9:38). His experience had been so extraordinary that he didn't know what to make of it until Jesus himself helped him to understand it. Once he fully absorbs who Jesus is, the beggar immediately worships him.

This story carries a strong note of realism. Some respond with amazement and gratitude, others with annoyance and skepticism. The Pharisees are learned men who are supposed to see, but do not. Conversely, because of Jesus, the beggar who was blind can now see. Instead of being grateful for what he had done for this poor man, the Pharisees take this moment as a chance to criticize Jesus for working on the Sabbath (Jn 9:16). Their reaction illustrates the fact that we often see only what we are willing to see and most of the time we only see what we are used to seeing. Psychologists today might describe this tendency as "confirmation bias." We can resent people who tell us things we would rather not know. Sight in this sense is, of course, not just a matter of visual perception but concerns acknowledging what is real. Jesus goes so far as to describe his mission this way: "those who do not see may see" (9:39), that is, that they will come to believe and thereby have "eternal life." *Believe* here does not mean just believing *that* what Jesus taught is true, but more important, believing *in* the person of Jesus. It involves trust in and loyalty to Jesus, not just having either certain intellectual convictions or ethical principles.

Jesus's sense of mission was based in his intimate love of his heavenly Father. He acts as a witness to the love of God in his healings, parables, and teachings. Jesus's passion and death displayed his absolute loving obedience to the Father. His resurrection and ascension testified to the Father's fidelity to him and to the power of divine love over sin, death, and evil.

The disciples experience the love of Jesus but only come to a fuller understanding of what it means after his death and resurrection. In his final discourse of the Gospel of John, Jesus tells the disciples he will send them an Advocate: "If you love me, you will keep my commandments. And I will ask the Father, and he will give you another Advocate, to be with you forever." The Advocate will empower the disciples: "This is the Spirit of truth, whom the world cannot receive, because it neither sees him nor knows him. You know him, because he abides with you, and he will be in you" (14:15–17). Jesus later promises the disciples that "the Spirit of truth who comes from the Father . . . will testify on my behalf." The same Spirit will empower the disciples to testify on Jesus's behalf.

The Acts of the Apostles reports that Peter and the other apostles worked many "signs and wonders" (4:29–30; 5:12), especially healing many people. They acted as witnesses to Jesus by performing works of mercy as well as through preaching and teaching. As the Christian community grew, Acts explains, the "Hellenists [Greek speaking Christians] complained against the Hebrews [Jewish Christians] because their widows were being neglected in the daily distribution of food." The Twelve came to see that they were neglecting the "word of God in order to wait on tables." They called a meeting to select "seven men of good standing, full of the Spirit and of wisdom," who could take care of the needs of the community so the Twelve could devote themselves to "prayer and to serving the word" (Acts 6:1–4). This is how the early church established a new kind of ministry—the diaconate—dedicated to providing concrete assistance to the poor or otherwise needy of the community. Deacons were also to preach and act as emissaries for the apostles.

The first deacon, Stephen, is described as a man full of "grace and power" who "performed wonders and signs" among the people (Acts 6:8). His opponents accuse him of blasphemy, stir up both the authorities and the people against him, and have him arrested. In a trial before the council, false witnesses charge Stephen with saying that Jesus threatened to destroy the Temple and cancel the law of Moses. He defended himself in a speech that enraged the council, and some of its members dragged him out of the city and stoned him to death.

Stephen's martyrdom is depicted to echo that of Jesus, except that he acts in fidelity to Jesus as Jesus had acted in fidelity to the Father. In Luke, Jesus's last words are "Father, into thy hands I commit my spirit!" (Lk 23:46); in Acts, Stephen prays as he is being killed, "Lord Jesus, receive my spirit" (Acts 6:59). Jesus prays from the cross: "Father, forgive them; for they know not what they do"; in Acts, Stephen prays: "Lord, do not hold this sin against them" (7:60). Witnessing to Jesus here is conceived as participating in his Spirit.

Early Christians recognized that witnesses to Christ would suffer, but they also trusted that those who remained steadfast in faith would prevail. We see this theme in the First Letter of Peter, which was probably written by a Christian living in Rome sometime in the last three decades of the first century. It was addressed to a mainly Gentile Christian community in Asia Minor whose members were struggling as part of a minority religion. The author assures his readers that faith tested by trial gives glory to God. Rather than getting discouraged, he writes, "rejoice in so far as you share Christ's sufferings, that you may also rejoice and be glad when his glory is revealed" (4:13).

Suffering is temporary, but the reward awaiting those who are steadfast is eternal. Just as Christ suffered and then came into his glory, so faithful Christians will enter into the eternal glory of God. In the meantime, they are to "live as free men . . . [and] as servants of God" (2:16) and be humble and patient when treated unjustly (2:21). At the same time, they are to be "prepared to make a defense to any one who calls you to account for the hope that is in you." (3:15). When Christians act as "servants of God" by giving explicit verbal testimony to their faith, they must do so with "gentleness and reverence."

Throughout the centuries, this message of hope has encouraged many Christians laboring under difficult circumstances. In the early fall of 1966, King, for example, felt increasingly burdened by both the militant strains of the Black Power movement and the growing violence of the Vietnam war. He saw more than ever that fidelity to nonviolent love does not make life easy:

> We are gravely mistaken to think that religion protects us from the pain and agony of mortal existence. Life is not a euphoria of unalloyed comfort and untroubled ease. Christianity has always insisted that the cross we bear precedes the crown we wear. To be a Christian one must take up his cross, with all its difficulties and agonizing and tension-packed content, and carry it until that very cross leaves its mark upon us and redeems us to that more excellent way that comes only with suffering.[4]

This dramatic advice of 1 Peter and the stirring words of King might seem completely irrelevant to the daily life of ordinary Christians today, yet in fact all of us are called to act as witnesses within our own particular circumstances. Every one of us is presented with opportunities to extend ourselves in small but significant acts of self-giving love. We are always given the opportunity to engage in small acts of dying to the self that have been called "white martyrdom."

At the same time, steadfast fidelity has often been misinterpreted to mean that Christians must always "suffer in silence." There are appropriate times and places for doing so, but this phrase has often been misused to convince people that they should not object to blatant injustice. Applying this concept the wrong way can violate not only our duty to love our neighbor but also our responsibility to exercise stewardship toward ourselves. No one ought to tell a battered wife, for example, to "turn the other cheek" to her husband. Denying, minimizing, or covering up this kind of injustice makes one complicit, reinforces the harm, and creates conditions for future abuse.

What we deliberately witness to reflects our conception of justice. Christians tend to think along two lines about the kind of justice God wills for perpetrators: one works by exclusion and the other by transformation. The exclusion approach to divine justice says that God will separate the good from the bad in the next life, and then vindicate the good and destroy the bad. This is the view of common sense. A woman once told me: "I'm convinced my ex-husband will never make it to heaven. I can't imagine God would make me spend the rest of eternity with him after what he did to me." This man had put his wife through years of suffering, and her feeling about

---

[4] King, "Beyond Discovery, Love," Dallas, Texas, September 25, 1966, op. 8, King Papers, cited in David T. Garrow, "King and the Spirit of Leadership," *The Journal of American History* 74, no. 2 (September 1987): 445–46.

him was understandable. She assumed, however, that God's judgment can only go in one of two directions: either inclusion or exclusion, good people in one place and bad people in another, eternal reward for the former and eternal punishment for the latter.

The transformation approach, on the other hand, claims that God brings good out of evil and seeks "a new heaven and a new earth" (Is 65:17). God does not want to eliminate oppressors but to help them become healed, converted, and properly developed human beings. The transformation approach is based on the redemptive suffering of Christ, who incarnated the healing and forgiving love of God.

Redemptive good will does not jettison justice; on the contrary, it demands it, particularly justice in the Christian sense of right relationship. King developed this transformationist agenda on a large scale. He urged African Americans during the civil rights movement to see their suffering as a vehicle through which God was at work to save the soul of the nation. Nonviolent protesters, he said, were acting as prophetic witnesses to the power of redemptive good will. He believed their suffering—and their willingness to turn the other cheek—would stimulate the building of an integrated society based on equal respect, racial equality, and economic justice.

Bearing witness to redemptive love creates the momentum for repentance, corrective justice, and social reconfiguration. The transformationist does not envision the powerful as merely passive beneficiaries of a redemptive process made possible by those who suffer. Oppressors can only partake of the process if they take active steps to acknowledge the injustice they have done to the oppressed, renounce their oppressive ways, enter into solidarity with their victims, and work with them to dismantle whatever gets in the way of their ability to build a better world. If they fail to do so, they will be like the rich young man who walked away from Jesus because he was unwilling to change (Mk 10:17).

Theological Reflection on Sacraments and Sacramentality

We turn now to theological reflection on the sacramental character of witnessing. Christians usually think of sacraments as ritual actions, like the pouring of water at baptism or the breaking of the consecrated host during the Eucharist. A sacrament is defined by the Catholic Church as a sacred sign that makes present what it signifies. St. Augustine understood a sacrament to be a visible sign of invisible grace.[5] In a broad sense, then, a sacrament is any reality that symbolizes and points to the presence of grace in our lives.

---

[5] See *City of God*, X.6.

Many experiences are sacramental in the sense that they help us become more aware of the presence of God's love in our lives. Grace is an undercurrent of love in the lives of ordinary people who quietly and unselfishly serve others. We function as witness to grace, at least implicitly, whenever we act unselfishly for the good of others. Older college students, for example, act as witnesses to younger students when they attend events like a Hunger Banquet or the Take Back the Night program that raises awareness about sexual assault. They act as witnesses to grace when they lead service trips to Appalachia or immersion trips to Mexico or staff a campus volunteer outreach program. Students are witnesses to one another when they spend Saturday evenings volunteering at a suicide hotline rather than partying with friends. They act as witnesses of grace to one another when they give their time and energy to others without calling attention to themselves.

If a sacrament is a symbol of God's presence in the world, then as theologian Karl Rahner maintained, there is only one *absolute* symbol of God's presence in the world: the humanity of Christ. Jesus Christ, the Word made flesh, is the "primal sacrament," *the* concrete manifestation of God's presence in the world. As the tangible, historical continuation of Christ's presence, Vatican II described the church as the sacrament of "communion with God and the unity of the human race" (*Lumen Gentium*, no. 1). The sacramental nature of the church calls it to be a witness to the truth of the gospel. It fulfills its mission only to the extent that it functions as an authentic witness to the gospel. It does so most directly in worship but most convincingly, at least to many people, in its ministries of service to people who are underserved by our larger society.

Our exemplars understood the sacramental character of the church's service. Claverie regarded the church in Algeria as a sacrament of salvation among Muslims.[6] Romero expressed concern that in the midst of all the conflict and turmoil, he and his brother priests not lose sight of what is most important: "being signs of the Kingdom of God, because this is why we are in the Church: to give witness of a transcendent presence amid our work on earth."[7]

If the church celebrates the grace that is already present in the world, then each of the sacraments magnifies and deepens our awareness of what God is already doing in our lives to bring us into faith, hope, and charity. By drawing us into a deeper friendship with God and one another, the sacraments empower us to serve one another, cultivate communities of love, and work for the transformation of the world. The church exists to be a

---

[6] Jean-Jacques Pérennès, *A Life Poured Out: Pierre Claverie of Algeria*, trans. Phyllis Jestice and Matthew Sherry (Maryknoll, NY: Orbis Books, 2007), 158.

[7] Oscar Romero, *A Shepherd's Diary*, trans. Irene B. Hodgson (Cincinnati, OH: St. Anthony Messenger Press, 1986), 488.

witness to the love of Christ, and to do so not just with words but "in truth and action" (1 Jn 3:8).

The church is enacted in sacrament, and sacrament builds up the church. Fellowship within the church both participates in and testifies to the eternal fellowship of the Father, Son, and Spirit. The church's liturgy—its public worship—is meant to empower the community and its members to enter more deeply into friendship with one another and with God. This does not just happen automatically; we have to choose to participate and to receive the grace made available in the sacrament.

We can speak of sacramentality in a broad sense as a way of seeing the world as the bearer of God's grace. A piety attuned to sacramentality notices, celebrates, and embraces the presence of grace in our everyday lives. Dorothy Day exhibited sacramentality when she described the spiritual life as focused on the "sacrament of the present moment."[8] This sounds simple, but it is no easy task. We usually fail to notice the grace we encounter in our daily lives. We often do not notice what is right in front of us because we do not have "eyes that see" (Lk 10:21).

The church exists to help us cultivate a sacramental attitude toward our neighbors, our culture, and ourselves. At its best, the church enables us, as Jesuits like to say, to "seek God in all things."[9] Particular sacraments are institutionalized expressions of this deeper sensibility. Sunday worship is meant to be an "eye opening" experience that shapes the rest of our week and helps us to live grace more deeply. This is why Peter Maurin thought the works of mercy depended on "cult, culture and cultivation."[10]

The practices of the Christian community—its liturgy, preaching, prayer, fellowship, and service—are intended to enable us to make the gospel visible in our homes, schools, workplaces, and wider communities as well as within our own parishes and congregations. Churchgoers often underestimate the sacramental significance of Christian fellowship. Parishes do provide opportunities for fellowship, for example, in groups formed around Bible study, service, religious education, self-help, and other commitments. Most Christians, though, seem to want their involvement in church to be "low investment" in time and energy.

Fellowship within the church is supposed to strengthen and guide us in our activity in the world. It is intended to inspire a sense of mission. The word for the Catholic liturgy, *mass*, comes from the Latin word *missa*, which means "dismissal." It is now taken to refer to "mission," the act of

---

[8] *Dorothy Day: Selected Writings*, ed. Robert Ellsberg (Maryknoll, NY: Orbis Books, 1992), 104.

[9] See Peter Schineller, "St. Ignatius and Creation-Centered Spirituality," *The Way* 29 (January 1989): 46–59.

[10] In Dorothy Day, *The Long Loneliness* (New York: Image, 1959), 216.

being sent forth into the world. Both Catholics and Protestants view the Lord's Supper as spiritual nourishment for service of the neighbor in the world.

We can receive spiritual nourishment by engaging in both contemplative and active practices. The word *contemplation* usually evokes something like the image of a solitary hermit living in the forest or a Buddhist monk sitting in the lotus position with eyes closed. But contemplation in a broader sense means "to take delight in" concrete moments of grace. After a nice ferry ride to Staten Island, Day observes: "how little we appreciate the beauties under our noses."[11] Day's appreciation of beauty in nature or art had a contemplative tone. This points to what theologian Karl Rahner called the "mysticism of everyday life."[12] We experience a contemplative moment whenever we behold the manifestation of the goodness, beauty or truth of divine love in the world. Taking in natural beauty, Day wrote, helps "to restore the sacramental aspect of things."[13] Christian witnesses at their best are grounded in contemplative sensibilities and experiences. We can exercise a contemplative awareness in church services, on retreats, and in private prayer, but also in washing dishes, sweeping floors, and making beds in a shelter. This opportunity is what enables Jesuits to strive to be "contemplatives in action" and for Dominicans to practice the "contemplation of the street."[14]

Contemplative activities help us feel more grateful for the goodness we have witnessed in our lives. The church identifies this goodness as a sign of God's love for the world when it gathers believers together for the Eucharist, the sacrament of Christ's love for the world. In the Eucharist the church celebrates Jesus's offering of his body to be broken for our sake and for the sake of the world.

One beautiful expression of how the Eucharist provides a witness to the love of God comes from the practice of celebrating mass on makeshift altars set up on both sides of the US-Mexico border.[15] In 2012, bishops, priests, and laypeople gathered near Anapra, New Mexico. On this particular occasion they worshiped on All Soul's Day, the day of prayer for

---

[11] Dorothy Day, *The Duty of Delight: The Diaries of Dorothy Day*, ed. Robert Ellsberg (Milwaukee: Marquette University Press, 2008), 46.

[12] Karl Rahner, "Experiencing the Spirit," in *The Practice of Faith*, ed. Albert Raffelt and Karl Lehmann (New York: Crossroad, 1983), 81.

[13] Day, *The Duty of Delight*, 290.

[14] On the latter, see Timothy Radcliffe, OP, "'A City Set on a Hill Cannot Be Hidden': A Contemplative Life."

[15] Dioceses without Borders has been sponsoring binational border masses and posadas since 2002 at various sites along the wall between southern Arizona and Hermosillo, Mexico.

the dead, to commemorate the thousands of migrants who died trying to cross the border.

The shared liturgy on the border presented a material sign of the spiritual unity affirmed and affected in the Eucharist. The congregation sang a prayer of eucharistic unity:

> One bread, one body, one Lord of all,
> One cup of blessing which we bless,
> And we, though many, throughout the earth,
> We are one body in this one Lord.

Writing about this mass, Bishop Ricardo Ramirez of Las Cruces, New Mexico, explained that while physically separated by a fence, the worshipping congregation was united by a shared faith that transcends all their differences. "It is this oneness," the bishop wrote, "which provides hope for those who have no human reason to hope and nowhere else to turn for support." This hope inspires a commitment to inclusive solidarity: "On both sides of the border we feel each other's agony, each other's pain, each other's anguish, each other's sorrow and grief." This solidarity generates both compassion and a commitment to social justice: "They, on account of the extreme violence of the drug wars and poverty; we, on account of seemingly unending wars and a government that is becoming increasingly less caring [and] less compassionate, which makes life ever more difficult for the little people, the poor, the elderly, the unemployed and the immigrant."[16]

Every stage of the eucharistic celebration can be inflected in ways that signified Christ's compassion for immigrants and the injustice of the laws that lead to their degradation. The whole sacrament points to Christ's desire to satisfy our hunger and thirst. The offering of gifts and the Eucharistic Prayer symbolically underscore Christ's solidarity with immigrants. Christ says, "This is my body, given to you." In the act of consecration the celebrants ask the Holy Spirit to transform the bread and wine into the body and blood of Christ. This moment calls to mind in a tangible way God's presence in the immigrant. As the bishop puts it, "God acts as an immigrant because he enters into our world as the bread and wine are transformed into the body and blood of our Lord."

The consecration is followed by the prayer known as the Anamnesis, a recollection of God's saving deeds. We remember these deeds so that they can shape our lives today. The Our Father calls to mind in yet another way

---

[16] Bishop Ricardo Ramirez, "At Border Mass, Eucharist Unites Where Fence Divides," *The Catholic Spirit*, November 20, 2012.

our unity as children of God. Worshipers exchange the sign of peace on both sides of the border by touching the palms of their hands through the fence. This peace is prophetic: "The fence at which the Eucharist without borders is celebrated contradicts aspects of our common ground as the Body of Christ," the bishop explains.[17] Yet in receiving the Eucharist together, participants sacramentally overcome the division symbolized by the border and witness to the unitive power of divine love.

The unity symbolized by the Eucharist is also displayed when we engage in the works of mercy. Pierre Claverie believed that the church's role in colonialism demands that its clearest witness to the gospel be concrete acts of serving the neighbor. The goal of Christian participation in interreligious dialogue with Muslims is not to generate more converts for the church but rather to enable one another to participate more deeply in the love of God and love of neighbor. Conversation can deepen Christian understanding of Islam and vice versa. Christians, for example, have a lot to learn from Muslims about the meaning of fidelity, religious devotion, and what it means to believe in a God of mercy, justice, and peace. Muslims can learn about what it means to love one's neighbor, to enact mercy, and to embody a prophetic peace from Christians like Day, King, and our other exemplars.

In the long run the path of mutual respect, dialogue, and friendship offers the best hope for the reconciliation of Christians and Muslims. This agenda does not suggest that Christians downplay their faith in Christ as Savior or ignore the last words Jesus speaks in Acts of the Apostles: "You will receive power when the Holy Spirit has come upon you; and you will be my witnesses in Jerusalem, in all Judea and Samaria, and to the ends of the earth" (1:8). Yet focusing on concrete acts of love as manifestations of grace helps to broaden the meaning of "bearing witness" to Jesus.

The Virtue of Integrity

We can act as witnesses to Christ only if we live with integrity. This is why Day wrote in her diary: "We must constantly return to a sense of the necessity of keeping our own integrity. We are each one . . . alone, and can only try to change ourselves first of all. How far we are going to reach others is something we cannot know."[18] The stronger our integrity, the greater our capacity to act as a witness. The term *integrity* has its roots in the Latin word *integritas*, "oneness, wholeness." The opposite of integrity is disintegration or chaos. T. S. Eliot once wrote, "Hell is the place where nothing

---

[17] Ibid.
[18] Day, *The Duty of Delight*, 52.

connects to nothing."[19] If so, then integrity is the place where everything is connected to everything else.

In ordinary moral discourse we usually think of integrity as a matter of acting honestly, fulfilling our commitments, and keeping our word. The person of integrity refuses to compromise important moral principles, even to achieve desirable consequences. The opposite of integrity can be dishonesty, insincerity, inauthenticity, intentional deception, hypocrisy, moral corruption, or some other form of ethical inconsistency. If we hear someone say a colleague has no integrity, we will probably immediately assume that he or she has cheated, stolen, lied, or otherwise committed a breach of justice.

Yet integrity is more than abiding by the minimal standards of legal propriety or even ethical duty. Integrity is used to characterize people who have a clear sense of purpose and who lead lives of internal order and harmony. We have integrity to the extent that the "parts" of who we are cohere with one another. We are not one person Monday through Thursday and another person on the weekend.

The virtue of integrity plays an important role in shaping decisions in everyday life. As a virtue, integrity is concerned not only with what we do, but also with our choices, intentions, motives, and overall character. If we ask, "Do I want to be the kind of person that does X?" I am raising a question about my personal integrity. When we ask, "Do we want to be the kind of community that does X?" we are reflecting on the demands of communal integrity.

Integrity is a form of fidelity. If we respect the integrity of a particular friendship, we will ask whether particular acts or attitudes are consistent with the kind of relationship we want to have with that person. This consideration helps us see, for example, that lying is wrong not only because it violates a moral norm but also, and more importantly, because it betrays the mutual respect that marks true friendship. The virtue of integrity reminds us that we must be a good friend if we want to have good friends.

A well-formed conscience attunes us to the demands of integrity. Dietrich Bonhoeffer believed that conscience comes from a "depth which lies beyond a man's own will and his own reason and it makes itself heard as the call of human existence to unity with itself." He believed that the pain of a guilty conscience is an internal alarm that alerts us to something we have done that contradicts our wholeness and internal unity.[20]

Integrity has a spiritual as well as a moral dimension. Abraham Heschel described faith as a willingness to perceive the wonder that is here and be

---

[19] Introduction to Dante's *Inferno*, in T. S. Eliot, *Selected Essays* (London: Faber and Faber, 1999), 242.

[20] Dietrich Bonhoeffer, *Ethics,* ed. Eberhard Bethge, trans. Neville Horton Smith (London: Collins, 1963), 242.

"stirred by the desire to integrate the self into the holy order of being."[21] Whereas egocentrism sees everything in terms of whether it is useful to the self, faith seeks to integrate the self into the divine. Our faith grows when we allow ourselves to be integrated into divine love.

Some postmodern critics consider integrity to be an old fashioned virtue based on a false view of the self. They consider it a naïve ideal based on the mistaken assumption that each of us has a stable if not changeless identity. They argue that we are composed of many ill-fitting "parts" that can never be coherently integrated with one another. According to these critics, the Christian ethic of integrity tries to impose a false, authoritarian unity that suppresses the real self with all its complexity.

Yet we can ask these postmodern critics if being authentic (in the sense of "true to oneself") is always good. Authenticity is certainly good for someone who has a thoroughly good character. But it seems compromised to the extent that our character is defective. In a sense, purely selfish people can be true to themselves as long as they act selfishly, and they are false to themselves when they act for the sake of others.

Christian faith suggests that our "true self" is the one who God created us to be and the one who God is now inviting us to become. Our true self can be distinguished from the flawed person we have become as a result of our disordered choices, acts, and habits. In various ways, our attitudes and dispositions—our "loves"—tend to be disordered. "Even the best human love is filled with self-seeking," Day observed.[22] Heschel expresses this problem aptly: "The course in which human life moves is, like the orbit of heavenly bodies, an ellipse, not a circle. We are attached to two centers: to the focus on our self and to the focus on what is beyond our self."[23]

The only integrity that makes one a truly coherent person is truly centered on divine love; our response to divine love, implicitly if not explicitly, is always mediated by our relationships with other people. God quietly and gently pulls us—whether we are aware of it or not—to love both ourselves and our neighbors the right way.

Conversion is a lifelong processing of growing in integrity. God seeks slowly to transform each of us from the (more or less) false, mixed up, and egocentric selves we are to the (more or less) true, coherent, and self-giving selves we are created to be. We move into our true happiness and fulfillment to the extent that we allow grace to move us down this path throughout the course of our lives. Christians conceive of this goal, in Paul's terms,

---

[21] Abraham Heschel, *Moral Grandeur and Spiritual Audacity*, ed. Susanna Heschel (New York: Farrar, Staus, and Giroux, 1996), 330.

[22] Ellsberg, *Dorothy Day: Selected Writings*, 87.

[23] Heschel, *Moral Grandeur and Spiritual Audacity*, 329.

as having "the mind of Christ" (1 Cor 2:16). This process integrates different aspects of our identity and the many goods we love into a coherent way of life.

Integrity corrects internal confusion and self-contradiction. Consider the case of an alcoholic who goes through a period of sobriety but then gets highly stressed at work and relapses. Or consider the case of a college student who wants to be faithful to her boyfriend but then, when he is out of town, hooks up with his roommate. The former wants to be sober, but only when he is calm and life is going well; the latter wants to be faithful, except when she gets lonely. These are examples of what St. Augustine called the "divided will." He displayed it when, after years of struggling, he prayed, "Grant me chastity and continence, but not yet."[24] King registered something of this confusion in contemporary terms when he noted that "each of us is something of a schizophrenic personality, tragically divided against ourselves."[25]

The virtue of integrity is ultimately a matter of love. Christian spirituality calls us to pay attention to our deeper, more truly loving self—our core self as it responds positively to grace—and to allow this gracious love to grow and shape the rest of our lives. "Blessed are the pure in heart, for they will see God" (Mt 5:8).

The virtue of integrity pertains to two closely related but distinct domains: one operates within the self and the other in our actions. First, what we might call practical integrity refers to the coherence between what we say and what we do. It is captured in the aphorism, "practice what you preach." The person of practical integrity acts distinctively in different roles but is the same person in all of them.

A major obstacle to *practical integrity* is the tendency to compartmentalize our lives in ways that separate who we are in one context from who we are in others. Compartmentalizing divides "Joe the excellent student" and "Joe the dutiful son" and both of these from "Joe the mad partier" and "Joe the pick-up artist." A man or woman can be respectful, conscientious, and morally sensitive from Monday through Friday, but then on the weekend get drunk and pick up others for sexual gratification with no thought to their feelings or needs.

Second, what we might call *internal integrity* is characterized by harmony in our willing, thinking, and feeling. Aristotle thought the truly virtuous person does what is right with pleasure and without internal conflict.[26]

---

[24] Augustine, *Confessions,* trans. Henry Chadwick (New York: Oxford, 1991), 145.

[25] Martin Luther King, Jr., *Strength to Love* (Cleveland: William Collins and World Publishing, 1963), 49.

[26] Aristotle, *Nicomachean Ethics*, trans. David Ross (New York: Oxford, 2009), Book I.8, 1099a20, 14.

Few people ever get to that point; most of us are internally at odds with ourselves in various ways. We all have trouble overcoming deep-set attitudes and undesirable old habits.

Christian faith suggests that our capacity to act as a witness to Christ comes from an internal integrity grounded in our participation in divine love. Internal integrity cannot be produced by momentary acts of willpower alone but are made possible by grace working in and through our choices and actions. Christian integrity is an ordering of the whole person *by* and *to* the love of God. If a divided will produces stunted and misshapen hearts, a will united by grace produces fully developed and properly shaped hearts. Grace is a healing and forgiving power that seeks to make us more fully developed human beings.

We do not and cannot undergo this transformative process alone. The church is meant to be a community that helps us grow in our receptivity to grace. The lives of holy men and women remind us that the process of spiritual growth involves renunciation and self-discipline as well as inspiration and consolation. As Day said, we must "be pruned as the vine is pruned."[27] Later in her life, she observed: "Change may mean growth but it hurts."[28] Christian hope understands true selfhood is attained completely only in union with God. Elements of what Paul called the "old creature" linger even as the "new" is emerging (see 2 Cor 5:17). But while we may always experience some kind of internal conflict, abiding in Christ reduces its intensity and its power to distort our love.

Growing in the Capacity to Witness

Previous sections have suggested that we can grow in our capacity to act as witnesses by becoming more dedicated followers of Christ, engaging in the works of mercy, deepening our sense of sacramentality, and building greater personal and practical integrity. This section adds three additional ways in which we can grow in our capacity to act as witnesses: becoming more educated, cultivating a sense of vocation, and engaging in spiritual practices.

Becoming More Educated

We can grow as witnesses by becoming more informed and articulate about our Christian faith and more willing to share it. The explicit offering of

---

[27] Day, *The Long Loneliness*, 269.
[28] Day, *The Duty of Delight*, 576.

Christian witness is called evangelization, which refers to communicating the good news in an appealing and appropriate manner. Witnessing to divine love in deed is most important, but witnessing by means of words can also be helpful.

As Pope Paul VI pointed out in 1974 in *Evangelii Nuntiandi*, "Even the finest witness will prove ineffective in the long run if it is not explained, justified . . . and made explicit by a clear and unequivocal proclamation of the Lord Jesus" (no. 22). As we saw earlier, the First Letter of Peter reminds Christians to be always "ready to make your defense to anyone who demands from you an accounting for the hope that is in you" (1 Pt 3:15). Most people do not have the luxury of extensive theological training, but we can all set aside some time during our week to read, reflect, and talk about the theological basis of our central convictions. In becoming more educated in scripture, spirituality, and other theological disciplines, we can become more effective witnesses to the gospel. Greater knowledge helps us not only think about our faith but also make wiser choices.

Cultivating a Sense of Vocation

Second, our capacity to act as witnesses can be enhanced by cultivating a sense of our lives as vocations or callings. Secular culture now uses *vocation* to refer to either paid work or meaningful activity. Christianity understands vocation in deeply religious, theocentric terms. We are called by God to participate in the missions of the Son and the Holy Spirit. To say that we are "called" suggests that it is God, not us, who determines the meaning and shape of our lives. This message is shockingly at odds with our assumption that the good life is one of strict autonomy and self-determination.

The Protestant tradition has from its inception emphasized that all Christians have particular vocations. Martin Luther and John Calvin both thought that any occupation—whether as a nurse, a police officer, or a farmer—can be a calling as long as it is a way of serving one's neighbor. As theologian Doug Schuurman explains, this view holds that "what people do in the home, workplace, and community—in all aspects of life—must be permeated with the Spirit of Christ."[29]

In Catholic circles vocation has traditionally referred to God's calling one to ordination or vowed religious life. This ecclesial sense of vocation is what led Dorothy Stang to the Sisters of Notre Dame de Namur and Pierre Claverie to the Dominicans. In the last half century or so, though, the Catholic Church has also come to speak about the vocation of the laity

---

[29] Douglas Schuurman, *Vocation: Discerning Our Callings in Life* (Grand Rapids, MI: Eerdmans, 2004), 36.

(EN, nos. 897-913). Dorothy Day was ahead of her time when she wrote: "We each have our vocation—the thing to do is to answer the call. We each have something to give."[30]

The Second Vatican Council saw that by virtue of baptism, all Christians, laypeople as well as priests and religious, are called to seek holiness in the service of one another. Mother Teresa writes: "The president of Mexico sent for me. I told him that he had to become holy as a president: not as a Missionary of Charity, but as a president. He looked at me a bit surprised, but it is like that: we have to become holy, each of us, in the place where God has put us."[31]

Now both Catholics and Protestants use vocation or calling to refer to any way of honoring God through serving our neighbor. Whoever we are, we all have one fundamental calling: to participate in the mission of Christ in the Spirit through loving our neighbor. We cannot be Christian in a vague and general way; we can do so only in the concrete circumstances of our own lives. We are called to cooperate with divine grace in every aspect of our lives—as the Catechism of the Catholic Church puts it, "works, prayers, and apostolic undertakings, family and married life, daily work, relaxation of mind and body" (no. 901). Christians believe God gives us talents not for our own sake alone, but also for the good of our neighbor and the renewal of the world. This means, for example, that teachers and students ought to see the classroom as a place to care for their neighbor, and that employers and employees can exercise their talents in ways that serve rather than exploit others.

There are many gifts, St. Paul said, but one Spirit (1 Cor 12:4). So our general vocation has to fit our particular talents, needs, opportunities, and aspirations. One person might be suited to be a fire fighter, another to be an accountant, and another to be a teacher. This rich Christian sense of the diversity of particular callings frees us from the misconception that there are two types of Christian: heroes like Day or Romero who give their all, and the rest of us mediocre people. There is nothing mediocre about allowing one's daily life to be a transparent reflection of divine love. Even though we cannot do everything Day said, each of us is expected "to do our part, at this time and in this place."[32] Sometimes this can involve very mundane, tedious tasks like raking leaves, doing dishes, and cleaning the bathroom. These, too, are ways in which we serve one another. We ought to measure ourselves, Day advised, "as to what God wants of us, what talents he has

---

[30] Ellsberg, *Dorothy Day: Selected Writings*, 329.

[31] *Mother Teresa: Essential Writings*, ed. Jean Maalouf (Maryknoll, NY: Orbis Books, 2008), 132.

[32] Ibid., 46.

given us to use, and not to compare ourselves or judge others, whether better or worse."[33]

The notion of vocation does not suggest that we shouldn't be ambitious, strive to get ahead, or move beyond our current station in life. Fidelity to Christ requires openness to where the Spirit might be leading us. The Spirit often works by engaging our deepest passions. This is what leads a police officer to go to law school at night or an entrepreneur to expand her business. Commitments like these can be part of our calling.

Our exemplars developed their abilities to meet the needs of others, went where they sensed they were most needed, and were supported by their friends and communities in doing so. At times they had to follow their "gut instincts," but they did so in informed and thoughtful ways. This is true, for example, of Claverie's initial decision to learn Arabic, King's choice to pursue a career in ministry rather than academia, and Stang's willingness to become a missionary in Brazil.

Discerning where the Spirit is leading us is often no simple matter. We need to pray but also to engage in honest, open, and realistic conversations with thoughtful friends whose judgment we respect. We can't make complex and emotionally weighty decisions as if we were just reading a spreadsheet or solving a math problem. This is why making major life decisions is a process of engaging in discernment rather than just reasoning. Jesuits take Paul's "fruit of the Spirit" as a helpful guide to this process (Gal 5:22–23). Our best decisions usually result in positive internal states like peace of mind, gratitude, and consolation; unsound decisions are often attended by inner disquiet, confusion, and restlessness. Paying close attention to where the Spirit is moving us plays a key role in helping us to grow as witnesses.

Engaging in Spiritual Practices

Third, we can grow in our capacity to act as witnesses through engaging in various spiritual practices. Christians have traditionally recognized three spiritual practices—prayer, fasting, and almsgiving—as useful means to spiritual growth. These practices help us function as good witnesses by strengthening our faith, hope, and charity. While they may sound old fashioned, they have stood the test of time as ways of deepening Christian discipleship. A "disciple" is someone who wants to be taught by a teacher, and discipline is a kind of internal order that gives strength and stability to our characters.

The capacity to act as a witness can be cultivated through personal prayer. Prayer is popularly described as a way in which we recharge our

---

[33] Day, *The Duty of Delight*, 165.

spiritual batteries, but it is more than a hobby or some kind of recreational activity. Prayer is a raising of the mind to God. "As breath is to the body," Day wrote, "prayer is to the soul."[34] To pray is to "practice the presence of God."[35]

Jesus prayed often. The Gospel of Luke says that he "often withdrew to lonely places to pray" (5:16). He tells his disciples that they "ought always to pray and not lose heart" (Lk 18:11). He told them that when they pray they ought to go into their rooms and pray alone (Mt 6:6). Since he attended the synagogue, went to the Temple, participated in Jewish festivals, and honored other Jewish religious practices, we can infer that he was not opposed to public worship in general but to pretense and hypocrisy in its exercise.

The most elaborate and communal form of Christian prayer is liturgical worship. The Acts of the Apostles says that the early Christian community "joined constantly in prayer" (1:4). The earliest Christian communities remembered Jesus telling his disciples to break bread together, "in memory of me" (Lk 22:19; 1 Cor 11:24). The night Jesus was arrested, he "came out, and went, as was his custom, to the Mount of Olives; and the disciples followed him" (Lk 22:39).

The litmus test of prayer and worship is whether they lead us to act justly and compassionately. This is an ancient biblical principle. As the prophet Hosea put it: "For I desire steadfast love and not sacrifice, the knowledge of God rather than burnt offerings" (6:6). One expression of steadfast love is reconciliation. Jesus taught that if we wish to worship rightly, we ought first to go reconcile with anyone who has something against us (Mt 5:23–24).

Worship is meant to support rather than compete with personal piety. In the Christian perspective, religion without spirituality is mere formalism, and spirituality without religion is mere private piety. Christian faith seeks to form people who are spiritual because they are religious, and vice versa.

Fasting is a second important spiritual practice that strengthens one's capacity to act as a Christian witness. The Christian tradition has long regarded abstaining from food or drink for a set time as a way of expressing, deepening, and renewing our relationship to God. Individuals and communities in the Bible fast to show repentance for their sins, to grieve for their dead, and to underscore the intensity of the desires they express in prayers of petition, for example, for a loved one to recover her health.

After his baptism Jesus goes into the desert and fasts for forty days (Mt 4:1–11). Satan first tries to seduce a hungry Jesus with bread, but it doesn't work. "One does not live by bread alone," Jesus tells him, "but by every

---

[34] Day, *The Duty of Delight*, 458.

[35] Ibid., 67.

word that comes from the mouth of God" (Mt 4:4; citing Dt 8:3). When his disciples are criticized for eating and drinking rather than fasting, Jesus explains that just as wedding guests do not fast when the bridegroom is present, so his followers do not fast when he is with them (Mt 9:14–17; Mk 2:18–22; Lk 5:33–39). They will have plenty of time to fast, he implies, when the bridegroom departs.

Because he embodies the bounty of God, Jesus promotes feasting more than fasting. He feeds the hungry crowds (Mt 15:32; Mk 8:2–3), and he presents his body as food for his disciples (1 Cor 11:23–26). In John's Gospel, Jesus describes himself as the "bread of life" (6:35) who wants us to be nourished, fulfilled, and have "abundant life" (10:10). Dorothy Day writes: "We know him in the breaking of bread, and we know each other in the breaking of bread, and we are not alone anymore. Heaven is a banquet and life is a banquet too, even with a crust, where there is companionship."[36]

Throughout the history of the church, Christians have practiced fasting for a variety of reasons: to commemorate the death of Jesus, to learn how to resist temptation, to offer penance, to become more open to God's will, to cultivate the virtue of temperance, to witness to the self-sacrifice demanded of Christians, to identify with the poor, and to prepare to receive the Eucharist. In his description of the holy monk Zosima, Dostoevsky describes the goal of fasting as spiritual freedom:

> Obedience, prayer, and fasting are laughed at, yet they alone constitute the way to real and true freedom: I cut away my superfluous and unnecessary needs, through obedience I humble and chasten my vain and proud will, and thereby, with God's help, attain freedom of spirit, and with that, spiritual rejoicing![37]

The Christian tradition has produced many holy men and women—from St. Teresa of Avila and St. Francis de Sales to Pedro Arrupe and Dorothy Day—who have testified to the value of fasting for spiritual growth. Yet in our age, when eating disorders torment so many people and even have become a public health issue, Christians need to be alert to the ways in which fasting can be employed for the wrong reasons or taken to unhealthy extremes.

Religious fasting has nothing to do with weight loss, physical fitness, or improving external appearance. Fasting ought never be done out of disgust with the body, a general suspicion of sexual appetite as inherently sinful,

---

[36] Day, *The Long Loneliness*, 276.

[37] Fyodor Dostoevsky, *The Brothers Karamazov*, trans. Richard Pevear and Larissa Volokhonsky (New York: Random House, 1990), 314.

or a desire to dominate ourselves. St. Paul places a high value on the body when he describes it as the "temple of the Holy Spirit" (1 Cor 6:9). The principle of sacramentality suggests that the body is a symbol of divine grace in the world and ought to be loved appropriately. The incarnation points to the goodness of the body as something that can even be a bearer of the divine nature. The "Word made flesh" offers a countercultural witness to the tendency of consumer society to reduce bodies to "eye candy" or what is useful.

Fasting can be not only a form of personal spiritual discipline but also an expression of love of neighbor. During a session of the Second Vatican Council, Dorothy Day joined a number of other women in Rome to fast for the sake of peace and "victims of famine all over the world."[38] In 1966, a year after the closing of the council, Pope Paul VI, in the apostolic constitution *Paenitemini (On Fast and Abstinence)*, urged Christians in economically better-off countries to offer both a "witness of asceticism" (including fasting) that strives not to be simply "worldly" but a "witness of charity" to brothers and sisters who suffer from hunger and poverty. Some Christians go without a meal to build empathy with the hungry; others take the money they would have spent on food and donate it to Bread for the World, Catholic Relief Services, or another organization.

Finally, in addition to prayer and fasting, Christians practice almsgiving, providing goods that meet some specific needs of our neighbors, for example, food or water or clothing. Of these three spiritual practices, almsgiving makes the most sense to our pragmatic culture. Though the term *almsgiving* is archaic, the practice is attractive because it makes a difference to its beneficiaries. If done in a spirit of respect, care, and tenderness, philosopher Simone Weil wrote that almsgiving "enshrines the real presence of God and constitutes something in the nature of a sacrament."[39]

Prayer combined with good works is better than prayer by itself, and even better are prayer, fasting, and almsgiving practiced together. In the second century before Christ the Book of Tobit observed: "Prayer with fasting is good, but better than both is almsgiving with righteousness" (12:8). Writing during World War II, Day explains:

> We will try daily, hourly, to pray for an end to the war. Let us add that unless we combine this prayer with almsgiving, in giving to the least of God's children, and fasting in order that we may help feed

---

[38] Dorothy Day, "On Pilgrimage," *Catholic Worker*, November 1965.

[39] Simone Weil, *Waiting for God*, trans. Emma Craufurd (New York: Harper and Row, 1951), 152.

the hungry, and penance in recognition of our share in the guilt, our prayer may become empty words.[40]

Prayer focuses on God, fasting on the self, and almsgiving on the neighbor. Almsgiving has two dimensions: the spiritual dimension draws us closer to God, and the humanitarian dimension directs us to other people. Christian almsgiving should not be an exercise of condescending pity that treats the recipient of one's action as a mere object, but rather an act of genuine love of neighbor.

Jesus wanted his disciples to practice prayer, fasting, and almsgiving, but he did not want them to do so in a way that is arrogant or that puts others down. Spiritual practices properly exercised inspire humility, not pride. Christian almsgiving, like prayer and fasting, are meant to intensify our sense of our common neediness, weaknesses, and absolute dependence on the mercy of God. They build solidarity, not superiority.

Temptations of Witnessing

Christians who serve as witnesses can be tempted to smugness, intolerance, and a desire to dominate the other. Some Christians seem to think that only they have the truth, and no one else does. Years of ministry made Pierre Claverie especially sensitive to this temptation. He understood that believers who see themselves as "bearers of a divine message with a universal scope" are not "naturally inclined to tolerance."[41] When we assume we alone possess the whole truth, we tend to use any power available to us to make others submit to that "truth." We may even be drawn into an attitude of "totalitarianism and exclusion."[42] Monotheism—the belief that there is one God and no other—seems to make its adherents particularly prone to this temptation.

A keen appreciation of the ineffability of God guards against this temptation. Claverie professed a strong faith, but his deep sense of the mystery of God led him to make the following observation: "I do not presume to possess God, neither through Jesus, who reveals God to me, nor through the dogmas of my faith."[43] A similar point was made by Cardinal Joseph

---

[40] Day, *All the Way to Heaven: The Selected Letters of Dorothy Day*, ed. Robert Ellsberg (Milwaukee: Marquette University Press, 2010), 130.

[41] Pierre Claverie, OP, "Humanity in the Plural," in Jean-Jacques Pérennès, *A Life Poured Out: Pierre Claverie of Algeria*, trans. Phyllis Jestice and Matthew Sherry (Maryknoll, NY: Orbis Books, 2007), 261.

[42] Ibid.

[43] Ibid.

Ratzinger, the future Pope Benedict XVI, when he wrote: "The nature of faith is not such that at a given point one might say: I possess it, others do not. . . . Faith remains a path."[44]

God communicates with us in subtle but profound ways—in Jesus, in sacraments, in the depths of our conscience, in conversations with friends, in encountering the other, in our communities of faith, in our families, in experiences of beauty in art and nature, and also in dialogue with members of other religions.

Decades of living as a member of a small Christian minority in a dominantly Muslim country led Claverie to see that people with radically different experiences have important insights that can enrich others: "Each of us is in need of the truth that others have found."[45] This principle provides the rationale for a social vision rooted in democratic pluralism and an attitude of deep respect for the truth as it emerges in open, honest, and respectful dialogue. It requires one to avoid any attempt to manipulate or coerce others into religious conformity.

Claverie believed that we must fight intolerance through a variety of means, including education, direct encounter, friendship, dialogue with the other, and working together in practical enterprises for the common good. Yet he insisted that Christians must not deny the truth of the gospel to avoid offending Muslims. Instead of trying to win debating points, he said, we ought to try to understand one another. We can do this only if each party realizes that the other has some insight that needs to be heard. Christians "do not own the truth," Claverie insisted. "It is the truth that takes hold of us and leads us to discover itself ever more deeply."[46]

We act as witnesses by being both open to the truth revealed by the religious other and faithful to the deepest convictions of our own tradition. Claverie's Christian humility was grounded in his profound sense of the incomprehensibility of God. There are objective truths, he believed, but they "exceed our grasp." We can attain them "only at the end of a long journey during which we piece this truth together by gleaning from the different cultures and instances of humanity what others have sought and obtained in their journey toward the truth."[47]

Christians with a deep sense of the mystery of God keep in mind that our profession of faith and theological formulations always fall short of the realities to which they refer. The Christian commitment to interreligious

---

[44] Joseph Ratzinger, *God and the World: A Conversation with Peter Seewald* (San Francisco: Ignatius Press, 2001), xxx.

[45] Claverie, "Humanity in the Plural," 261.

[46] Ibid., 148.

[47] Ibid.

dialogue is grounded in the theological conviction that in grace the Holy Spirit communicates with people everywhere—whether or not they are Christian—within the terms made available by their own particular cultures and historical locations. God does not leave the whole world outside of Christianity completely in the dark.

An account of Christian witness that acknowledges the true breadth and depth of divine grace, moreover, cannot assume that only Christians and their churches offer an effective witness to the love of God. While the Holy Spirit prompts us to testify to the truth of our faith, we also need to recognize that the Spirit prompts sincere believers of other traditions to witness (in either word or deed) to the truth of their particular traditions. Signs of grace abound in the world, and Claverie thought Christians and Muslims can help each other "read" them correctly. Christians need Jews, Muslims, and people of other religious traditions to understand more adequately the wisdom of our own tradition.

The struggle for mutual respect begins as a process of spiritual purification, Claverie thought. When the church in Europe was historically entangled with the power of states, it focused on gathering and exercising its own institutional power so that it could exert some control over political events. Today the church exerts influence only through whatever moral authority it can elicit by the power of its own witness. It is better positioned to question political and socioeconomic forms of power on behalf of those who are excluded or oppressed.

Claverie believed that the marginalization of the church in Algeria—its postcolonial loss of status, influence, and social presence—taught Christians there how to serve the needs of the people through small institutions like libraries, rehabilitation centers for the disabled, and women's resource centers. His platforms for encounter and service helped to build bonds of trust between individual Christians and Muslims. Mutual respect and cooperation provide the context for a dialogue that makes possible a process of reciprocal conversion in which Muslims help Christians become better Christians and vice versa. This helps all parties grow closer to God. It was fitting, then, that Claverie was buried with a liturgical vestment that carried the Arabic inscription *Allah mahabba* (God is love).

Because of the terrible destructiveness of its colonial legacy, the church's central challenge today is reconciliation. We witness to the love of God and the unity of humanity by loving our neighbor in tangible ways. Christians can witness to the fraternal love of Christ while repudiating the domination that has often been attached to the colonial past of our tradition. This agenda can only proceed if Christians can show that they can act without any intention of wanting to control the other. We must address the suspicion and resentment generated by centuries of conquest, colonialism, and war. Fear, anger, and distrust continue to intensify not only since 9/11, but also in the wake of the Boston Marathon bombings of April 15, 2013, the Charlie Hebdo shootings of January 7, 2015, and the attocities of ISIS in 2014–15. The church must do whatever is possible to act as peacemaker, to overcome divisions based on religious antagonism, and to work as a source of healing and inclusive solidarity for those who have been wounded, excluded, and oppressed.

Conclusion

As a form of service, witness testifies to God's love for all human beings. Through the power of grace we can witness to this love in word and deed. Integrity is the virtue that gives credibility to our witness. We can grow as witnesses by becoming more informed, cultivating a sense of calling or vocation, and engaging in healthy spiritual practices that lead us to become more wise and compassionate people. The virtue of humility helps us counteract temptations to arrogance, intolerance, and domination.

13

Evaluating the Models

This chapter offers an overview of some of the key insights about service that can be gleaned from the models of service presented in the previous six chapters. It first examines ways in which Christians differ among themselves over service and then addresses the question of whether one particular model of service is most important. It maintains that compassion is the paradigmatic form of service, accompaniment its most personal form, and witnessing the most excellent form. This chapter then discusses the virtue that underlies all forms of service, love, and then its dependence on practical wisdom.

When Christians Disagree about Service

Some forms of solidarity can be at odds with charity. Speaking the truth in advocacy for one cause might come at the cost of compassion for others. Stewardship of one's own resources might, on some occasions, compromise one's ability to extend compassion to others. The money parents are putting away for their daughter's college education, for example, could have been used to keep children alive in refugee camps in Kenya. Solidarity within our community might be at odds with challenging the choices of some of its members. In these and other ways, particular circumstances might mean that to act in one form of service conflicts with other forms of service.

We can distinguish these kinds of practical tensions from even more fundamental disagreements over what actually counts as service in the first place. Christians often disagree over what constitute appropriate and truly Christian ways of serving God and our neighbor. Earlier chapters showed that models of Christian service are based on interpretations of the Bible and later church doctrines. They also reflect certain assumptions about what counts as either virtuous or vicious conduct. Christians can differ on any of these points, but also in politics, economics, and other domains. We can disagree, for example, over what the Bible teaches about property or war or how to be a good steward when it comes to climate change, meat consumption, and the use of genetically modified organisms.

What counts as compassion for one person might be unjust for another, or what one Christian praises as a legitimate act of advocacy seems to another to betray gospel values. How we interpret each of these models of service is inevitably shaped by the larger religious and political framework within which we act. We will look briefly at three areas that have a strong impact on how Christians think about service today: gender, politics, and theology.

Gender

How we interpret each of these models is shaped by our underlying assumptions about gender, particularly about what constitutes masculinity and femininity. Christians who take for granted more traditional gender roles often think of women as more prone to be compassionate or hospitable than men and, conversely, for men to be naturally more inclined to exercise stewardship and advocacy. Popular images of men as dominant, competitive, and controlling suggest that they more easily specialize in courage and wisdom. The popular image of women as more naturally drawn to nurturing and cooperation implies that they can more easily develop the virtues of patience and love. Promoting male headship in the home is one way in which some churches have lent their support to this way of distinguishing masculine and feminine styles of service.

This culturally normative conception of gender supports a hierarchy of power within the church and society that leads to the subordination of women and the marginalization of gay people. It has coopted the language of love to justify keeping some people up and others down or out.

Christianity played a major role supporting this normative conception of gender, but in recent decades many Christians have played a forceful role in challenging it. The former is much more common, yet the gospel does present resources for a prophetic alternative. All people are equally created in the image of God, equally baptized into the church, and equally redeemed in Christ. Women as well as men have a right and a duty to participate responsibly in the decision making that shapes our communities.

Recent challenges to gender stereotypes carry implications for how we think about service. As the churches and the wider society have become more convinced of gender equality, we have seen gender-assigned forms of service begin to erode. Women are now pilots and CEOs, and men now work as nurses and take more responsibility for family life, domestic chores, and childcare. Christians are more free to exercise these models of service regardless of gender.

Politics

Second, how we think about service is also shaped by our assumptions about politics. In the broad sense, politics concerns not just elections and lawmaking but how we conceive of and contribute to the common good of our communities. As we saw in the chapter on compassion, some Christians have a tendency to separate service from politics. They regard service as the domain of individual agents, free of any political or social significance. Many students, for example, plunge with enthusiasm and commitment into service programs and volunteer organizations but make sure to keep at arm's length from any political conversations on campus.

Political power is often described as a way in which some people control others. Like the prophets that preceded him, Jesus denounces powerful people who benefit from exploiting the weak and excluding others. Honor for Jesus and Paul is found among the humble, weak, and lowly (Mt 18:1–4; 2 Cor 12:9). Jesus announced the in-breaking of the reign of God by paying attention to people who were despised and by restoring their physical integrity, peace of mind, and rightful place in their communities. He subverted systems of domination and subordination, especially those enforced by violence. He announced good news that brought forgiveness, healing, and companionship.

The gospel suggests a normative framework for what constitutes a human community. It can be said to be political in the broad sense that it offers criteria for what constitutes a good human *polis* or political community. The best long-term service Christians can perform for the world is to embody in the church's own politics and structures the message of love that is the heart of the gospel. Pope Francis prays for the conversion of the papacy and is working for the reform of the Catholic Church's bureaucratic apparatus. Since the problem of clerical sexual abuse has been made public, theologians and bishops have written eloquently about transparency, accountability, collegiality, and the dignity of the laity. But these values have yet to be put into the procedures, practices, and institutions of the global church. A more credible witness would offer a more effective and appealing alternative to the logic of domination and exclusion that governs so much of both the church and the world.

Theology

Finally, Christians also disagree about what counts as genuine service because of implicit or explicit *theological* differences. For example, some Christians promote the death penalty based on their view of a God who insists that perpetrators be punished for their crimes with proportionate suffering. They believe that if someone intentionally takes the life of an innocent person, his or her life ought to be taken by the state. They regard supporting capital punishment as a way of serving both the families of victims and the larger good of public order.

Sister Helen Prejean, CSJ, on the other hand, offers an alternative theology, pointing to Christ, who died on the cross to show that God offers forgiveness to all transgressors and wants the healing rather than destruction of perpetrators.[1] She understands herself as serving the church and our society by working to abolish capital punishment and more broadly, to reform the criminal justice system. Prejean's opponents, however, believe her advocacy is badly misplaced, violates the demands of retributive justice, and lacks compassion for the families of the victims of capital crimes. These two radically opposing approaches to capital punishment reflect fundamentally different views of God, Christ, compassion, and justice. Similar divergences can be traced in other morally or politically charged issues.

One way to characterize this kind of divergence focuses on the meaning of God's redemptive and salvific love. A previous chapter discussed "verticalist" Christians who focus on individual salvation and see the Christian life as primarily a matter of sacramental worship, private prayer, and personal morality. This framework shapes their approach to stewardship, hospitality, and the other models of service. They think churches ought to focus on what helps believers attain salvation of their souls.

A more "horizontalist" approach to Christian faith understands the gospel as primarily committed to compassion expressed in social justice. Christianity ought to be more concerned with fighting oppression and suffering in this life than helping people get to the next one. In this view, we ought to concentrate on corporal works of mercy when they are most urgently needed and on long-haul social transformation through political activism.

A middle way between these extremes, the Christian integrationist, is seen in exemplars like King, Stang, and Romero. They regarded salvation as transforming the whole person and the whole world. Salvation concerns the whole person, King wrote; not only soul but also body, not only our spiritual condition but also our material condition. King criticized any church, black or white, that is "so absorbed in a future good 'over yonder' that it forgets the present evils 'down here.'" He insisted, "If the church does not recapture its prophetic zeal, it will become an irrelevant social club without moral or spiritual authority."[2] Not too long before he was killed, Romero delivered a speech along similar lines at the University of Louvain, Belgium. He pointed out that, contrary to otherworldly piety, "Christian faith

---

[1] Helen Prejean, *Dead Man Walking* (New York: Vintage, 1993).

[2] Martin Luther King, Jr., *Strength to Love* (Cleveland: William Collins and World Publishing, 1963), 150, 101, 62.

does not separate us from the world, but immerses us in it." For this reason the church cannot be seen as a "fortress apart from the city, but rather [as] the follower of Jesus, who lived, worked, struggled, and died in the midst of the city, the polis."[3]

The church must, of course, avoid being coopted by partisan political interests. Yet while it has no properly political competence or mission, the church is responsible to form the consciences of Christians in a way that their political decisions meet the standard of justice, human rights, and the common good. As Romero puts it, "Faith ought to inspire Christian political action but not be confused with it."[4]

This more balanced theological perspective helps us avoid three unhelpful tendencies when it comes to faith: privatization, secularization, and Pelagianism. First, it resists a form of Christianity that reduces faith to private piety. Christian faith without charity—the love of God and love of neighbor—is dead. Charity, in turn, is stunted if it is expressed only in private acts of kindness. Authentic Christian charity is not complacent in the face of social injustice.

Second, the integrated position also resists the reduction of Christian service to humanitarian concern or social work. The church is not just another NGO. Christian activists engaged in the world of secular politics can easily drift into assuming that salvation is advanced by social reforms based on building a consensus around public values. They can lose a sense of the richness, distinctiveness, and countercultural character of Christian faith expressed in St. Paul's advice to the Romans: "Do not be conformed to this world, but be transformed by the renewing of your minds, so that you may discern what is the will of God—what is good and acceptable and perfect" (Rom 12:2).

Third, the integrated position resists an ancient Christian heresy called "Pelagianism," which basically assumes that we can save ourselves if we strive to be good. Many socially committed Christians try hard to do good deeds and to cultivate attitudes that will make them better people. They deserve a lot of credit and ought to be encouraged. Yet it is a mistake to think that even the best of us "build the reign of God." God is the one who builds the reign of God, and we are called to participate in God's work—but we can only do so appropriately if we realize that in the end we are radically dependent on divine grace and must count on divine forgiveness when we fall short. We should of course spare no effort in doing everything we can to make the world less unjust and more peaceful, but at the end of the day

---

[3] Archbishop Oscar Romero, *Voice of the Voiceless* (Maryknoll, NY: Orbis Books, 1985), 178.

[4] Ibid., 100.

the reign of God is a gift of Christ and the Spirit, not our achievement. An integrated spirituality thus generates a twofold imperative: "Pray as if everything depended on God and work as if everything depended on you."[5]

Connecting the Models

We now turn to the question of how these models are connected to one another. The first point to note is that these models are essentially complementary. Acting within any of the distinct models often leads us to practice others. For example, if your friends have become victims of burglary, you will want to meet with them, listen to their story, and comfort them. You might invite them to your home to share a meal, or go to court to testify on their behalf, or help them fill out complicated insurance forms. Compassion here leads to hospitality, witness, and advocacy.

Another example of this interconnection is seen in solidarity. Other things being equal, the more seriously we are committed to solidarity with a particular community, the more we will want to take care of our resources so we can put them at the disposal of its members (stewardship), welcome members into our space (hospitality), pay attention to struggling community members (compassion), speak up about their plight (advocacy), and communicate truthfully within that community (witnessing). Similar kinds of interconnection can be seen in all of the other models of service, as well.

Compassion: The Paradigmatic Form of Service

I would now like to suggest that compassion is the most paradigmatic form of Christian service, accompaniment its most personal form, and witnessing its most excellent form. Compassion is a nearly universal human value today and appeals to something deeply human in us. As we have seen, it also lies at the heart of the Christian ethic. Jesus, the incarnation of God's mercy for human beings, taught, "Be merciful, just as your Father is merciful" (Lk 6:35). The church is at its best when it acts compassionately.

Compassion is especially powerful in one-on-one interaction and what Day and Maurin called the "art of human contacts."[6] The other models of service are compromised when their practitioners lack compassion.

---

[5] Attributed to St. Ignatius Loyola; cf. Joseph de Guibert, SJ, *The Jesuits: Their Spiritual Doctrine and Practice* (Chicago: Loyola University Press, 1964), 148n.55.

[6] Dorothy Day, *The Long Loneliness* (New York: Image, 1959), 167.

Advocacy without compassion, for example, becomes strident and rude, hospitality becomes mere tolerance and dutiful performance, and solidarity becomes in-group favoritism.

We can distinguish *direct* and *indirect* forms of compassion. One can give a cup of water to a thirsty child, but also raise money to have a well dug so that the child's village can have water for the next decade. The former expresses direct compassion, the later indirect compassion. If indirect compassion involves persuading donors or lending agencies to release funds that will pay for wells, then it also requires advocacy. A utilitarian might say that advocacy is better than compassion because it is more important to secure a supply of water for many children for many years than to give one glass to a child in a single moment. But since compassion creates the intention for both commitments, they cannot be cleanly separated.

Direct compassion is critically important, but it is obviously not a sufficient response to all forms of human suffering. To make this point, activists ask us to consider the following scenario. Imagine people living in a village on the edge of a river. One day some of the villagers see a baby floating down the river. A few of them jump into the river to rescue the baby. The next day other villagers rescue two more babies, and the day after that even more.

As the number of babies floating down the river increases, some of the villagers decide to row upstream to find out what is causing them to be in the river in the first place. Some villagers, though, complain that such a venture will leave fewer people in the village to save the babies who might be drifting by at any moment. Both sets of villagers are doing what they think is most compassionate. The rescuing villagers engage in direct compassion to address an immediate crisis, and the investigating villagers look for the cause in order to come up with a long-term plan to prevent it from recurring. Rescue and prevention are both important. The former is more immediate, but the latter has a potentially greater scope.

Compassion needs advocacy, but advocacy also needs compassion. I have known a number of young people who get involved with a particular community organization and then become so inspired that they begin to work there and make its cause their own. Over time, they get pulled into the bureaucracy and spend more and more time in meetings, writings grants, filling out paperwork, and connecting with local government officials. As their work for the organization takes on a life of its own, they have less and less to do with the people they initially wanted to serve. When interpersonal connections are lost, advocacy for people can easily get replaced by advocacy for the institution, and compassion can be replaced by loyalty to the organization. People who get trapped in this way can only be reinvigorated if they rekindle the particular interpersonal ties that energized them in the first place. This is why solidarity of accompaniment is the lifeblood of long-term and sustainable advocacy.

Accompaniment: The Most Personal Form of Service

If compassion is the paradigmatic Christian response to human suffering, accompaniment is the deepest and most personal form of Christian service. Because we are social beings, we thrive on friendship and community. All of the other forms of service can flow in one direction, but accompaniment by its very nature involves mutuality, cooperation, and partnership. Accompaniment is constituted by ongoing relationships, not just one-time encounters. It is seen in reciprocal concern and shared agency, not just when a strong person helps a weak person. It is mutuality, not unilateral service. In Christian terms it goes beyond the one-time helping of the Good Samaritan to the intimate gathering of disciples at the last supper.

Accompaniment is most personal because it occurs only when all parties are engaged in mutual availability, vulnerability, and belonging in what Greg Boyle calls a "covenant of equals."[7] It enables companions to delight in one another's good fortune and to grieve at one another's suffering. It displays the meaning of St. Paul's advice to Roman Christians: "Rejoice with those who rejoice, weep with those who weep" (Rom 12:15). Delighting and weeping both flow from the union that comes from love. Accompaniment is the most personal form of service because it only flourishes in community. Its participants envision community not as a collection of individuals seeking their own self-interest, but as a people whose identity is based on their relationship with one another. In a Christian context, the church is the People of God formed as members who accompany one another in a shared journey in the spirit of Christ.

Theologian Roberto Goizueta maintains that the "paradigmatic form of human action is not simply that of 'being with' another but, rather, the act of 'walking with' the other."[8] "Walking with" involves not traveling in independent and parallel zones but rather interacting with one another, sharing a common goal, and growing in friendship along the way. "Walking with" always includes a spiritual dimension: companions enable us to grow closer to Christ. This is especially the case when it comes to accompaniment with the "least" of our brothers and sisters. "Truly I tell you, just as

---

[7] Gregory Boyle, *Tattoos on the Heart: The Power of Boundless Compassion* (New York: Free Press, 2010), 77.

[8] Roberto Goizueta, *Caminemos con Jesús* (Maryknoll, NY: Orbis Books, 2003), 206.

you did it to one of the least of these who are members of my family, you did it to me" (Mt 25:40).

Witnessing: The Most Excellent Form of Service

Effective witness is the most excellent form of service in that it refers us to God, invites us to faith, and exemplifies what it means to love our neighbor. If, as Christians believe, the God of Jesus Christ is real, then it has to be the highest, and indeed, an incomparable good for human beings. If this is the case, then the faith, hope, and charity that draw us to God have to be the most important human virtues. If they are the most important virtues, then witness to them has to be the most excellent form of service.

What Dorothy Day called the "primacy of the spiritual"[9] suggests that effective religious witness provides the most important form of service because it draws us more deeply into the very purpose of our existence and the source of our fulfillment. The New Testament places a high value on the public proclamation of the gospel in word and sacrament (Acts 6:1–4). Humble care for the neighbor is the primary way in which we serve God, but this capacity is rooted in a living faith that must be nurtured, protected, and guided. Perhaps this is why Day believed that the "first job of the Christian, it seems to me, is to grow in faith in God—in His power, in the conviction that we are all held in the hollow of His hand."[10]

People of good will can be deeply offended by proselytism, and wise believers have a sense of when, where, and how to testify to the truth they accept in religious faith. We ought to be open to sharing the "reasons for our hope" (1 Pt 3:15), but this does not mean we ought to judge people, preach at them, or try to pressure them to go to church. Some of the most effective Christian witnesses are, for whatever reasons, not comfortable with talking for any length of time about religious matters.

As discussed above, we act as witnesses when we serve authentically. The truth of Christianity is displayed above all in action: "you will know them by their fruits" (Mt 7:17). Service is what shows that Christianity is real, neither an abstract set of beliefs nor just a moral code. Dag Hammarskjöld recognized that Christian faith has to be made real in *action*. As secretary-general of the United Nations he spent a lot of time shuttling from one disaster to another, but his posthumously published journal shows him to be a man of deep spiritual sensitivity and Christian commitment. Hammarskjöld's spiritual life supported his diplomatic life, and vice versa.

---

[9] Day, *The Long Loneliness*, 176.

[10] Dorothy Day, *The Duty of Delight: The Diaries of Dorothy Day*, ed. Robert Ellsberg (Milwaukee: Marquette University Press, 2008), 329.

"In our era the road to holiness necessarily passes through the world of action."[11] Yet his action was nourished by years of meditation and private immersion in a "center of stillness surrounded by silence."[12] Contemplative solitude gave him a freedom from self-concern that allowed him to serve as an international agent of justice and peace.

We can act as witnesses without even being aware of doing so. A good mother teaches her children how to treat other people primarily by modeling appropriate behavior herself. Sometimes she has to explain things, but most of what she teaches is unspoken.

The witness of practice takes place whenever someone does a good deed. Good people testify to the goodness of God, even if they don't explicitly believe in God. We can testify to goodness in acts of compassion or friendship whether or not we have correct beliefs, let alone a metaphysical theory, about the ultimate basis of that goodness.

The witness of practice is implicitly present as a dimension of all other forms of service. The dedicated advocate who defends the widow and the orphan testifies not only to the value of justice but also, at least implicitly, to the justice of God. The relief worker who accompanies migrants in a strange land not only displays personal compassion but also points to the compassion of God. These reflections lead us to conclude that compassion is the most paradigmatically Christian form of service, accompaniment its most personal form, and witness its highest expression.

But what is the core that runs through all of these six forms of Christian service? Indeed, what is the central uniting feature of *any and all* forms of Christian service? We have seen that each of these models can lead to any or all of the others. But what is the element that runs through all of them? The answer is love, understood as the *agape* of the New Testament or *caritas*, its Latin translation. Love in this sense refers not to a feeling of attraction or affection but to an affective affirmation of the goodness of another person. Thomas Aquinas described love in this sense as the crown and the root of all the virtues. King described *agape* as the "love of God operating in the human heart" and an "understanding and creative, redemptive good-will" for all human beings.[13] Day too described love as not just sentiment but "a matter of the will."[14]

---

[11] Dag Hammarskjöld, *Markings*, trans. W. H. Auden and Leif Sjoberg (New York: Knopf, 1964), 122. Cited in Roger Lipsley, *Hammarskjöld: A Life* (Ann Arbor: University of Michigan, 2013), 665.

[12] Dag Hammarskjöld, text for visitors to The Meditation Room, UN Headquarters (1957).

[13] King, *Strength to Love*, 50.

[14] Robert Ellsberg, ed., *Dorothy Day: Selected Writings* (Maryknoll, NY: Orbis Books, 1995), 7.

What is distinctive of human love is that it must include the will—our capacity to choose and desire the good. Day believed that if you "will to love someone (even the most repulsive and wicked), and try to serve him as an expression of that love—then you soon come to feel love." Love can thus begin with action. "If you help people, you soon begin to love them."[15]

When you appreciate the worth of other people, you want what is good for them. When what is good for them involves addressing something that harms them—hunger, disease, loneliness—we speak of acting compassionately. This is what we mean by direct service. Christians are so big on compassion that many of us think it is the same as Christian love or *agape*. Love, however, does not stop when pain and suffering are alleviated. Love appreciates the goodness of the one it embraces and seeks to promote his or her good wherever it can. Love promotes the good of others; it naturally wants to help our loved ones lead good lives.

We see this kind of pro-active benevolent love, for example, when citizens get together and work to obtain funding to build a city park so that children will have an attractive and enjoyable place to play. We see it when neighbors offer hospitality to visitors from other cultures. We see it when parents push for enrichment programs in schools so that students can have more exposure to music and fine arts. We see it when neighbors build local solidarity by throwing block parties. Finally, we see it whenever people quietly testify to the goodness of God by acting for the good of their neighbor in concrete, unassuming ways.

Unselfish love is not only a commitment to the good of the other. It is always also, whether we notice it or not, an expression of the power of divine love active in the world. Love, King writes, "is at the center of the cosmos. It is the great unifying force of life." Because "God is love," a person who loves has "discovered the clue to the meaning of ultimate reality."[16]

Dorothy Day never tired of telling her readers that "love is the measure."[17] Whatever we do with or for others is rooted in some kind of love. Sometimes that love is generous, emotionally mature, and well ordered; at other times that love is reserved, emotionally underdeveloped, or otherwise disordered. In any case love of some kind lies behind our compassion, hospitality, or other modes of serving others.

Love is the virtue that shapes how we use all of our gifts. When St. Paul wrote to the troubled Christian community in Corinth, he wanted the people to understand the role of spiritual gifts as serving the body of Christ.

---

[15] Day, *The Duty of Delight*, 25, 50.
[16] King, *Strength to Love*, 145.
[17] See, for example, Day, *The Long Loneliness*, 244.

Love is the virtue that shapes how we use all of our gifts. This is why Day wrote: "I have always prayed for an increase of love and surely this prayer is granted, 'Ask and you shall receive.'"[18]

Paul's words to the Corinthians point to the centrality of love for Christian service. "If I speak in the tongues of mortals and of angels, but do not have love, I am a noisy gong or a clanging cymbal" (13:1). We should not confuse cheap talk with real love. Love comes even before religion, faith, and the church: "And if I have prophetic powers, and understand all mysteries and all knowledge, and if I have all faith, so as to remove mountains, but do not have love, I am nothing" (13:2). Love is also the basis of all authentically good works, including those that are the most costly: "If I give away all my possessions, and if I hand over my body so that I may boast, but do not have love, I gain nothing" (13:3). Well-ordered love frees us from narcissistic self-absorption and allows us to bear with one another: "Love is patient; love is kind; love is not envious or boastful or arrogant or rude. It does not insist on its own way; it is not irritable or resentful; it does not rejoice in wrongdoing, but rejoices in the truth" (13:4–6). Finally, love provides the only lasting way to face the suffering that life imposes on us: "It bears all things, believes all things, hopes all things, endures all things" (13:7). Day observed that we can be tempted to sink into sadness as we get older and see more and more suffering. The only way out, she wrote, is to "overcome it daily, growing in love, and the joy which goes with loving."[19]

Faith, hope, and charity tell us that this world is God's, not ours, and that ultimately we live by the providence and grace of God. Earlier chapters of this book show how every model of service runs the risk of certain characteristic flaws. Each of these temptations reflects some kind of distortion of love. We can serve our neighbor in ways that are narrow minded, selfish, or destructive. Some forms of compassion can reinforce privilege, demean its recipients, and create unhealthy dependency. Advocacy can be tainted by self-righteousness; stewardship can be cramped by stinginess; hospitality can be a vehicle for cliquishness; solidarity can trigger fanaticism; and witnesses can act out of Pharisaic self-righteousness. We are all tempted to be small minded, biased, and selfish and to shrink the scope of our service to people who are like us or who share our values or who can be useful to us. The way to prevent this from happening, or repair it as best we can, is to cultivate a more appropriate order of love that puts first things first. Practical wisdom, Thomas Aquinas thought, is the virtue that puts the right order in our actions.

---

[18] Day, *The Duty of Delight*, 410.
[19] Ibid., 310.

Practical Wisdom

Jesus taught that we love the right way when our love is grounded in heart-felt trust in the healing, forgiving, and redeeming power of God. Gratitude generates a desire to serve God, and to the extent that we seek to serve God we will love our neighbor without either hesitation or ulterior motives.

This is not to say we can help everyone all the time. We are finite beings with limited resources, and we can only do so much. We have to learn how to balance our responsibility to loved ones with our responsibility to more distant neighbors. Since we can't do everything, we have to decide how to put our resources at the service of those who need them the most and to those for whom we are most responsible. We must, in other words, find a way to balance compassion, hospitality, and stewardship in the context of our particular lives. Each of our exemplars had a unique way of incorporating these types of service into the specific landscape of his or her life. Day expressed hospitality in one way, Claverie in another, and Romero in yet another.

The context-sensitive nature of service underscores the importance of practical wisdom, the virtue that enables us to exercise good judgment about what to do in specific circumstances. Practical wisdom helps us know when to be present in silence with someone who is struggling and how to speak a word of hope to someone who feels alone and disconsolate.

Practical wisdom is an intuitive ability to see what is going on in a particular situation and to judge accurately what needs to be done about it. True compassion is always the appropriate direct response to people who are in pain, but we need good judgment to know how to act most constructively.

Christianity ought to help us become not only more faithful, hopeful, and loving, but also wiser human beings. Christians see their lives shaped by divine grace and so are called to look for redemptive possibilities in contexts that might otherwise seem hopeless. For all their differences and mistakes, we see a common thread of practical wisdom in many of the actions of Dorothy Day and Martin Luther King, Jr., Mother Teresa and Dorothy Stang, Oscar Romero and Pierre Claverie.

Conclusion

The Introduction to this book posed two large questions: First, what difference does service make to Christianity? Second, what difference does Christianity make to how we engage in service?

In response to the first question, we can say that service lies at the very core of the Christian life. Christianity without service is shallow and empty. Anyone who professes Christian faith without in any way serving others has, at the very least, a radically deficient faith. As the First Letter of James puts it: "Faith by itself, if it has no works, is dead" (2:16). The test for the authenticity of our faith lies not in what we profess but in how we act, particularly in response to the marginalized. As Day put it, we love God only as much as we love the least in our midst.[1]

To say that authentic faith gives rise to service does not mean that every Christian has to volunteer at a soup kitchen, homeless shelter, or hospice. Many people lead lives of demanding service without doing so. Parents raise children, families care for a severely disabled relative, and adult children do everything they can for an elderly parent suffering from dementia. We don't have to volunteer at a House of Hospitality to act with love. As Day pointed out: "You can do this work wherever you are" as long as you do not turn your back on "the urgent needs of others."[2]

I think of a good friend who for years deliberately structured every day around visiting his mother in her nursing home. His visits led him to get to know other patients in that community, to befriend them, and to become an important presence of love and joy in their lives. I also think of a student who spent her adolescence taking care of three multiply handicapped younger siblings. When I asked her how she dealt with spending many weekends in hospitals while her sisters were getting surgery, she shrugged and said, "Well, when I needed to be with my family at the hospital, my real friends just hung out there with me."

There are countless ways of performing works of love. Many of them are spontaneous, but others are done deliberately and repeatedly. Some can be

---

[1] See Dorothy Day, *The Duty of Delight: The Diaries of Dorothy Day*, ed. Robert Ellsberg (Milwaukee: Marquette University Press, 2008), 318.

[2] *Dorothy Day: Selected Writings*, ed. Robert Ellsberg (Maryknoll, NY: Orbis Books, 1992), 165, 176.

performed by anyone, but others require great skill. This book has attempted to show that the practice of love constitutes a form of human excellence that depends on friends and community that can help the exercise of virtues like mercy, justice, and patience. It also suggests a bold hypothesis: that faith is the heart that pumps the lifeblood of Christian service throughout the body of Christ. This means, as Dorothy Day once put it, that, "The first job of the Christian, it seems to me is to grow in faith in God—in His power, in the conviction that we are all held in the hollow of His hand. . . . This faith, we must pray for, does away with all fear, which paralyzes all effort."[3] This lies at the heart of the distinctive Christian approach to service.

The answer to the second question—what difference does Christianity make to how we engage in service?—could be either nothing or everything. It is *nothing* in that a good doctor or teacher who is Christian performs the same tasks, shows the same professional concern, and exerts the same effort as good doctors or teachers who are not Christian. Christian faith doesn't give any special knowledge of how to serve that other people don't have access to. Nor does it give any special sensitivity to human pain that cannot be attained by anyone else.

In another sense, though, the answer is *everything*. Christianity makes all the difference when service is rooted in a vital and dynamic Christian faith motivated by love, modeled on Christ, and sustained by Christian community. Such a faith, Christians believe, is empowered by grace, inspired by the Holy Spirit, and fed by the Eucharist. Service that develops in this rich context can be willing to act with the radical generosity of Claverie, Romero, and Stang. Their cases suggest that Christian service is not just a matter of developing humanistic concern and then adding a transcendent meaning to it. They understood that Christian service, including the struggle for social justice, is sustained by the virtues of compassion, humility, and patience incarnated in Jesus.

Personalizing Service

The models of service examined in Chapters 7–12 provide a kind of inventory of values that can help us understand and assess our own particular strengths and weaknesses. This book has prepared us to ask ourselves six questions: (1) Are we good stewards of the gifts we have been given? (2) Do we show hospitality to those who visit our homes and communities? (3) Are we compassionate to people who are in pain, wounded, or troubled? (4) Do we speak up when we are confronted with injustice, whether on behalf of others or ourselves? (5) Do we support the communities of which we

---

[3] Day, *The Duty of Delight*, 329.

are a part and pay attention to the least of our brothers and sisters within them? Do we pay appropriate attention to outsiders and their communities? And (6) Do we act in a way that presents a positive witness to the gospel?

Dorothy Day held that we need only a "heart of grace, a soul generated by love. And [we] can be that servant."[4] But not everyone can perform every form of service equally well. Martin Luther King, Jr., was right to insist that "everybody can be great" because "everybody can serve."[5] But we also know that we can't all serve in exactly the same way. Our models of service cannot function in a "one size fits all" manner. Each of us has to personalize them so that our actions are appropriate to our needs, talents, opportunities, and circumstances.

We do best when we serve in ways that engage our strengths and don't set us up for frustration and failure. Most people are inclined to some ways of serving more than others. Someone who is very empathic, for example, might be more drawn to the works of mercy like feeding the hungry or counseling the afflicted. Someone who is highly outspoken and passionate about fairness might be more prone to engage in advocacy. Yet as Day points out to her activist friend: "Not everyone has the vocation to take a stand, to cry out, as you are doing."[6]

The kind of service that is right for us also offers new challenges. Most of us get energized by being stretched the right way. Sometimes we face challenges that demand skills that we have not yet developed or talents we do not yet possess. Service is fundamentally a cooperative enterprise, and communities enable us to work with people whose gifts complement our own. Colleagues and friends also can help us grow, sometimes in unexpected ways. Romero learned from his friend Rutilio Grande, even after his death, about how to live and work in solidarity with the poor. Day credited Peter Maurin for giving her a vision and sense of direction.

Each of us can think of our lives as an opportunity to personalize Christian service by creating our own particular blend of these models of service. They are all noble. Trying to live up to any of them requires focus, self-discipline, and commitment of energy, time, and resources. How we best serve depends on our particular capacities and sense of priorities, what we most care about, where we find opportunities to serve, and where we think our abilities and skills can be most effective. Martin Luther King, Jr., could not have done what Mother Teresa did, and vice versa. As Paul

---

[4] Ibid., 266.

[5] Martin Luther King, Jr., "Drum Major for Instinct," in *A Testament of Hope: The Essential Writings and Speeches of Martin Luther King, Jr.*, ed. James M. Washington (San Francisco: Harper, 2003), 265.

[6] Dorothy Day, *All the Way to Heaven: The Selected Letters of Dorothy Day*, ed. Robert Ellsberg (Milwaukee: Marquette University Press, 2010), 230.

liked to say, there are many gifts but one Spirit (1 Cor 12:4). While all of these forms of service are relevant in a general way to every Christian life, we have to figure out which are most pertinent to us at any given stage of our life journey.

Faith, Love, and Accompaniment: Dean Brackley, SJ

A dramatic example of what it means to personalize service comes from the life of the late Dean Brackley, SJ. Brackley was a member of the New York Province of the Society of Jesus. As a young man he became acquainted with Dorothy Day. After formation, ordination to the priesthood, and doctoral studies, he began to work for a church-sponsored community organization called the South Bronx People for Change. He also taught theological ethics at Fordham University.

On November 16, 1989, an event took place in El Salvador that would deeply affect the rest of Brackley's life. Late in the evening heavily armed soldiers from the Salvadoran military burst into the Jesuit residence of the University of Central American in San Salvador. They dragged six Jesuit priests out of their beds and shot them at close range. To eliminate potential witnesses, the soldiers then killed their housekeeper and her daughter.

News of the massacre quickly spread around the world. When Brackley heard what happened to his brother Jesuits, he volunteered to move from New York to El Salvador to continue their work. His offer was accepted. In January 1990, Brackley moved into a war zone and lived in the very residence where his Jesuit predecessors had been slain. The armed conflict continued for two more years, but he remained undaunted. The war ended in 1992, but the socioeconomic oppression that occasioned it did not. Brackley spent the rest of his life working with the poor of El Salvador. In addition to teaching at the university and fulfilling many pastoral responsibilities in local parishes, Brackley spent a great deal of time speaking with delegations that came to visit communities in El Salvador to learn about their struggle for human dignity, justice, and peace. He died of cancer in El Salvador on October 16, 2011.

Brackley displayed tireless devotion to the "promotion of faith and the service of justice," the title of a talk by Peter Hans Kolvenbach, SJ, at Santa Clara University in October 2000. Kolvenbach wanted Jesuit schools and universities to expand service beyond the acts of charity that characterized the old noblesse oblige. Kolvenbach wrote that, "Students, in the course of their formation, must let the gritty reality of this world into their lives, so they can learn to feel it, think about it critically, respond to its suffering, and engage in it constructively." Interpersonal contact can inspire a desire for solidarity and a willingness to make a preferential option for the poor. An education informed by contact with underserved people can help young adults learn to "perceive, think, judge, choose, and act for the rights of others, especially the disadvantaged and the oppressed."[7]

Brackley represented this gritty, praxis-based approach to formation and education, which he believed ought to be not just part of a high school or college curriculum but, more broadly, a dimension of the life of anyone striving to be authentically Christian. He embodied the "downward mobility" that puts a person's intellectual, moral, and spiritual capacities at the service of the marginalized.[8]

Years of experience convinced Brackley of the intimate link between Christian faith, solidarity, and service. Before he died, he sent this email to his friends:

> The faith factor is decisive, as you know. When I ask you and Monseñor Romero to pray, I mean: Let us pool our faith. Mine is weak enough, but with all of us, that is another matter. God wants to give life more than we want life. St. Ignatius wrote to Francisco Borja: I consider myself wholly an obstacle to God's work in me. In other words, the exercise of faith, our fundamental human challenge, gets us out of the way of God's work. So, let us pray. I cherish your friendship now more than ever. Un fuerte abrazo. Dean.[9]

This excerpt from Brackley's final letter to his friends reflects his deep sense of the religious and spiritual roots of Christian service. Experience taught him that faith is not merely an add-on to the moral life but a critically important feature of our humanity. He did not, however, naively think that it is easily attained or developed. Indeed, like Day, Romero, and our other exemplars, he saw allowing our faith to grow as our fundamental challenge. Brackley did not see Christian faith as a blind leap made by heroic individuals, but rather as a deep trust shared among friends who accompany one another in Christian communities. Solidarity in faith empowers solidarity in service.

---

[7] Peter Hans Kolvenbach, SJ, "The Service of Faith and the Promotion of Justice in American Jesuit Higher Education," in *A Jesuit Education Reader*, ed. George Traub, SJ (Chicago: Loyola, 2008), 155.

[8] Dean Brackley, "Higher Standards for Higher Education: The Christian University and Solidarity," speech at Creighton University, November 4, 1999, available online.

[9] In Pat Marrin, "The Jesuit Who Replaced Slain Salvadoran Priests Dies," *National Catholic Reporter*, October 17, 2011.

Practical Paths: Three Examples

Engagement in community can be pursued in the context of particular parishes or congregations or through church-affiliated groups. By way of illustration, I mention three different types of Christian groups that have had a strong impact on their participants: the Jesuit Volunteer Corps (JVC), JustFaith Ministries, and the Saint'Egidio Community.

The JVC was founded over fifty years ago to help laypeople deepen their commitment to a "faith that does justice." It works in collaboration with the Society of Jesus to enhance the capacity of local organizations to serve the marginalized of their communities. Volunteers serve for a year, typically after they graduate from college. Every volunteer works in a school or community organization, lives in a small community, and undertakes a commitment to incorporate the following four Ignatian values into his or her daily life: living simply, working for social justice, engaging in prayer, and participating in community life.

A JVC volunteer could be placed, for example, in one of the tuition-free Jesuit Nativity middle schools or one of the twenty-six Cristo Rey high schools across the country. Some are placed in advocacy and service organizations like the Campaign for Fair Sentencing of Youth in Washington, DC, Homeboy Industries in Los Angeles, or Women Against Abuse in Philadelphia. JVC supports its volunteers with workshops, retreats, spiritual direction, and community gatherings.

A second kind of opportunity is based in parishes, congregations, or Christian organizations. JustFaith Ministries, for example, provides programs for parishes that allow members to develop a greater commitment to some kind of social ministry. It invites parishioners to enter small communities that can help them deepen their understanding of what it means to be friends with people from marginalized communities. The groups' regular practice of reading, discussing, and engaging in work for social justice helps their members continue to extend their commitment to care. JustFaith Ministries provides introductory workshops, curricula, a helpful website, and other resources for parishes that want to establish their own JustFaith communities.

A third kind of opportunity is provided by organizations like the Community of Sant'Egidio. After the Second Vatican Council, a small group of teenagers led by Andrea Riccardi and some friends in Rome got together to see if they could incorporate the gospel more authentically into their daily lives. They gathered to pray and discuss how they might move beyond merely nominal, culturally comfortable Christianity. They were especially taken with the way of life of the first Christians as depicted in the Acts of the Apostles (see Acts 2:43–47). They were especially impressed with how the first generation of Christians lived in their own homes but met regularly for prayer, reflection, and service of the poor. They also took great inspiration from St. Francis's spiritual practices of simplicity, love of the poor, and peacemaking.

The Sant'Egidio Community began to teach underserved children in the slums on the outskirts of Rome. As it gained members, the community reached out to the Roma (gypsies), the elderly, and AIDS patients. It also became involved in anti-death penalty advocacy and in peacemaking. It was instrumental in the 1992 peace negotiations that ended the brutal and protracted civil war in Mozambique.

The name of this organization is taken from the Church of Sant'Egidio in Rome, where its members used to meet and that now functions as the group's headquarters. The community has attracted more than sixty thousand people in seventy-three countries. The key values of the community are communal prayer, communicating the gospel, solidarity with the poor, ecumenical bonds among different Christian traditions, and interreligious dialogue—goals also pursued by our examplars.

Conclusion

These are but three examples of specific organizations or programs that seek to help people grow in their capacity to serve others. They help to translate individual good will and generosity of spirit into practical commitments. The desire to serve cannot just reside in our hearts or heads. We need to take concrete actions, even if only in modest ways. Small steps along the way can over time cover a great distance. The important thing is to do them with care. Each practical commitment is a "step along the way, an opportunity for the Lord's grace to enter and do the rest."[10]

Christian service is not captured in any one of these models, but each of them points to what it means to love. Stewardship is love taking care of the people who have been entrusted to us; hospitality is love welcoming friend and stranger into our space; compassion is love responding to the concrete human needs of particular people; advocacy is love defending the innocent and speaking up for those who have been silenced; solidarity is love building inclusive community; and witnessing is love manifested in word and deed. Love is the heart of service and the measure of all that is valuable about being human.

---

[10] Bishop Ken Untener, "A Step along the Way," November 1979.

Each practical act of service that we perform is a "step along the way" because in it we come closer to finding ourselves by giving ourselves away in love and friendship. This "giving ourselves away" lies at the heart of Christian spirituality as well as ethics. There is, then, no better way to close this book than with a meditation that Dorothy Day recorded in her diary: "The difference between dead-weight knowledge and a living rich experience can never be enough expressed. Everyone knows too much, feels too little. . . . Pray to become aware, to will to live in Presence. Necessary to continually renew your intentions—pure intention: kneel down every now and then."[11]

---

[11] Day, *The Duty of Delight*, 85.

Index